MW01537472

Irony and the Poetry of the First World War

Irony and the Poetry of the First World War

Susanne Christine Puissant

palgrave
macmillan

© Susanne Christine Puissant 2009

Softcover reprint of the hardcover 1st edition 2009 978-0-230-57693-3

All rights reserved. No reproduction, copy or transmission of this publication may be made without written permission.

No portion of this publication may be reproduced, copied or transmitted save with written permission or in accordance with the provisions of the Copyright, Designs and Patents Act 1988, or under the terms of any licence permitting limited copying issued by the Copyright Licensing Agency, Saffron House, 6-10 Kirby Street, London EC1N 8TS.

Any person who does any unauthorized act in relation to this publication may be liable to criminal prosecution and civil claims for damages.

The author has asserted her right to be identified as the author of this work in accordance with the Copyright, Designs and Patents Act 1988.

First published 2009 by
PALGRAVE MACMILLAN

Palgrave Macmillan in the UK is an imprint of Macmillan Publishers Limited, registered in England, company number 785998, of Houndmills, Basingstoke, Hampshire RG21 6XS.

Palgrave Macmillan in the US is a division of St Martin's Press LLC, 175 Fifth Avenue, New York, NY 10010.

Palgrave Macmillan is the global academic imprint of the above companies and has companies and representatives throughout the world.

Palgrave® and Macmillan® are registered trademarks in the United States, the United Kingdom, Europe and other countries.

ISBN 978-1-349-36673-6   ISBN 978-0-230-23421-5 (eBook)
DOI 10.1057/9780230234215

A catalogue record for this book is available from the British Library.

Library of Congress Cataloging-in-Publication Data

Puissant, Susanne Christine, 1977–
    Irony and the poetry of the First World War / Susanne Christine Puissant.
        p. cm.
    Includes bibliographical references and index.
        1. English poetry – 20th century – History and criticism.
    2. World War, 1914–1918 – Literature and the war. 3. War poetry, English – History and criticism. 4. Soldiers' writings, English – History and criticism. 5. Irony in literature. I. Title.
PR605.W65P85 2009
821'.9109352403—dc22   2008042703

10 9 8 7 6 5 4 3 2 1
18 17 16 15 14 13 12 11 10 09

Transferred to Digital Printing in 2009

For Sven and Noa, and for my parents

Contents

Preface and Acknowledgements

Irony and the Poetry of the First World War is a study of one of the most distinctive features of war literature, which has often been mentioned but which has never been analysed in detail. In it I have concentrated on the English literary legacy of the First World War, which has attracted an international readership over the past ninety years. My debt in writing this book is therefore not only to the many literary critics of the literature of this first modern war in the history of mankind, but also to the poets themselves and their outstanding achievements. All of them are mentioned in the chapter notes and the bibliography.

Yet I owe my primary inspiration for this book to the memories of my family. At least two of my great-grandfathers were wounded in the First World War but survived. Their experiences shaped the youth of my grandparents, who again had to live through the tragedy of the Second World War. At every stage of writing I have benefited from their encouragement and love.

Above all, I would like to thank Jacobs University Bremen for granting me a scholarship, without which this book would never have been possible. I have received invaluable comments from Thomas Rommel, Peter Paul Schnierer and Ludwig Pfeiffer. I am also deeply grateful to Anna Saunders for her support with the final version of the manuscript. Special thanks are due to my editors at Palgrave Macmillan, Paula Kennedy and Steven Hall, for their guidance and expertise.

My greatest debt is to my husband Sven Christian Puissant, who encouraged me to keep writing, fought innumerable battles against the oddities of computers with me, and cheerfully baby-sat our daughter when deadlines were pressing. For his love, patience and emotional and intellectual support he deserves the major share of the credit.

S.C.P.

1
Introduction

1.1 Irony and war

When the First World War finally ended with the Armistice on 11 November 1918, the nations involved had lost millions of citizens, of whom at least 744,000 were British and Irish soldiers (Harris, 2003, ch. 8). To this number must be added 14,661 merchant seamen and 1,117 civilians, and for the British Empire as a whole the number of deaths is approximately 947,000. This loss constituted 'a fracture in time and space that separated the present from the past' and consequently the war entered postwar consciousness as a 'gap in history' (Hynes, 1991, p. xiii), indicative of modern experience. Long before the Armistice, even before the end of the first year of the war, disillusionment had set in as it became obvious that the war would not be over before Christmas.

Although the British army did not have to struggle with large-scale mutinies, her allies did[1] and the general feeling of tiredness and despair spread quickly, especially in the trenches of the Western Front. In order to guarantee constant enlistment, Great Britain was flooded with political propaganda based on ideas of patriotic duty and chivalric ideals which had little to do with the experience of the soldiers at the front. Despite the propaganda effort, the number of volunteers was by no means enough to cover the immense losses, meaning that conscription became necessary in 1916. After Lord Derby's scheme in October 1915, it was introduced with the Military Service Act of 1916. Not only was the mere proposal of conscription regarded by many as un-English, but it also appeared to represent a lack of faith in the patriotism of the people. By forcing men to sacrifice themselves for their country, the glory of that sacrifice would be stained. Whereas the majority of scholars

1

still perceive the battle of the Somme in July 1916 with its immense losses as the decisive event for a general change of attitude towards the war, Hibberd argues that it was the introduction of compulsory military service which gradually reshaped public opinion. In a paradigmatic change, propaganda no longer aimed to attract young men to sign up but instead focused on the bravery and hardships of the troops as a sacrifice for their country (Hibberd, 1993, p. 230).

Once at the front, the reality of war was perceived by most of those actively involved to be totally different from this portrayal but also from what could have been expected from previous wars, especially after the introduction of tanks and gas warfare. The Western Front on the allied side alone comprised over 12,000 miles of trenches stretching from the North Sea to the Alps. Seen from the air, the trench systems looked like a gigantic labyrinth dug out at surprising speed. Although the Great War has been identified as the great tragedy of the twentieth century,[2] it is important to note that the war as such had been more than a mere slaughter of the prototypical young infantry soldier. Whereas this is certainly one side of the coin, the other is that the war was, at least partly, greeted with enthusiasm, as a process of liberation and as the only means for the renewal of an overcome society. A comment by Julian Grenfell in October 1914 may serve as an indicator for these sentiments despite his exaggerations: 'I adore war. It is like a big picnic without the objectlessness of a picnic. I have never been so well or so happy.' Even if this attitude was atypical, it has not been without parallel, especially in the minds of those who compared the war to hunting or other favourite sports and pastimes. The idea of change brought about by war thus drove many middle-class young men, including most of the major war poets, to the war offices in order to enlist and by doing so take their part in the 're-creation' of England.

An important key to this ambivalent position of the population at the beginning of war lies in the fact that many of those educated in the famous public schools before the war – among them many poets such as Rupert Brooke, Siegfried Sassoon or Robert Graves – were extremely bored by the way of life during the pre-war years, a 'world grown old and cold and weary' (Rupert Brooke, *Peace*, l. 5). They welcomed the war as the long-desired change or even as a 'disinfectant that would cleanse the present' (Hynes, 1991, pp. 12, 19). Accordingly, *Peace* praises war as the only appropriate means against the decadence and emptiness of the pre-war years. 'Peace' in this sense is not opposed to 'war', but rather stands for an inner peace of mind ('hearts at peace'). The 'death' of the past was believed to be a necessary step towards a new future for both

England and art, a future that would free the artist from the narrow traditions of the past. War was welcomed not as the end of civilisation, but as 'the end of civilisation's illnesses' and thus a new beginning.

It was the excitement caused by the idea of a dangerous life combined with an idealistic patriotism showing itself in the love of a particular English landscape or the pride of a regiment that culminated in the belief of sacrifice in battle for a just cause as the most desirable way to end one's life. At first, 'there was no thought of what war meant, but an overwhelming desire to put the presumptuous German Kaiser in his place, to right the wrongs done to the small countries of Europe, and to show a Britain still victorious and free...' (Hynes, 1991, p. 31). The British fleet had always been identified with the Empire itself, and thus the militarisation of Germany and its growing Navy seemed to be aiming at the core of the nation. Additionally, Germany's march through neutral Belgium according to the Schlieffen plan was perceived as a general insult to all neutral countries. As a consequence, the majority of the population supported the war effort when Britain officially declared war on Germany on 4 August 1914.

England before the war, however, was not as fundamentally stable as has often been assumed. In 1912, miners went on a long and economically devastating strike, followed by further strikes in schools, the building trade and transportation. There were militant suffragist campaigns and the crisis about Home Rule for Ireland threatened the surface stability from within. One could even speak of a civil war, a class war, and a gender war hovering over the English society of the pre-war years. Culture likewise took up this general notion of aggression with exhibitions of futurist paintings and performances of aggressive compositions. Together with Ezra Pound's and Wyndham Lewis's Vorticism, an art war was fought against English institutions and traditions. However, the 'modernist' disease with which the English population was struggling was soon identified as distinctly German, so that the war against Germany also became a war against Modernism. As a result of the rupture that went through Europe, Futurism, Vorticism, and Imagism hardly survived the war as artistic movements. Notwithstanding these interior political and cultural turmoils of pre-war society, the majority of the population believed, or at least hoped, when the war broke out in summer 1914, that the crisis would be over by Christmas. Furthermore, their anxieties were geared towards a unification of the various opposing political groups and a homogenisation of English society.

All of these factors, together with the shocking but at the same time fascinating experience of the First World War, led to an immense production of poetry that tried to come to terms with the circumstances of daily life in the trenches by using a 'new language of truth-telling'[3] which can be characterised as ironic and/or satiric discourse. This is due to the fact that the First World War was, and has been perceived as, an ironic or at least absurd event in its very nature (see Fussell, 1975) ever since its beginning: nearly eight million people had to die because of a minor incident involving only two persons, namely Archduke Ferdinand of Austria and his Serbian murderer. Furthermore, although air bombardment was supposed to shorten the war, it rather helped to prolong it, as did other technical developments.

The war's horrors, especially those of the trenches of the Western Front, finally led to the breakdown of the mimetic discourse. 'Modern war necessitated different, and more thoughtful, modes of poetic response' (Bridgewater, 1987, p. 224). Both traditional vocabulary and poetic style became inadequate when confronted with front-line experience surpassing everything known up to that time. Above all, the war reversed the idea of progress that had dominated nineteenth-century British thinking. Modern warfare forced many authors to adapt their notions of poetry to the new situation and reject those abstractions that made war seem familiar. In order to grasp the ambivalent situation of modern war, poets drew back on various poetic means of expressing ambiguity. In addition to irony and its enhanced form of sarcasm, cynicism, satire and parody were among those frequently used stylistic devices to comment on the absurdity of war. They often took on a cathartic role to counter the tensions, fear and grief of front-line experiences by allowing the expression of personal attitudes towards war. 'In the process, irony, which is one expression of sensibility at odds with its surroundings, became for many the rhetorical mode and mood.'[4] For many war-time poets both at home and at the front, the only other option would have been silence. By raising their voices, the poets chose to become politically active, even though they might not have realised this at the time.

The huge amount of poetry that evolved out of this situation of horror can be situated in a central position between the decline of realistic and pastoral modes of writing at the beginning of the twentieth century and the rise of Modernism quickly gaining ground after the end of the First World War.[5] War poetry and modernist literature no longer relied on a shared set of norms, but had to conjure up the experience of violence and loss responsible for the rejection of faith in nineteenth-century notions of progress and happiness, both of which were destroyed by the war.

Accordingly, Stuart Sillars distinguished three main roles performed by war-time authors: 'to reassure in reversal; to see in a larger context actions which in themselves are complex and confusing; and to change dismay into anger, and direct it at an appropriate target (...) in the hope that something positive might come of it' (Sillars, 1987, p. 5). In this context, the technique of irony seems to have served various purposes. On the one hand it helped to create a diction and/or imagery appropriate for describing situations in which people were looking for shelter from bombardment under the ground where they were then exposed to explosions of mines, or in which soldiers bumped into the enemy during patrol duty because they got lost[6] in the labyrinth of the trenches. On the other hand, it became a way of thinking, or rather of psychologically dealing with the absurdities of war such as the impossibility of distinguishing between the world of the dead and that of the living in the trenches. Thus the First World War led to a rupture between the traditional world in which fighting was still largely associated with chivalric ideals – with heroism and glory as in the diction of patriotic propaganda – and the rejection of these ideas due to the disillusionment that had already taken place during the war and reached its peak after the Armistice in November 1918. As a consequence, irony gradually became the dominating means to fill this gap.

Due to the large-scale shift in attitudes towards the war among both combatants and civilians, the development of English poetry of the First World War has been characterised by Paul Fussell and others as a 'movement from a myth-dominated to a demythologized world' (Bergonzi, 1965, p. 198), a movement from the pastoral world of the Georgian poets to the bleak sarcasm of those poets who tried to overcome the war's incommunicability. The initial excitement expressed for instance in Rupert Brooke's sonnet cycle *1914* was 'to be replaced by sick disillusionment as the appalling realities of modern warfare were experienced'. However, this development from enthusiasm to bitterness has been disproved as too simplistic by modern literary scholarship. In most cases, a clear-cut line between affirmative and critical poems is hard to draw, as many of the poems discussed in the following chapters will show.[7]

The poetic debate on the poetry of the First World War, however, also had political implications: it not only challenged post-romantic and Victorian literary conventions, but also questioned England's imperialist positions and, in doing so, the purpose of the whole war. Again, however, one should not equate the use of irony with antiwar or anti-imperialist thinking.[8] The identification of various targets of irony in the following chapters will reveal that the use of irony served as an outlet for a multitude of sentiments, as a means of confronting one's experiences and fears rather than attacking possible scapegoats.

The poetry of the First World War differed from earlier poetry in that it was not only about a certain form or style, or the evocation of a specific emotion, although all these aspects certainly continued to play a role. The aesthetic ideals of earlier poets did not suddenly cease to be of value, but the war seriously challenged some of the most basic assumptions of aesthetics. Although many poems are neither propagandist nor moralist manifestos, but literary artworks, they can be called 'manifestations of conscience' (Lane, 1972, p. 11) in their depiction of largely intolerable situations. For most of the later generation of the so-called war poets, poetry was not only a form, but also a medium of transmitting a specific message, as well as adding a meaning to their daily experience. It gradually turned into 'a way of looking at things, as well as a way of rendering them' (Lane, 1972, p. 12).[9] Poets like Sassoon and Owen therefore do not fit any category of 'myth destroyers'; instead, 'their myth was a faith in the endurance of man's humanity: a myth rich and valid, but perilous as any other, as history demonstrates' (Lane, 1972, p. 174). Neither can these poets be called pacifists[10]; for what they renounced was not war as such, but the way this one in particular was fought.

The various ironic techniques used by the war poets range from rewritings of ancient myths, such as the one of Abraham and Isaac, in Owen's version of which Abraham finally sacrifices his son, to contrasting visions of the pastoral and/or romantic tradition with the reality of war and its consequences in Harold Monro's *The Poets are Waiting*, to the satiric contempt for ridiculous military orders and patriotic discourse most explicitly expressed in the work of Siegfried Sassoon. As a result of this diversity, Linda Hutcheon warns against confusing irony with other discursive strategies, especially humour. Not all uses of irony are amusing, nor is all humour ironic (Hutcheon, 1994, p. 5). Thus it is necessary at this point to briefly clarify the theoretical bases for the following interpretations.

Scientific analysis of irony can mainly be divided – though with overlap – into three main branches: linguistic, philosophical, and psychological approaches, of which the last-named are the youngest, for philosophical ideas about the phenomenon date back to ancient Greece. While linguistic approaches are the only ones dealing immediately with the relationship between irony and language, and are thus of particular interest for the analysis of poetic diction, psychological studies have provided useful insights into the encoding and decoding processes of irony. Philosophy, last but not least, brings into focus the personality behind the poem. According to philosophers throughout the ages, irony not only serves to express opinion and attitude on behalf of the poet, but is triggered by particular incidents and human constellations, which are again based on the political and cultural climate at the time of artistic production. By nature, irony is an interdisciplinary phenomenon and can thus only profit from interdisciplinary analysis.

The first among the approaches developed at the beginning of the twentieth century and useful for the analysis of war poetry is structuralism/formalism with its strong focus on the text itself. In order to detect irony in the texts it will be important to look for linguistic evidence in the form of internal semantic contradictions and discrepancies. The use of exaggerations, imitations of form, noticeable rhyme schemes, switches in the linguistic mode or a peculiar syntax all have to be considered as eventual markers of irony. Furthermore, it is important to note the rare (the fewer the signals, the better the irony) but possible indicators of irony in the form of exclamation marks, hyphens or inverted commas. All of these indicators are socially agreed upon and may vary from culture to culture, as none of them signify irony in and of themselves. The main disadvantage of structuralist approaches, however, is that they deliberately exclude the author, the reader, and the context from the process of interpretation.

Yet irony is more than a trope to be analysed and intentionalist theories will therefore also prove helpful here. They ask for the writer's purpose in using a specific form, mode and style of language, as well as asking whether a speaker is deliberately being ironic or whether he reports an (unintentionally) ironic event to make a certain point. In order to be able to gain insight into an author's intention one has to acquire biographical background knowledge as well as compare texts by the same author from the same period. In some cases this will be impossible due to lack of information, and in others the author might deliberately choose not to include any clues for the discovery of his/her intention in the text itself. An author might also be role-playing, providing for a whole range of possible interpretations due to ambiguous elements in the text. However, any reader taking an active part in the literary communication process will try to work out what a writer may have intended by choosing a certain diction and style. This is again similar to other forms of communication, as will be shown in the following paragraph.

Notwithstanding the above efforts of readers to discover the author's intention, it remains striking that an audience might perceive a text as ironic or satiric despite a lack of information about this intention.[11] Why this is the case has been the focus of various psychological approaches, which, however, often neglect possible evidence for irony in the text, as their main focus is on the communicative context. Most psychological theories are strongly based on the assumptions of speech act theory,[12] combining psychological and linguistic aspects such as Grice's cooperative principle.[13] These theories perceive irony to be a case of violation of the maxims of relevance and coherence. The main problem that arises here is that many utterances can be irrelevant or incoherent without being ironic. Furthermore, speech act theory again focuses more or less only on the ironist. However, it is important to concentrate on the interpreter, whose job is not only to comprehend the ironist's intention or the text's signals; he or she also has to recognise the evaluative content. On the basis of context, interpreters will evaluate the said and the unsaid, or rather the written or the unwritten, in their relation to each other as they interact in order to create the irony of a text.

To overcome these limitations, one also has to include reader-oriented theories in the analysis of irony. The various reader response theories have pointed out the influence of the social and political context on reading processes. These theories focus on the individual perception of funny or didactic elements which may vary considerably from culture to culture and from time to time. The detection of irony thus largely depends on the reader's sense of humour, background knowledge and previous reading experience, and the value systems prominent at the time of reading. It is thus possible that at certain times certain readers will not perceive the irony of a poem, whereas earlier or later readers once did or will do so. In order to argue against a total relativism of interpretation, most reader-response theorists – especially Iser (1972) – refer to elements in the text, such as 'gaps', guiding the interpretation process.

The importance of context with regard to writing and reading has already been mentioned, and the most recent historical and cultural approaches have tried to show how writers and readers are influenced by, but also influence, the culture of their time. However, most of these approaches assume too strong a determination of the author by the context, whereas the context of reading only plays a minor role in these theories. Furthermore, despite its undeniable importance, one has to be aware that context alone can never be sufficient to render something ironic. It is in itself constructed through interpretive procedures which rely on prior experience with interpretation and which are formed by interpretive expectations.

The First World War, as the first truly 'modern' war, provides the background for the frequent use of irony as it provoked all sorts of emotional and intellectual responses. Whereas the poets fought against the Germans and the ever-present vermin in the trenches, in their poetry they fought against the living conditions in the trenches, for understanding, and against the war itself. The specific irony of life at the front is given a voice in Frederick Manning's *Grotesque* in which soldiers sing 'as a choir of frogs/ In hideous irony, our patriotic songs'. In the following pages, however, we will establish whether this irony is only a 'higher rank phenomenon', or whether poets like Ivor Gurney or Isaac Rosenberg, who were never commissioned and served as private soldiers, ever use it and, if they do, whether their usage differs from that of officer-poets like Wilfred Owen or Siegfried Sassoon. Furthermore, it will be interesting to see whether the use of irony is a front-line phenomenon or whether it also plays a role in poems from the home front. Last but not least, the various forms of irony – situational, verbal, ontological – will be analysed with regard to their function and frequency. My distinction of these different forms will largely be based on Douglas C. Muecke's groundbreaking works *The Compass of Irony* (1969) and *Irony* (1970), in which he elaborates on irony's multiple shapes.[14] His ideas have subsequently been taken up in more recent works on the linguistics of irony such as Uwe Japp's *Theorie der Ironie* (1983), Linda Hutcheon's *Irony's Edge* (1994) or Edgar Lapp's *Linguistik der Ironie* (1992). However, for the analysis of literary texts with regard to communicative aspects, Marika Mueller's study on irony, *Die Ironie. Kulturgeschichte und Textgestalt* (1995), will become of particular importance as she follows an interactional–aesthetical approach. Consequently, she criticises Muecke's and other linguistic approaches as insufficient (Müller, 1995, p. 105f.) as they concentrate on a set of stylistic features while neglecting intertextual aspects and irony based on the interaction between authors, readers and texts. It is this interaction in particular which establishes literary communication in general and which provides the basis for any understanding of irony's purposes and functions.

1.2 Methodological reflections

From the preceding reflections on irony as a literary phenomenon it becomes clear that all attempts at an appropriate methodology must meet the following requirements:

1. There are a vast variety of ways in which irony presents itself. Thus one single method cannot be sufficient for its analysis.

2. If we consider irony as a means of expressing a particular view or attitude on something, in this case the First World War with all its consequences for the population at home and all those who took an active part in it all over the world, the required method's focus has to include the author who consciously used irony to make his or her point. The method required thus has to take into account the artist's intentions, at least where this is possible. Of course, an artist's intentions can never be the only evidence for an ironic reading, but biographical knowledge may help to define the range of possible interpretations.

3. From our own daily experiences with irony it is obvious that it is the context (both literary and social) that determines our understanding and interpretation of ironic utterances. An analysis of irony in literature therefore requires a theory that allows an evaluation of the context of both the production of the poem and of its various readings, of intertextual references and of biographical data.

4. If irony is used deliberately by various authors to express an opinion, one can presuppose that they expect their audience to dissolve the irony and in doing so draw conclusions about the author's point of view. The process of interpretation thus gains a special importance as an act of decoding the message of the poem. A methodology for the analysis of irony necessarily needs to allow insights into reading processes. From these considerations it becomes clear that the required method needs to be one that focuses on both the poet and the reader while at the same time considering the contexts of literary production and reception, as well as the variety of shapes which irony can take in different literary texts. This implies that neither the various approaches in the tradition of the New Criticism or Formalism nor pure Reader Response Theories will be sufficient for the analysis of irony.

To solve the dilemma of either focusing too much on the linguistic aspects of irony or starting from a too rigorously deterministic perspective, Roger Sell proposes a 'historical yet non-historicist literary pragmatics' which 'does *not* confine writers or readers to some single communal formation' (Sell, 2000, p. 255). This implies that authors as well as readers are influenced, though not totally determined, by the historical and cultural contexts surrounding them. The contexts of writing and reading, however, might greatly differ between various cultural and historical communities[15] so that the text might be interpreted differently according to the communicative contexts in which both writer and reader find themselves.[16] Additionally, interpretive strategies vary from interpretive community to interpretive community. Consequently, misunderstandings of

ironic utterances may be due to the differences in discursive communities and are not necessarily a question of competence in the understanding of irony itself: 'The communicative context of a poem and the
interpretation of a poem have a reciprocal relationship, for one implies
the other. Consequently, when different critics derive different interpretations from the same text, it is often because they identify or otherwise
apply different communicative contexts to it' (Adams, 1985, p. 42). Yet,
even though 'the pragmatic structure forces the reader to conform his
interpretation to the communicative context' (Adams, 1985, p. 45), the
text itself inevitably limits the possibilities of interpretations.

    Following Bühler's *organon model* (1934), Sell perceives every commu-
nicative situation as a triangular relationship between sender, receiver
and topic or text of the communication. In an extension of Bühler's
original model, Jacobson added language itself as a fourth component
of communication – the code transmitting the content (Jakobson, 1960,
pp. 350–377).[17] For the analysis of poetry and literary texts in general,
this modification takes into account the particular language of a poem
by a particular author. Fictional communication in this respect does
not differ from real-life communication: 'One of the functions of language is communication, and verbal communication is always loose.
This is fundamental to the communicative potential of ordinary language, and is exploited for particular effects in literature' (Fabb, 1997,
p. 267). However, one has to be aware of the fact that, while ordinary discourse is more or less direct, the communicative act established
via literature is diverted: a text may reach a readership to which it was
not particularly addressed. Whereas the attribute of directness might
at least partly have been valid for early forms of literature – personal
texts passed on via letters or written on commission – the introduction
of the printing press led to an increased audience in the first place and
to the conservation of texts from past epochs in the long run. At the
same time, texts are not exhausted by one single act of reading, whereas
spoken discourse is usually only valid for the moment. And finally, as
writing requires a careful modelling of language, literary discourse can
be considered as more reflexive. In his study, Bühler furthermore distinguished between various functions of language, such as expression,
appeal, and representation, to which Jakobson added a poetic function.
Yet even this last poetic function of language cannot serve to distinguish fictional communication from ordinary language use in everyday
speech, as so-called 'poetic' elements feature prominently in all types
of discourse. The 'poetic' function only serves to direct our attention to
the language of the message as such.[18]

By being an interpersonal activity, a 'deed' or action according to Greek *pragma*, literary communication expresses attitudes the author wants the reader to take on by engaging him in an emotional discourse which involves judgement and moral statements.[19] As such, irony is neither a limited rhetorical trope nor an extended attitude to life, but a discursive strategy operating at the level of language and form.[20] However, these attitudes need not be accepted by the reader in order to understand the text itself. The following chapters will show that the authors of the First World War poetry deliberately entered the political discourse of their time in the hope of changing common perceptions of war in general and this one in particular by making use of the illocutionary potential of utterances. By depicting the circumstances of trench warfare, gas attacks or injuries resulting from the war, on the illocutionary level the poetic utterances attempt to warn, to make aware and to increase understanding. Furthermore, the poets are able to communicate both their own and someone else's attitudes towards a specific aspect of the war at the same time. This is what Sell calls the 'pragmatic potential' of literary utterances, a term which in my opinion is more useful for the analysis of war poetry than the terminology of speech act theory.

Due to the individuality of human beings, human communication can never be predictable in its outcome. As we have seen, it is always based on situational contexts representing extracts of the participants' worlds[21] which, especially in the case of literary communication, only partly overlap. Successful communication, however, always relies on the existence of mutual insight. In the case of literature, this becomes a difficult prerequisite as it is a communication between partners who do not know each other. Sperber and Wilson speak of *mutual manifestness,* defining it as follows: 'A fact is *manifest* to an individual at a given time if and only if he is capable of representing it mentally and accepting its representation as true or probably true' (Sperber and Wilson, 1995, p. 39). On the part of the addressee this implies the construction of assumptions on the basis of personal knowledge, the surroundings and the given and implied context in the text itself. In some cases of literary communication, an author might not pay attention to the needs of readers, or he/she might deliberately refuse to reveal information and thus hinder the process of inference on the part of the reader. In these cases, the utterance will remain ambiguous and will be interpreted as either ironic or non-ironic by various readers.

Yet what about an author's original intention? 'Since the hearer actively seeks the speaker's intention, and since recognizing the communicative intention entails recognizing rhetorical intentions, the rhetorical effects can be almost irresistible' (Adams, 1985, p. 66). Sperber and Wilson furthermore distinguish between an *informative intention* 'to make manifest [...] a set of assumptions' (Sperber and Wilson, 1995, p. 58) and a *communicative intention* as one that makes 'it [...] manifest that the communicator has this informative intention' (ibid., p. 61). By discovering the communicative intention, the reader is not yet neces-sarily able to get the informative intention. However, most informative intentions, they point out, can only be conveyed via a communicative intention.

In order to further minimise misunderstandings, Sell points out the need for 'mediation' (Sell, 2000, p. 3) between any writer and reader as the literary scholar's main task,[22] which should not, however, be mis-taken for a smoothing out of historical or cultural differences. Mediation draws on expert knowledge from various fields of enquiry, such as his-tory, the social sciences, semantics, and philosophy to fully understand the communicative potential of a poem. In particular cases this might also mean that contradictions on the semantic level do not necessarily need to be solved, but instead can be interpreted as a particular means for the expression of an attitude (see also Berntsen and Kennedy, 1996, pp. 13–29).

To sum up, communication theory first points out the use of irony by an author as a risky business, and secondly works to minimise this risk by maximising its detection and interpretation. Furthermore, Sell's the-ory accounts for the affective element of (ironic) communication: it relies on strategies of building bonds between the communicative part-ners regardless of cultural or historical differences.[23] It is the flexibility of imagination and empathy that enables human beings to communi-cate with each other across cultural or historical boundaries,[24] so that even today English the First World War poems can be fruitfully read by non-English scholars.

What Sell's theory of literature as a form of communication does not cover, however, is the problem of irony's various forms and functions.[25] As the poems to be discussed in the following chapters will show, there cannot be one single working definition of irony or ironic voice. Verbally, an author might express his or her attitude towards the war by choosing a particular linguistic form that can determine its interpret-ation as ironic or satiric. Another option would be to represent some-one else's thought while dissociating oneself from it. Alternatively, an author might turn someone else's words against that very person by exaggerating them. And as for situational irony, the possibilities to con-vey irony are innumerable. The question is now whether the various forms of irony are used for distinct purposes. With literature being a 'deed', an author's utterance has to be interpreted as following a certain purpose like any other human action. However, if we perceive communication to follow a specific aim in history,[26] i.e. being 'intentional and motivated',[27] we also have to assume that poets strategically use one or the other form of irony for its specific function. Instead of trying to find one single definition or function of irony, it will thus be necessary to analyse each poem according to the dominant aspects of its irony with the help of all theoretical approaches available.

As has already been pointed out, structural–linguistic approaches are mainly interested in rhetorical and stylistic variants of irony according to a catalogue of irony-signals while neglecting intertextual irony or ironical parabasis. Discourse analysis and speech act theory might prove helpful with regard to communicative strategies, but both approaches hardly focus on literary communication. As the interpretation of irony always requires culture-specific competence, historical or biographical insights might be required in some cases, and others will necessitate psychological or philosophical approaches. Only a combination of the various disciplines under the umbrella of communicative theory as an interactional aesthetics will reveal the multiple facets and thus the full communicative potential of the poems.

1.3   The material

1.3.1   Censorship

At the outset of the war allied military leaders prevented newspaper reporters from visiting the front and whatever was published had to undergo powerful censorship in order to prevent outrageous reports. As the First World War – at least up until 1916 and the introduction of conscription – had mainly been a war fought by volunteers,[28] the British government was anxious that 'bad' reports, containing, for example, descriptions of the common soldiers' living conditions at the front, might prevent people from enlisting. The aim of censorship was thus mainly to secure public interest in the war effort by encouraging accounts of the heroic British soldier fighting a just war and by suppressing negative or critical voices about the war. For reasons of preventing decreasing enlistment rates and general public support for the war effort, censorship not only affected newspaper reports and radio broadcasting, but was also applied to the soldiers' personal communications home via letters. 'Groups opposed to the war were harassed, books were suppressed, and printers intimidated by the police. News about the results of the fighting was delayed and falsified. Conditions in the trenches and hospital were romanticised in photographs and films' (Tylee, 1990, p. 53). Despite its primary concern with troop movements, place names or other intelligence matters, censorship attempted a systematic starvation of the population at home regarding the truth about what was going on at the various fronts. Casualty lists came closest to reality, although figures were often less than accurate and many people wanted to read them as documents of soldierly heroism. Only gradually did the reality of war find its way into family homes – via soldiers on leave, nurses' reports or the sight of dramatically wounded soldiers – despite the fact that a report by a *Times* war correspondent was published on 24 November 1914 that spoke of the bleak realities of trench warfare. Yet the question was also whether one wanted to see and hear.

In Britain the Defense of the Realm Act (DORA),[29] first introduced on 8 August 1914, listed all issues correspondents were allowed to write about, and, more importantly, those they were not to write about. Apart from regulations concerning daily life in Britain, talking about naval or military matters in public places or spreading rumours about military movements was prohibited. The formulation of the regulation was vague enough to allow a variable interpretation by the police. The use of invisible ink was equally prohibited when writing to or from abroad, and any civilian breaking these laws was to be immediately tried by the government. Censorship of newspapers by the War Office Press Bureau under F. E. Smith was perceived as a necessary and legal instrument of the government, and, although private letters were not explicitly mentioned, the application of censorship to personal communications went without saying. Although the Act was rarely applied in practice, it constantly threatened editors with the closure of their papers, fear of which often caused them to refuse to publish too overtly critical material.

It did not take long for soldiers on both sides of the front line to figure out that their letters were being monitored, and so it is not surprising that they resorted to coded language as a means of telling the truth about modern warfare. Implied attitudes towards the war must thus be decoded in many of the poems to be discussed in the following paragraphs. One means of doing so was to resort to the various forms of irony. 'If men', says Shaftesbury (1981), 'are forbid to speak their minds seriously on certain subjects, they will do it ironically.' As in the Middle Ages and the times of the 'wise fool', laughter served as protection from censorship and social or legal repressions. The poet as fool was thus the bearer of the objective but abstract truth and as such provided a serious

challenge to wartime society as irony reversed hierarchies. 'The subversive functioning of irony is often connected to the view that it is a self-
critical, self-knowing, self-reflexive mode that has the potential to offer
a challenge to the hierarchy of the very "sites" of discourse, a hierarchy
based on social relations of dominance' (Hutcheon, 1994, p. 30). Irony
reverses this hierarchy of power into one of knowledge, where those
who use it dominate over the ones who get it, yet those who get it are
superior to those who remain ignorant of the ironical edge of an utterance. It is thus elitist in function as it expresses a sense of superiority
on the side of the ironist.[30] However, one could equally argue that it is
the discursive community that is being inclusive or exclusive – in some
cases by deliberate choice of sharing or not sharing an ideology.

Both sides, the government and the opposition, were prepared to risk
open confrontation about the war issue. Although the war critics were
confronted with lifelong imprisonment if their case was heard by court
martial, the government at the same time was keen on upholding the
British reputation for freedom of speech and thus tried to avoid publicity
through court cases. Only gradually did it become apparent to those in
power that a change of attitude was needed to achieve the cooperation
of the press with regard to the public support of the war. It is probably
an indication of the strength of literary opposition to politics that its
voice grew louder the longer the war lasted. However, censorship also
had a great impact on the poetic legacy of the war as we have to assume
that a great amount of poetry was lost because it was never published
or did not even make it beyond the front lines but was confiscated and
destroyed before reaching relatives or friends back at home.

1.3.2   A literary war

Even though the large number of anthologies of the First World War
poetry has constantly guaranteed the availability of war poetry over
the past 90 decades, they have also, together with literary criticism,
shaped its perception. The choice of material largely followed the politics of the time, so that history dominates our knowledge of the poems
up until today.[31] James Campbell identifies two main principles which
have been governing the interpretive ideology for decades: 'an aesthetic
criterion of realism and an ethical criterion of a humanism of passivity'
(Campbell, 1999, p. 213).[32] As a result, the canon of war poems was and
is often limited to poets with first-hand experience of battle as the only
'truthful' perception of war while at the same time excluding all other
poems on the topic by women and other noncombatants. Only recently
did the equation of trench poetry with war poetry come into question,

especially after Catherine Reilly's bibliography of the First World War poetry (1978) revealed that the majority of poetic reactions to the war were written by civilians rather than combatants. Furthermore, it should not be forgotten that the majority of poets were officers, while the war was mainly fought by privates. It is therefore necessary to take into account the possibility of ordinary soldiers having totally different reactions to some of the issues of war, even if records are few.[33]

While the first histories of the First World War had already been published before hostilities ceased, the interwar period was highly dominated by the autobiographical literature of famous war veterans like Siegfried Sassoon or Robert Graves. After the end of the Second World War, which constituted another great shock and which again left many nations bereaved of their young men, literary scholars in the 1950s and early 1960s mainly focused on the individual biographies of certain poets. By adopting the attitudes of these poets towards war rather than critically evaluating them, this biographical approach led to the creation of the popular war myths which even today have not lost their popularity and still continue to shape the perception of this 'war of all wars'.[34]

However, as works of art in which the balance between personal experience and aesthetic reflection may vary from poem to poem, the poems should not be mistaken for historical evidence. Despite their aim of being as realistic as possible, the war poets added one feature which is important for all kinds of poetry, their imagination. Ironically, it was exactly the 'disastrous lack of imagination on the part of those who could either have prevented it, or could have curtailed it' (see Bridgewater, 1987, p. 223), that led to the horrible outcome of the War. By dealing with particular instances from a highly individual perspective, these poems do not allow us to generalise about the war, but rather represent 'slices' of reality. Nevertheless, they creatively illuminate the war from a partial witness's point of view and thus prove to be valuable documents of the war experience of the infantry soldier, the nurse or the pilot. Modern historiography during the last two decades has therefore focused increasingly on these individual voices, and especially on those of poets, as essential for a truthful account of the war. It is in this context that we have to read Wilfred Owen's famous statement in the *Preface* to his first volume of poems: 'All a poet can do today is warn. That is why the true Poets must be truthful' (Stallworthy, 2003, p. 192). And so Keegan (1988, p. 31) points out: 'Allowing the combatants to speak for themselves is not merely a permissible, but, when and where possible, an essential ingredient of battle narrative and battle analysis.'[35]

However, biographical criticism often neglected the fact that the poetry of war was first and foremost a fictional[36] construction of war which engendered the general identification of the First World War with the so-called 'Western Front'. This is mainly due to the fact that it was there that the industrial development of the nineteenth century showed its most fatal consequences. It turned warfare – which at the beginning of the First World War was still largely associated with chivalric artillery battles – into a large-scale technical *Materialschlacht* with armies devoid of mobility as a result of their technological equipment. Despite the importance of the Western Front as a major area of war, it should not be forgotten that the war was fought just as fiercely in other areas of the world, especially because the First World War was fought not only between nations, but between colonial empires.

The war of 1914–1918 was thus many wars rather than one single one. If this dissertation focuses mainly on poetry written by members of the Infantry, i.e. poetry about war in the trenches of the frontline stretching from the North Sea to the Alps, this is largely due to reasons of quantity. During the four long years of static warfare in the trenches, soldiers spent many hours waiting for the next attack, during which they dedicated themselves to reading, drawing, or the composition of poetry. Furthermore, by the time of the outbreak of the First World War the percentage of literacy had risen to heights it had never reached before. The 1870 education act and the improvement of the schooling system had played their part most effectively so that the generation in the trenches had already grown up with the knowledge of a long English literary tradition which certainly influenced even amateur writing.

The dominance of poetry written by the infantry might be attributed to various reasons. Members of the air force, for instance, perceived war differently and regarded it as less horrible, as most of the pilots saw their service to be testing new limits, even if this included the risk of death. In their not yet fully developed machines survival depended on the individual skill of the pilot and only few flying aces lived to see the end of the war. Yet death was 'clean' in being more or less instant and it was impossible to blame someone else for it. Thus there was no immediate psychological necessity to transform one's experiences into poetry.

As for warfare at sea, its results did not meet with expectations. Although there were some major naval battles (and thus high losses), such as the Gallipoli campaign in the Mediterranean, or the battles around Jutland, the role of the Royal Navy was by no means decisive for the war, especially after the high losses of 1916 and Germany's decision to concentrate almost entirely on submarine warfare in the North Sea

(Keegan, 1999, p. 296). Again death seems to have been perceived as less 'dirty' than in the trenches. Soldiers on bombarded ships simply drowned and thus perished from sight instead of rotting in the sun or mud and remaining visible for weeks.[37] Furthermore, the menace of submarine warfare was an indistinct one due to the invisibility of the enemy and as such difficult to describe. Among both the air force and navy of all nations involved there was thus no pressing need for poetry as a means to come to terms with the horrors of modern warfare.

Thirdly, as the casualty rate was highest in the infantry, which was consequently strongly dependent on new recruits, the number of volunteers with a higher education or even a university degree was considerably higher in the infantry than in the navy, which strongly relied on family traditions for its recruits. Additionally, the numbers of soldiers involved in war at sea and in the air were miniscule compared with the vast infantry, due to the fact that volunteers were not easily accepted in the rather traditional Navy and that the Royal Flying Corps was completely new in 1914 and remained an area of individual effort. Thus, although there are poems written by members of both these branches of the military, which will be considered in the following chapter, their quantity (and to some degree also their quality) cannot rival that of poetry written in the trenches between the North Sea and the Alps. It seems as if the boredom of trench warfare rather than the exciting nature of war in the air or the long tradition of pride in the British Navy triggered the production of an immense corpus of the First World War poetry.

Some of the poems to be considered here originated in the Middle Eastern involvement of the British Army. They focus on warfare in the desert regions of Egypt, Mesopotamia and Palestine and describe a totally different sort of war experience from that of the poetry of the Western Front. The difficulties and problems these soldiers had to face were not the constant noise of battle and the mud in the trenches, but lack of water, the burning sun, sand storms, and enormous flies. The spread of diseases such as dysentery at Gallipoli, malaria in Mesopotamia due to the lack of mosquito nets, and cholera at Salonika was hardly surprising and often proved more deadly than the enemy. Furthermore, the war on the Eastern Front(s) as such was different from that in France and Belgium for various reasons: it was a war of movement, it was less dominated by modern military technology, and it left space for individual action. Other than on the Western Front, the cavalry still proved useful in the East, where war was fought over tens of thousands of square miles rather than a few yards. However, despite the different location and experience of warfare, some of the works about war in the East are linked in topic to the poetry of the Western Front by the fact that the poets ascribed a large portion of their fate to the incompetence of their leaders.

Before hostilities began there had been a frequent and fertile exchange between the European nations, especially between Britain and Germany, with regard to literary production and culture in general. However, this literary traffic between the belligerent nations ceased completely with the outbreak of the war, and artistic production had to turn back to its traditional national roots. It is here that the distinct cultural peculiarities of the nations involved become most obvious. Whereas the English literary responses to war were dominated by pastoral imagery in contrast to the mechanism of war, the influence of avantgardist literary ideas was much stronger on German war poetry. The limits of literary exchange posed by the war may also serve as an explanation for the focus on English war poetry as distinct from poetry written during and about the war by citizens of other belligerent nations due to a lack of artistic exchange.[38] Whereas modernist literary and artistic circles all over Europe had used militaristic language and imagery before the war – as Pound's *Sestina Altaforte* (1909) shows – or even embraced war as a purifying force, the actual outbreak of war in fact implied the end of the movement or at least a major change in modernism as such.

The former enemies of modernist artists, against whom they had mobilised in their works, had been the hostile press, conservative academies and the reactionary critics as representatives of a self-satisfied bourgeoisie. Their aggressions first found an outlet in the riots after the premiere of Stravinsky's ballet *Le Sacre du Printemps* in Paris, but, with the outbreak of war, Germany's modernists were added to this list. Whereas the various groups' struggle for recognition led them to direct their aggression against one another, war affected all of them. Many of the members of modernist circles either volunteered or followed mobilisation orders, or they migrated into neutral countries. War thus not only destroyed modernism's former optimism about the future of art and war as the cleansing instrument of culture, but, by being limited to national tradition as a result of the impossibility of European artistic exchange, modernism became associated with decadence and subversion, so that what began as a radical artistic movement now largely suffered from a turn towards conservatism.

As a result, the beginnings of the First World War literature are marked by a struggle between modernist and conservative approaches to poetry, of which the so-called Georgian poetry is exemplary. While strongly relying on traditional, mainly Romantic, imagery and form, the Georgians also challenged aesthetic ideals by using colloquial and plain language. Although concentrating on rural themes, especially the stylised South of England landscape, they expressed an awareness of a changing country. Instead of describing an ideal world, they were aware of the social realities of pre-war England such as poverty, ugliness and unrest. Many of the so-called 'war poets' were influenced by Georgian literary ideas, amongst them Rupert Brooke, Siegfried Sassoon, Wilfred Owen, Robert Graves, Ivor Gurney and Isaac Rosenberg. However, even though Georgian poetry remained the most dominant lyrical mode during the first two years of war, and its colloquialism prepared the way for the further development of war poetry, most of the soldier-poets began to feel its inadequate nature for expressing war experience and thus the need for adaptation. The longer the war lasted, the stronger became the need for a 'turn of speech',[39] which in itself established new groups of poets, such as that of Graves, Sassoon and Owen. Edward Thomas and Robert Frost equally shared ideas about language and literature, whereas Ivor Gurney and Isaac Rosenberg were both privates and thus linked by class and rank, rather than their poetry. On the other hand, Owen's, Thomas's and Rosenberg's poetry includes elements of French Symbolism and thus links to literary modernism on a much wider scale than, for example Sassoon's war poetry. All of these groups, however, were more or less strongly influenced by their admiration for Thomas Hardy, especially for his Boer War poems and his long epic *The Dynasts*. Accordingly, the poetry of the First World War creates new effects of voice, imagery, rhyme, assonance and rhythm through its combination of traditional forms with historical events.

As already pointed out above, the concentration of analysis on English war poetry has its reasons in the distinctiveness of the English poetical tradition as opposed to that of Germany or France. 'English' in this respect refers to poetry in the English language, as only few poets wrote in their native languages such as Scots or Welsh. Yet American, Australian or Irish poetry about the war will also be neglected, although these nations played a major part in the literary development as well as the outcome of the war. This exclusion is due to the late involvement in the war for the American forces (America only declared war on Germany on 6 April 1917), the almost total lack of irony in Australian and New Zealand[40] war poetry, and the different nature of Irish war poetry.

Although many Irish volunteered to fight in the British army, only few poets qualify as 'war poets' in the strict sense of the words. First of all,

Irish war poetry was primarily written by non-combatants. Second, the question of Irish home rule was inevitably linked with the First World War (as was the Scottish opposition to English dominance) and thus featured far more prominently in the literature of the time. It is the Easter Rising in April 1916 that takes the place of the battle of the Somme in the collective memory of Ireland, an indicator of the general problem Irish soldiers had to face: whereas the rebels of the rising entered history as heroes, those who died at the Somme are simply remembered as 'bloody British' soldiers. Fran Brearton thus ascribes the rarity of Irish war poetry to the lack of a frame of reference that was able to include both the Somme and Ulster unionism (Brearton, 2000, p. 35).[41] Additionally, for most Irish soldiers, the enemy was England, not Germany, against which they fought in poetry as well as in real life.[42]

Thus, although the British Army was a container for many different nationalities and cultures as a result of its imperial past, the focus of analysis will be on English war poetry in the most narrow sense. This implies restrictions not only in nationality, but also in time. As the aim of this book is to show the immediate effects of the war on the conception and utilisation of irony and satire among both combatant and civilian authors, I will not consider those poems on the subject of war composed in retrospect. They are no doubt valuable documents of war experience, but are not marked or triggered by a sense of immediate danger, a fear of one's possible death or censorship. Instead, after November 1918, the impression of war was modified and interpreted by individual memory (see Bond, 2002, p. 7ff.). This exclusion, however, does not affect those poems written during war-time but published at a later date due to the author's death, censorship or editorial debates. Equally included will be the poetry from the so-called English home front as giving proof of the wide-ranging effects of the war on the population, be it the loss of family members and friends, the devastation caused by air raids in the southern parts of England, or the impact of food shortages on the public support of war.

1.4   Outline of chapters

Whereas the romantic period is often characterised as the high phase of irony, after which its use declines, many literary scholars identified irony as a driving force of modern literature in general and therefore as a characteristic, if not the most dominant, feature of the poetry of the Great War: 'Irony which is one expression of sensibility at odds with its surroundings, became for many the rhetorical mode and mood' (Eksteins, 1989, p. 19).[43] As will be shown, its use cannot be limited to a certain stage of the war, a certain area of production, or a specific group of poets such as that of middle-class officers. Instead, it was taken up as a particular poetic means for the expression of viewpoint right from the beginning of hostilities by authors like Rupert Brooke or Charles Hamilton Sorley, and by both male and female authors at the front and at home. What changed during the course of the war was the extent of ironic language and imagery and its targets. As a traditional means of defence against experiences which one cannot help or change, the ironic mode later allowed war poets such as Owen, Sassoon, Rosenberg and their contemporaries[44] to deal with the sometimes absurd reality of trench warfare that haunted them even when they were not on duty. The use of satire provided another important channel for the expression of anger over war in general and certain incidents in particular, because it enabled the poets to combine ridicule and contempt as they 'seek relief from insupportable nerve-racking experiences (...) by satirizing them' (Bridgewater, 1987, p. 217).

In order to fully grasp the phenomenon, it will be useful to take a closer look at some of the most recent developments in the theory of irony and satire. Due to the character of the poems to be discussed, Chapter 2 will mainly focus on situational irony, whereas theories of verbal irony and its usefulness in satire will be necessary for the discussion of poems in Chapter 3. In Chapter 4, attention will then shift to Romantic ideas on irony as an 'irony of existence', finding their way into those war poems dealing with the physical consequences of war such as general exhaustion, wounds, and finally death.

The structure of this book, however, will not so much rely on theoretical reflections, but is largely conditioned by the content of the poems. The first of the following chapters will therefore deal with poems that, for various reasons, do not directly address the war and its related topics. While nature has always been a prominent topic in the English poetic tradition, reflections on flora and fauna in the context of war provide a counterpoint to the devastation and chaos of the trenches, as they convey ideas of peace and tranquillity, at least at first glance. Furthermore, the foreign countryside of the Ottoman Empire provided a huge variety of issues for both amusement and diversion which helped the soldiers to distract themselves from the immediate context of war. In order to preserve their lives, soldiers largely had to rely on their comrades, and it is thus not surprising that comradeship plays a major role in the poetry of the First World War. However, the second part of Chapter 2 will also reveal that this was a subject matter it was difficult to be ironic about. It may then seem to be a large step from nature and comradeship to military technology, but the poems that will follow in the next sections of this chapter are not so different from those on nature and the countryside, in that they represent a fascination for something which is initially perceived as detached from the issue of war. The poetry from both the air force and navy does not focus so much on the war in general but instead is marked by pride in being a member of a military elite. However, this does not prevent the mockery of defective aircraft, the weather or ridiculous orders. The final section of this chapter will then pay attention to poems concerned with military technology in the widest sense, be it the invention and usage of tanks, gas warfare or a variety of guns and other killing instruments as objects of simultaneous fascination and terror.

When asked about the functions of either irony or satire, most people readily reply that for them these two devices convey a critique and opposition towards the issue of conversation. And, although this is not irony's sole function, it certainly is a prominent one, as the poems discussed in Chapter 3 will show. The first section focuses on the critique of the establishment and its role in the proceedings of the war. Both State and Church were identified by many as responsible for the prolongation of war and its transformation from a war of defence into one of aggression. It is in this poetry of critique that the myth of the slaughter of youth found its distinct basis, as it ascribed the huge losses to the incompetence of the military and political leaders as well as the propaganda of the churches. Furthermore, many soldiers accused women of both ignorance and patriotic sentiments with regard to the war. Whether this is true and whether the female perception of war really differs from that of male authors will be the subject of the third section of this chapter. A last section will then be dedicated to the role of the press and the way it is represented and opposed in the poetry of the time as spreading lies about the real nature of war.

Life in the trenches, of course, provides another large area of war experience for which an adequate language had to be found. Chapter 4 will therefore deal with irony as a means of coping with the situation of death, dirt and constant danger at the front, together with either heat or rain and bad food. Irony will be shown to have a psychological function, among others, which is closely linked to the Romantics' reflections on irony. The first section of this chapter will deal with two aspects of war which highly influenced the morale of the troops, namely rations and the weather. However, it will be shown that food rationing also seriously threatened the public support of the war at home in its later stages. The following sections will then be dedicated to the terrible wounds created by exploding shells, stray splinters or sniper shots which required a large amount of self-irony from the wounded themselves and those nursing them behind the front lines; even more so did the mental disabilities immediately caused or triggered by the war experience. While physical wounds had long since been accepted as side effects of war, mental illnesses were still either ignored or punished as a sign of cowardice at the beginning of the First World War. This divergence of perception and its gradual change during the course of the war is once more reflected in the poetry of the time in which irony helped to come to terms with the unknown and undesirable effects of war on the human psyche. The third section of Chapter 4 will then concentrate on poetry dealing with the worst of all consequences of war, namely death in battle and the loss it implies for family and friends. For those who experienced – often multiple – bereavement it was only a short step towards the characterisation of war, and this one in particular, as a futile undertaking. The last section of this chapter will therefore deal with the various arguments of the poets against this waste of life, ranging from political dissatisfaction and the critique of military strategy to personal disgust.

After this close analysis of a variety of poems targeting a huge set of war-related issues, the conclusion will attempt to bind together the results of the poetical analysis in order to formulate a theory on the functioning of irony and satire in the context of war, based not so much on individual philosophical or linguistic approaches as on an overarching theory of communication as presented above. The idea of literature as a communicative process will help us to understand and appreciate the multitude of possibilities irony offered poets (and readers) to come to terms with the experience of the Great War as the first technological war in the history of mankind.

The existence of irony in war poetry cannot be proved, but its function in achieving a particular end requires detailed analysis. As a consequence, the poems chosen will be taken from a large corpus of ironical poems from the period of war and its immediate aftermath. Accordingly, the criteria for their selection will not be based on one particular definition of irony (which was shown as inappropriate) or on content or authorship. Instead, the chosen poems will be exemplary for their particular focus on the war and its related issues. By no means do they constitute a complete catalogue of 'ironic war poems', nor is all war poetry considered to be ironic by nature. The perception of irony remains highly subjective based on both linguistic and social skills for the detection of incongruities, attitudes and intentions, for 'irony isn't irony until it is interpreted as such – at least by the intending ironist, if not the intended receiver' (Hutcheon, 1994, p. 6). Of course, it would equally be possible to come up with a similarly large number of non-ironic war poems, each of which would be interesting in itself, yet this would go beyond the scope of this study.

2
Evasion

Some of the poetry written during the First World War seems, at least at first sight, to have little to do with the war itself, and the only link to the conflict is the time of composition. The attempt to look away from war has usually been characterised as an escape, especially with regard to two of the most famous modernist poets, W. B. Yeats and T. S. Eliot. In the case of these two, it was a deliberate choice not to speak of war. The Irishman Yeats was too old to get personally involved in the war and therefore refrained from commenting on the conflict for reasons given in *On Being Asked for a War Poem*: 'I think it better that in times like these/A poet's mouth be silent, for in truth/We have no gift to set a statesman right.' His only poem directly addressing the war, *An Irish Airman Foresees His Death*, is not so much concerned with expressing the author's attitude towards modern war, but rather favours an emotional approach. Consequently, when Yeats edited *The Oxford Book of Modern Verse* in 1935, he only included four poems about the war – W. Gibson's *Breakfast*, Grenfell's *Into Battle*, Read's *The End of War*, and Sassoon's *On Passing the New Menin Gate* – arguing in the introduction that 'passive suffering is not a theme for poetry'.

In the case of T. S. Eliot, the reason for his silence about the war might be found in his American citizenship, although he was a resident in England throughout the whole of the war. *Prufrock and Other Observations* was published in 1917 but contains no reference to the conflict. However, many of the poems of the volume date back to 1910–1912 and were thus written before the start of the war. Despite Eliot's deliberate choice not to mention the war, he seems to have been impressed by the war's effect on culture and by the spiritual stagnation that was the result of four years of excessive destruction on the continent. *The Waste Land*, published in 1922, gives proof of these reflections.

However, for many writers at the time it was impossible to dissociate themselves completely from the war as it inevitably provided the background for all creative processes. Their attempts to focus on other aspects of life can hardly qualify as 'escapes'. Instead, these 'flights of fancy' rather served to repress the war experience in order to preserve one's sanity by concentrating on home and nature as symbols of peace and security, as well as memories of happier times. Ivor Gurney, for instance, like many others tried to detach himself from the war but in the end failed to preserve his sanity against the haunting spirits. Nevertheless, one of his poems is indicative of his attempt: 'The dead land oppressed me; I turned my thoughts away,/And went where hill and meadow/Are shadowless and gay.' Again and again, the poet was dragged back to the battlefield from which he tried to escape mentally but in the end failed to do.

Thus images of war – the barbed wire, the shells, or the wounds – are entwined with descriptions of flowers, animals or landscape impressions, suggesting the coming of new hope and joy, as will be shown in the following section. A second section will then concentrate on the important role of comradeship in constituting insider and outsider circles. Irony in this respect will be revealed as a way of dissociating oneself from ignorant outsiders as well as the only appropriate means to deal with personal loss. By their partial nature, these brief flights from the reality of modern warfare also highlight and intensify the individual attitudes of the poets towards the conflict. The large variety of emotions dealt with by the individual will be revealed as yet another trigger for irony in the sections on war at sea and in the air and on military technology. All three of these areas of military existence evoked a myriad of reactions ranging from pride and fascination to cool detachment, complete rejection and questions of personal guilt. As a distancing mode preventing the ultimate commitment of the self (Thurley, 1974, pp. 10, 16) to the world of war, irony served as a shield for the human psyche, enabling moments of beauty in the midst of chaos and destruction, as many of the following poems will show.

2.1 Nature and countryside

2.1.1 The Romantic tradition

Nature as a possible theme of war poetry is by no means far-fetched, as the war was an open-air event and death at the front reduced man to his original state of dust, thus reuniting him with mother earth. However, there is more to the relationship between nature and war than the pastoral tradition of poetic language. The connection between war and nature in patriotic poetry published in national papers such as *The Times* during the early years of war initially helped to support the national cause by justifying the suffering as a necessary sacrifice for England and thus calling young men to join up. Both male and female poets saw England, especially its southern parts, as being worthy of sacrifice. Apart from Rupert Brooke's famous war sonnets and other popular poems by various male writers, Constance Ada Renshaw's poem *The Lure of England* and Lily Marcus's *In the Trenches* particularly stress this aspect by focusing on the beauty of the countryside as a healing contrast to the destruction wrought by war. Yet, at the same time, this connection provided a means of measuring the disastrous results of war for nature and the population alike. Additionally, nature served as a psychological refuge and a source of hope. One means of preventing war from dominating one's thinking was to focus more strongly than ever before on an ideal British model world with flowers, fields, sheep, birds, gardens, and valleys as opposed to the destroyed forests and upturned fields of France and Belgium. Especially in Blunden's and Gurney's poems the imaginary flight into pastoral idylls functions as implicit critique on the war or as an attempt to handle its consequences for the human psyche (Löschnigg, 1994, p. 31).[1] A similar effort can be traced in Rosenberg's work which asserts the 'humane spirit against the power of war' (Graham, 1984, p. 136).

England's rural past and the countryside of southern England had already been a frequent subject for the Romantics as a stabilising or even curative power for the individual troubled by industrialisation and progress. The English naturalists, however, had introduced a second viewpoint, namely nature as an indifferent or even hostile force in opposition to mankind. While many of the Georgians, in the search for a distinctly English identity, had concentrated on the Romantic heritage in order to find in nature a frequent source for the myth of a prewar golden age, Georgian diction was later rejected as inappropriate in the context of modern war in which artificial trees were positioned between natural dead trees as a hiding place for snipers. A sign of life thus became a symbol of death, even though the First World War did not alter the basic language of national representation. However, it led to the adaptation of romantic imagery to its circumstances.[2] The poets' aim was to place their new experiences and visual impressions in the context of the familiar as a means of both achieving reassurance and expressing bewilderment.

The general attentiveness to nature reflects the strong influence of Romanticism on popular thinking. The landscape of Flanders and

Picardy enabled the soldiers to draw parallels with home. Larks and nightingales were as common in England as they were near the Western Front, and they soon became associated with morning and evening stand-tos. Similar to birds, flowers also became part of the symbolism of the war. It was the colour red of roses and poppies that reminded soldiers and poets of the blood of their comrades. At the same time, the English rose stood for a specific form of female beauty[3] and as such linked the soldiers at the front with their loved ones at home. In other areas of war, the comparison of landscape and nature with England caused equally strong emotions. In Palestine, Mesopotamia and Egypt, the historical significance of the sites engendered deep awe, while at the same time the desert was often perceived as more life-threatening than any human enemy.

There were, however, some ironical twists resulting from war. While spring was the most loved season in England, it was also the time for the most fatal offensives at the Western Front. The same holds for the beauty of sunrise and sunset, usually the time of attacks. The frequent portrayals of the shifting colour of the sky have their origin in the fact that the trenches only allowed an upward gaze as in Sassoon's *The Redeemer:* 'And dawn a watching of the windowed sky' or Manning's *The Trenches:* 'And the sky, seen as from a well'. Furthermore, the dead remained on the surface whereas the living had to shelter underneath in holes hardly suitable as housing for human beings. It is the ironic conjunction of aesthetically appealing elements with the anxieties and horrors of war that finally transforms traditional poetic techniques. All of these ambivalent images provide a source for the concept of situational irony that is used by the authors of the poems to be discussed in the following pages. It is therefore necessary to briefly reflect upon this particular form of irony.

Although irony has always been used in various forms in literature, it is not primarily a literary term, but one of philosophical origin. Aristotle in his *Nicomachian Ethics* gave the first definition of irony as a particular way of thinking. His prime example, of course, was Socrates, whose whole lifestyle was described as ironic. Right from the start irony was thus more than simply a rhetorical means, as we know it today from the reflections of Quintilian or Cicero. This diversity was then further elaborated upon during the history of irony in which the term was applied to both literary and ontological forms. The problem that arises out of this multiplicity is that even today there is no single form of analysis that is able to cover all aspects of the phenomenon. In general, linguistics and psycho-linguistics are occupied with what Muecke (1969) and others call 'verbal' irony, whereas all other forms of irony are mainly investigated by philosophy, psychology, sociology, or even history.

The easiest way to distinguish between the two forms of irony is by comparing the following two sentences: 'He is being ironical' and 'It is ironic that ...'. Some readers might now think of Alanis Morissette's famous song *Ironic*. However, this cannot serve as an illustrative example here as she reports incidents which are merely coincidental, rather than ironic, and therefore lead to one of the most frequent confusions of terms. Yet 'a traffic jam when you're already late' might well become ironic if the speaker were late for a meeting concerned with the avoidance of traffic jams. The example is thus indicative of the important role of the context with regard to the interpretation of an utterance as ironic. Whereas 'he is being ironical' implies a human subject, an ironist, 'it is ironic that' refers to a state of affairs. The result of this absence of the ironist is the semi-personification of fate, or, in the case of the war poets, war itself. This implies that the victim of the irony, i.e. the soldier enduring his fate, remains ignorant of what is already predestined. If he survives, he is not necessarily distinct from the observer, the poet, who only interprets a situation to be ironic in retrospect.

The general problem in literature now is that the poet might be an ironist being ironical by showing something ironic happening. A combination of both verbal and situational irony in literary texts is thus not unusual. Indeed, they often work together in order to increase the ironic effect. However, although both verbal and situational irony was already prominent by the time of Socrates, neither kind was called irony for a long time. Even today secondary literature often talks about dark humour, ridicule or mockery when referring to the phenomenon. In order to ease a distinction of the two forms, situational irony in literature can furthermore be described as impersonal. In most instances, the ironist is absent as a person, and we only have his presentation of what he perceives as an ironical situation. This form of irony is therefore sometimes also called dramatised irony because of the ironist's presentation of ironic situations or events.

All forms of irony are determined by the context in which they occur, and they strongly rely on an incongruency recognised by both user and perceiver as constituting a field of ironic stress (Allemann, 1970, p. 34) on the basis of common knowledge. In literature, this incongruency can be established on several levels: (1) it can be based on the words used. The incongruency would then be purely verbal; (2) the words used may not fit into the context in which they are used, which would imply a mixture of situational and verbal irony; or (3) the fictitious situation itself might contain oppositional or incongruent elements with regard to reality. This would best be qualified as situational irony, but one embedded in a literary context.[4] It is the last two forms that are of interest in this chapter concerning the strategies of evasion of many poets.

In their majority these ironic forms are ironies of gaps: by leaving out the action of war and instead concentrating on the essentials of human life (environment, basic needs, friendship, emotions) the poetry becomes charged with additional significance. What is describable begins to serve as a comment on the indescribable horrors of modern war by way of the perceiver. The irony as such is not inherent in a particular remark or situation, but it is the assumed general knowledge of the reader that leads to its discovery in a mutual understanding with the speaker. There cannot be situational irony without an observer who is able to perceive it. Based on this mutual understanding between poet and reader, irony reveals the absurdity of the war while strongly emphasising the meaningful elements of life by asking existential questions. Speculations on life and death, renewal, continuity, destruction and decay thus feature prominently in the following poems.

In order to prevent despair resulting more than once in madness or even suicide, as for instance in Sassoon's *Suicide in the Trenches*, many poets would subscribe to the idea that 'One must separate oneself from a world which is dead, illusory, unmanageable, contradictory, or absurd. But unless one commits suicide, one must also accept it. Accept it therefore ironically' (Muecke, 1969, p. 235). The resulting use of irony by many poets was not without parallel in real life, in which lovely summer nights were predestined for air raids and in which every autumn brought a harvest of casualties rather than crops. The following examples will reflect the various possibilities of combining war and nature to create an ironic potential.

For Edmund Blunden nature and countryside usually provide consolation and a way of escaping the war. However, in *Zero* (*Come on, my Lucky Lads*) he seems to negate this possibility altogether. Colourful sunrise is combined with the pyrotechnical effects of artillery fire during an attack. The poem's title *Zero* is indicative here as it refers to the 'zero hour' in military jargon. The result is a peculiar combination of awakening and death, a clash of images which is mainly responsible for the ironic effect of the poem.

Nature equally provides the material for an ironic reversal of romantic imagery in Owen's poem *Spring Offensive*. Man is still bonded to nature, but it is a violent, rather than a peaceful and harmonious, bond. The title of this longer poem is already charged with paradox. As a time of growth and renewal, spring suggests innocence, maybe even eroticism, to which the military offensive provides a stark contrast. The poem is loosely based on the assault at Savy Wood in March 1917 which preceded Owen's shellshock. It begins with an accurate description of facts, then shifts to static watching in the next stanza, and later makes a transition from the Arcadian atmosphere of shelter back to the horror of an infantry attack. Contrary to Owen's other works, however, it is difficult to locate the setting of the poem in the First World War as the only markers can be found in the title and the soldiers' 'pack-loads'. Even the presence of a human enemy in the poem can only be deduced from the word 'bullet' marking the climax of the poem. Throughout the poem the men seem to fight the surrounding natural world rather than the Germans, as Hipp (2002, p. 41) suggests: 'The first line of the poem establishes the opposition that the poem as a whole will explore. The men are "halted against the shade of a last hill." The use of the word "against" posits the conflict between the men who exist within a natural landscape and the landscape itself which will act against their actions.' The hostile world of the trenches as opposed to peacetime nature is further marked by the syntactical isolation of the word 'exposed'. As a formal as well as syntactical caesura, the participle reveals the soldier's transition from the quiet resting place, as described up to stanza 5, into the hostile world of the war marked by the explosion of shells. 'Nature and her beauties are hardly more than ironic facts in this paradoxical interlude of relaxation before certain nightmare; it is not anthropomorphism, but the heightened awareness of the condemned...' (Lane, 1972, p. 138). In this life-threatening environment, however, the soldier takes an active part as killer and as victim who 'leaps' over the flying bullets, an action the young veteran in *Disabled* failed to achieve.

As in many other nature-centred poems of the First World War, the sky and the grass take on an important role in *Spring Offensive* (ll. 11f.). The image of the storm is usually used to convey war's destructive potential,[5] or the sky above the fighting men is blank and taciturn. In its mystery, it refuses to give an answer to the soldiers' questions concerning themselves and God. Here, the flashing sky and the long grass are symbolic of summer but at the same time evoke imminent danger with the enemy lying just a few yards away over the ridge of grass. The grass thus takes on the additional connotation of a killing blade. As a consequence, both images become signs of destruction and violence as the poem progresses. This dichotomy of nature as both a redemptive and a destructive force is further elaborated upon in lines 13–31 of the poem. The buttercups colour the men's boots as they march along and the brambles cling to their trousers as if to hold them back. However, as the soldiers progress, the sky burns 'with fury against them' (l. 30) a moment later and the earth gratefully receives their blood. 'Nature is now unquestionably in its role as the men's enemy; its "fury" suggests an anger at the actions of the soldiers and punishment for their having disobeyed the implicit "command" not to have attacked' (Hipp, 2002, p. 42). In its ironic demystification of nature, the poem comes close to Charles Hamilton Sorley's earlier poem *All the Hills and Vales Along*, especially its penultimate stanza.

Other authors focused on daily life in the trenches which was not dominated by action but rather followed a fixed routine of stand-tos, cleaning of arms, sleeping, hunting vermin or simply waiting for the next attack. To pass the time, hunting rats turned into a favourite sport among soldiers at the Western Front and it is in this context that Isaac Rosenberg's poem *Break of day in the Trenches* can be situated. Rats were feared because they were disfiguring corpses by eating their eyes and livers. Furthermore, they spread infection and contaminated food. Yet hunting them was a futile business as one healthy rat couple could produce up to 900 offspring per year. Furthermore, they were ascribed prophetic qualities and many veterans swore that rats sensed the coming of heavy shell-fire and thus disappeared from view before the start of attacks. However, the speaker in Rosenberg's poem does not shoot the rat, but instead enters into an imaginative conversation with it. The focus on natural phenomena like the rat or a blossoming flower, however, reinforces the idea of the absurdity of war.

The first version of the poem was probably completed by the end of July 1916 but it was not until December that the poem first appeared in the Chicago journal *Poetry*. Its dialecticism might have been influenced by John Donne's poetry as the basic structure of the poem recalls that of *The Flea*: the soldier in the trench is juxtaposed between two modest natural objects, the rat and the poppy. The structure of the poem is subdued in favour of the imagination of the speaker pondering over the general nature of mankind and his own fate in particular. As such, Rosenberg's 'subject matter at last lends itself to his somewhat chaotic method of composition, where image is hurled upon image, the rhythms are highly irregular and form is not of prime importance' (Wilson, 1975, p. 211).

The pastoral background of the poem is furthermore reinforced by Rosenberg's choice of the aubade as the form of the poem. Accordingly, the poem begins quietly by mirroring the stillness of an ordinary morning in the trenches shortly before sunrise. Both the speaker and the reader are left unsure as to what the coming dawn will bring, even if the morning begins like so many others before ('the same old druid time as ever'). The overall impression is one of resignation to the dangers of the coming day. But the general tranquillity of slowly waking up is interrupted by the startled movement of the rat involving a shift of focus, as does the poppy at the end of the poem.

The rat seems to be an unusual poetic subject, but an even more unusual addressee. However, during war, the rat was a chance companion of the soldier with whom he shared his living space. Traditionally rats were seen to be demonic creatures (see, for example, Fussell, 1975, pp. 251–253), but this one in particular appears less noisome than expected and rather charming, sophisticated and well-travelled. The speaker even seems to prefer the company of the rat rather than talking to his fellow soldiers. This peculiar preference possibly has its origins in the author's own experiences among his comrades. Rosenberg himself was a Jew from a rather poor immigrant family – and maybe as such used to rats in ordinary life – while at the same time his family had always been part of the London artistic and intellectual community. His father was a strong pacifist and member of the Workers' Friend Club in Jubilee Street, which was based on libertarian principles of access to knowledge for all. Before enlisting for financial reasons, Isaac Rosenberg had been on the way to becoming a painter. Despite his background, he had succeeded in entering the Slade School of Art, London, due to two wealthy benefactresses. Rosenberg's religious and artistic background, as well as his lack of patriotic feelings, seems to have set the author apart from his fellow privates, as the author's letters and diaries reveal more than once.[6]

The general tone of the poem is that of the sardonic outsider. The rat itself rises above both the ideological barriers and the physical obstacles of human beings and is therefore characterised as both 'droll'/'queer' and 'sardonic'. By a reversal of roles, the rat even serves as a negative foil to the soldiers and reveals war's absurdity. Normally it is man who ponders over animals and nature, now the rat wonders about the unnatural terror of mankind. And in its grin is reflected the mockery of man's fate as victim and potential killer. The rat even becomes a sort of silent objective judge of mankind. Rosenberg was well aware of this double role of the soldier as he once described himself as a man who 'killed with slaughter mad' (Rosenberg, 1962, p. 78).

Rats usually hide in holes to escape dangers, but in times of war it is the soldier who has to hide in trenches. If he dared stick his head out too high, he would inevitably be shot, whereas the rat is able to move freely among the various fronts. According to Harold Bloom 'the rat's function is to emphasize by his very freedom the arbitrary separation between the two front lines, and by his low, ugly vitality to point up the fact of human death' (Bloom, 2002, p. 68. See also Löschnigg, 1994, p. 43). It is one of the absurdities of war that a measly rat is able to transgress boundaries at the face of which man fails. And furthermore: 'There is something ironic, too, in the idea that the two enemies – German and English – will be temporarily linked by their common acceptance of this measly rat' (Bloom, 2002, p. 75). War is reduced *ad absurdum* with the help of this imaginative conversation between rat and man strongly relying on situational irony (Simpson, 1990, p. 132).

With the verdict 'they would shoot you…' the poet returns to ordinary life again. This sentence with its many 'u' sounds echoing one another brings us back to the reality of trench life in which the rats – rather than the Germans on the other side of the trench – were the real enemies of the soldiers, spreading diseases, feeding on the dead and disturbing one's sleep. The question remains who 'they' are: in the context of Rosenberg's Judaism the righteous gentiles? In the case of war some soldier conspirators? Or the military leaders and politicians? While rats were usually shot by the soldiers for reasons mentioned above, the speaker of the poem gives us another reason for the rat's death sentence: its 'cosmopolitan sympathies'. In a context where it was strongly forbidden to meet the supposed enemy or even to enter into conversation with him the rat commits a serious crime. The word 'cosmopolitan' used here is richer in connotation than 'national' or 'allied' and it seems that the speaker, too, shares these sympathies and might just as quickly be shot down. 'In this perilous instant, rat, poet and poem take their lives into their own hands: this instant when the wakeful poet/ soldier dissociates himself (by virtue of his sympathies) from the company of haughty athletes, of either side, and soliloquies (…) in front of a scampering unidealistic rat – the only being around in the breaking dawn alive and sympathetic enough to 'share' his tremulous humanity. The irony of this could hardly be more heartrending' (Simpson, 1990, p. 132).

The rat will 'do the same' to all enemies at the front, a fact which exposes the distinction between enemy and ally or between nationalities to be artificial. In the rat's eyes these differences do not exist and are therefore absurd. As the conversation is imaginative, however, the rat becomes the objectification of the soldier's mood and thoughts. As in other poems of the time, as for instance Owen's *Anthem for Doomed Youth* in which men are like cattle, or Robert Nichol's *Noon*, the distinction between man and animal becomes blurred at the front; only the soldiers are less adjusted to life under the open sky than animals are.[7] It is one of the ironies of war that the rat has a greater chance of survival than the young athletes at the height of their youth, as is underlined in lines 14 and 15 of the poem.

In line 13, the poet uses the idea of sleep to suggest the possibility of peace. At the same time the reader knows that the 'sleeping green between' will soon be awake. As a euphemism for No-Man's Land it evokes the horror of exploding shells making sleep nearly impossible. A similar ironic device is the poppy. It grows on the parapet over which the soldiers climb to meet the enemy during an attack and would, in this case, be trampled down at once. By pulling it out and sticking it behind his ear, the speaker seems to save the flower from this fate. However, in doing so he already triggers the flower's dying process. The poppy is not safe at all, even without the occurrence of an attack. Like the flower, the soldier is pulled from the soil, separated from family and friends and located in a life-threatening environment. Just like the flower, he will soon turn into dust.

In popular myth poppies were thought to feed off the blood of the dead ('poppies whose roots are in man's veins'), turning their petals red. Additionally, poppies are short-lived flowers and thus mirror the life of the soldier at the front whose life expectancy during an attack was only a few minutes. The dust that covers the poppy recalls the literal dust of the hot summer of 1916 while at the same time it is the dust into which all men will turn after death according to the biblical image of Genesis. Furthermore, 'a little white' sounds very similar to 'only a little while (and then I'll be dead)'. The flower will soon be totally white as its blood runs out of it, just as it will run out of the soldier. 'Rosenberg announces his own impending death in these lines as clearly as if he had arranged to be shot in front of us' (Stephen, 1996, p. 217). Thus the most ironic word in the poem is the word *safe* in the penultimate line. In their fate, man and nature are inevitably bound together in the poem.

The effect of Rosenberg's poetry in large parts relies on his handling of nature images. As the previous example has shown, the poet focuses on details to highlight specific aspects of the war instead of elaborately describing landscapes. One of Rosenberg's first attempts at this technique originated in South Africa, *On Receiving News of the War*, in 1914. War in this poem is both a linguistic fact and part of nature symbolically expressed in the word 'snow'. As Kedzierska (1995, p. 22) points out, 'winter itself becomes metamorphosed' into a 'god-like ruler of the world' when it attacks in the middle of the hot summer of 1914.

While the poem is free of the initial euphoria expressed in many other poetic responses at the beginning of the war, its irony is not one of protest. It rather patiently accepts what is to come as a natural course of events which has to be endured, even though it might be ghastly.

In the following two poems, *Louse Hunting* and *Returning, we hear the larks* the poet again uses similar devices of fragmentariness by reducing the world of the trenches to its non-human inhabitants. These aspects distilled from nature function as a source for his irony. In *Returning, we hear the larks,* this irony is based on the dominant sound of birdsong in the midst of devastation and death. The sparse descriptions and the frequent enjambments create a fearful expectancy of danger. Suddenly a change occurs. However, this time it is not a flying shell or the explosion of a mine, but the sound of a bird that 'drops' into the silence and releases both soldier and reader from their heightened awareness. The poem represents one of the rare instances in Rosenberg's work where nature is represented as a friendly entity, represented by the Shelleyan lark.[8] However, the general impression is one of arbitrariness – nature as well as the outcome of every new day at war is unpredictable. Larks featured prominently in English poetry from Shakespeare onwards, suggesting the coming of a new day with new hope. In Rosenberg's poem, however, the bird serves as symbol for the fragility of the peacefulness that might just as well turn into horror again. The emotional response of the soldiers to the song of the lark creates the impression of safety which daily experience teaches them to be an illusion. 'Rosenberg can infuriate by not seeming to know what he is writing about; at times he can convert that and make himself the spokesman for all the ironies of war that can never be explained' (Stephen, 1996, p. 219). Sassoon's *Thrushes* even reverts this irony into bleak sarcasm as his bird rises over a field of corpses.

Instead of focusing on the misery of the men, *Louse Hunting* portrays their futile attempts to kill lice in a quasi-ritual dance around the fire. 'Without the typical orchestration of guns and political character, war emerges as a private affair of the hunters who in the course of their struggle become themselves hunted' (Kedzierska, 1995, p. 30). It is the grotesqueness of the hunters' futile battle against inhuman nature that brings home Rosenberg's critique of the war. As in many other poems, the vermin are presented as the real enemy of the troops on both sides of the trenches as they were spreading trench fever and fighting against them was as ridiculous as the whole war. At the same time, the 'lice, as Rosenberg sees them, are a comic definition of man's smallness because of the scale of the soldier's battle against them' (Graham, 1984, p. 150).

As such they also provide the subject of another of Rosenberg's poems, *The Immortals*, a poem which plays with a reversal of dimensions and perspectives on the verbal level. There is a general incongruency between the violent language of warfare and the insignificance of the enemy which increases the comic success of the poem. In stanza 2 'red', for instance, suggests the blood of the enemy but it is the blood the louse has sucked out of the members of the speaker's own army. Again, war is not mentioned at all and the reader is left in the dark regarding the nature of the enemy. To explain the verbal irony here speech act theoreticians would argue that the poem flouts the maxims of both coherence and relevance as set up in Grice's cooperative principle. Thus the traditional communication model has to be extended to two levels here: on the superficial level someone is talking about killing lice, on the underlying level the topic is war. In order to understand the content of the poem and perceive the irony, it is necessary for the reader to be able to distinguish between these levels on the basis of his or her background knowledge about the living conditions in the trenches of the Western Front during the First World War.

Throughout the poem, the speaker talks about a threatening and dangerous opponent, but only in the last line is the enemy identified as a tiny louse which serves as a symbol for the absurdity of warfare in general. While the Germans are reduced to artificial and therefore less frightening opponents, the natural enemy, the louse, rises to supernatural power in the description of the speaker. It is an immortal Devil from whom nobody can escape. Instead of saving their energy for the next attack, the soldiers constantly fight against the daily terror in their own trenches which takes the form of little insects and other vermin. It is only lice which the soldier feels a desire to murder, and thus the ideas of the militarists are mocked by experience. Graham (1982, p. 152) argues accordingly: 'For the central myth of "the enemy" we have lice, for the belief in the effectiveness of aggression we have a fury that is unending and impotent; for the celebration of the joy of killing we have the tormenting nightmares of slaughter. A wisdom has been gained but it is not the discovery of glory or nobility. It is the mastery of disgust.' Again, this can be identified as a typical instance of situational irony for the purpose of targeting war in general. The mystification of the louse thus serves to demystify the war.

However, although the irony becomes rather overt in the context of Rosenberg's other war-related works, a non-ironic interpretation of the poem might also be possible in retrospect. The title of the poem, *The Immortals*, may equally refer to the long-lived war memories of the

First World War veterans. Psychological studies of neurasthenia have revealed that even after the end of the war many of the soldiers continued the killing in their minds. Possible misinterpretation results from the reader being determined by the historical context of communication and background knowledge, and is augmented by the violation of the rules of ordinary conversation, which increases the readers' difficulties in understanding the text.

The experience of vermin was by no means limited to the Western Front, nor was the use of irony in order to deal with it. The overt irony of H. W. Berry's *Somewhere East of Suez* in this respect is surprisingly similar to that of the above poems by Rosenberg, although the poetic quality of the poem is no match for Rosenberg. Again, war provides the reason for the speaker's situation but is not the foremost topic of the poem. Indeed, the soldier is plagued by mosquitoes and sand-flies rather than the enemy, in this case the Turks. As in Rosenberg's poem, nature in the proper sense of the phrase gets the best of man, his blood. By sucking him dry and taking his most valuable essence, the insect is portrayed on the same level as the human 'profiteers'. They are neither better, nor worse. In both cases, resistance is futile as the sheer quantity of 'the enemy' is against the soldiers. For effect, the poem successfully combines biblical imagery with war slang, such as when the slain mosquito 'goes West' (l. 24) in order to create a peculiar synthesis of humour, anger and curse. As such, the poem shows that it was not the experience of trench warfare at the Western Front that led to the creation of a certain kind of 'ironic discourse', but that irony as a psychological means of dealing with the various war-related conditions and situations was far more widespread. It rather seems to have been part of a cultural system that was available to all classes in all areas of war and independent of poetic circles.

While the abovementioned poems represent the supremacy of nature over mankind, the role of earth is a different one in *Dead Man's Dump*. Especially its third stanza portrays earth as a jealous and hungry monster. The deaths of the soldiers seem to be part of a larger plan. In the end, enemy and friend lie identically together (see also Owen's *Strange Meeting*), with bones crushed by the limber rolling over them as if they were nothing more than dry branches randomly spread in the countryside. Even the single grave, preserving at least some kind of honour in an intact setting, is exchanged for a garbage heap of corpses in times of war. 'The earth that ought to have been (as in pastoral) a consoling home for the living and a regenerative grave for the dead had become instead a grave for the living and a home for the dead' (Gilbert, 1999, p. 184). However, despite this bleak vision of the relationship between nature and mankind, in *Spring 1916* nature still seems to possess a regenerative potential for Rosenberg as it did for the Romantics. Flowers and bushes blossom every year although there are only few men left to appreciate the sight. On the other hand, this image of returning spring in the midst of destruction underlines nature's independence from all human affairs.

2.1.2 Rural life

While the above poems largely drew their ironic potential from both the continuation and reversal of romantic traditions, another option was to set (fictional) English rural idylls in sharp opposition to the world of war or to present war as an intruder into French/Belgian agriculture, as does Sassoon in the first stanza of *Battalion Relief*: with its double-edged title, the author already positions the poem in an ironic discourse in which the soldiers are going to relieve the troops, but at the same time will experience the opposite of relief once they arrive at the front line. The naïve talk of the recruit, as well as the impressions of summer in Flanders, furthermore provides a sharp contrast to the seriousness of the situation. Thus the phrase 'harvest soon,/up in the line' (l. 5f.) suggests more to the informed reader than just bringing in the crops. It will also be the time of bringing back the dead, cut like crops fully ripe at the height of their youth. When the poem was written in July 1918, it was still not clear who would win the war and when it would be over, but it was obvious that it would cost many more lives even if it were 'done/by Christmas-Day' (l. 6f.).

Indicative of the opposition of peaceful England to the world of war is the work of Edward Thomas. For a long time he had not been considered a real 'war poet' as most of his poetry was written in England before he went on active service in France. Robert Frost, however, recognised the subject of war in Thomas's poetry at a very early stage: 'Because all his poetry was written after the outbreak of war, it is all, in an important sense, war poetry. Behind every line, whether mentioned or not, lies imminent danger and disruption.'[9] When the war broke out, Thomas was already 36 years old and as such exempt from conscription when it was introduced in 1916. Nevertheless, he enlisted in 1915 as a private[10] and was commissioned as a second lieutenant a year later. Unfortunately he was killed after only three months of active service in France at Arras on 9 April 1917. Most scholars have argued that the war provided a release for Thomas in the sense that it freed him from his private troubles. Without the war, he probably would have committed suicide as he had been suffering from depression for a long time before the war. His poetry suggests that he actively sought death or at least oblivion in the war. In addition to these private reasons for enlistment, his motives were not patriotic in a traditional sense, but he rather felt a deep love for English culture and the southern countryside (similarly to Rupert Brooke) which he was aiming to protect. Although his poem *This is No Case of Petty Right or Wrong* ends with an expression of hatred for England's 'foes', Thomas does not share the notion of British superiority as spread in nationalist propaganda.

Thomas was often accused of indifference and complacency for his marginalisation of war and the absence of political themes in his poetry, but his contribution is a different one. By showing the (often indirect) effects of war on the agricultural or natural cycle, his poems contain an imminent critique of war as destructive, even without explicitly mentioning it. His poem *February Afternoon* represents the combination of nature, mythology and war typical for Thomas's art. At the same time the poem challenges Rupert Brooke's sonnet *Now, God be thanked who has matched us with His hour* in both structure and content. By the presentation of war as monotonous, the sense of resignation becomes ever stronger in the poem until it culminates in the accusation of God as blind and detached. His eco-centric vision of the world attributes an equal, rather than a superior, position to humanity with regard to nature.[11] Consequently, Thomas's conception of England is not based on its population or civilisation, but rather on its countryside and the poetry that it inspires.

Instead of commenting on the war by focusing on the action at the front, Thomas's most famous poem *As the Team's Head-Brass* centres on the effects of war on rural life at home. In doing so, however, he does not follow the pastoral traditions of his time. Thomas's portrayal of rural England is never idyllic or idealised, but rather a neutral one as it shows the hard work farming implies. This aspect is shared by the ironic poems of Rose Macauley, published under the collective title *On the Land*, in which the author deals with her experience as a land-girl. These poems reveal that 'farming was [only] romantic for those who had no real knowledge of it' (Khan, 1988, p. 97).

In *As the Team's head-brass* the speaker of the poem enters a conversation with a ploughman about life during war-time. Yet this conversation between the two is highly ironic, as speculations about losing a limb in a light-hearted tone are opposed by the bleak reality of the death of the farmer's friend. At the same time, this death seems to become insignificant in the context of nature's routine, represented by the blizzard and the farmer's seasonal work, contrasting sharply with death at the front. At the same time, the poet uses ambiguous vocabulary in the last two lines of the poem, referring to the ploughman's work as well as the soldiers in France. While 'crumble', 'topple over' and 'stumbling' in the context of farming refer to means of increasing the fertility of the soil, they evoke death in the context of war. The plough turns up the soil as do shells and grenades. However, the overall statement of the poem is one of neutrality rather than critique – it 'denies the concept of war as making a monumental change'.[12]

Everything that happens is presented as having consequences, for better or worse. If the young man had stayed at home, the broken tree would have been removed, but at the same time this would have prevented the conversation from taking place, and consequently the poem probably would never have been written. The poem clearly states that human beings are denied insight into the whole picture and as a result it is not up to them to judge the war. Life and death are both part of the natural cycle and even this war of all wars cannot destroy this routine. There would always be lovers in the wood, just as there would always be farmers cultivating the land. The irony of the poem therefore does not serve the purpose of criticising the war, or at least the conditions under which the soldiers were spending their lives, as it does in some of Rosenberg's and Owen's poems. 'For Thomas, the war was evidently not political or moral; and he could not have done justice to it if it were' (Pikoulis, 1987, p. 127).

Both Edmund Blunden and Wilfrid Gibson used a similar technique of drawing parallel pictures of rural life at home and the reality of life at the front. But while Blunden focuses on specific natural details, showing his love for the English countryside, Gibson additionally combines his front-line descriptions with colloquial language and satire, as can be seen in *The Question*. Although the speaker's thoughts dwell on a rural world back at home while he himself is away at war, his musings are by no means consoling. Before he left for the front, an old cow of his had fallen sick, and so he had to leave it in the care of a man called Dick. Even when he is confronted with the enemy, the idea that he does not know the fate of the cow haunts him, just as the war will haunt him back at home should he survive it. The death of the cow at the same time sheds light on the millions of deaths at the front which often remained unknown. Especially the last stanza is heavily charged with irony when the speaker talks about his 'lucky chance of being shot' as if this were a minor incident compared with the death of the old cow. The life of man is no longer superior to that of farm animals, but they share the same fate for different causes. And, while the cow fell sick because it was old, the soldier might never reach old age himself.

While nearly all of the poems discussed above perceive nature as either a place of refuge from the war, or in neutral terms as a parallel existence even in shell-cratered France and Belgium, the negative aspects of nature should not be forgotten. For those fighting on the Western Front as well as in the East, it was the weather that caused major problems. In Palestine, Mesopotamia, Egypt and Turkey, however, it was the heat and the resulting lack of water, whereas in France and Belgium too much water soaked the ground and turned it into knee-deep mud. In winter, the cold equally caused all sorts of illnesses from trench foot to pneumonia. Considering these facts, it is not surprising that country life largely lost its idyllic connotations but became suitable for ironic reversals when faced with the realities of war.

2.1.3   Anti-landscapes

These ironic reversals, however, were by no means limited to selected elements from natural life such as plants, animals, farming or the various times of the day. When extended to the soldiers' environment in its entirety, irony transformed it into the unknown, the unbelievable, the surreal. This otherness finds its most striking example in Owen's *Strange Meeting*, set in a hellish netherworld. The poem's ghostly tone largely results from Owen's extensive use of half-rhyme and an archaic diction. This diction especially clashes ironically with the image of war Owen wants to portray.[13]

Whereas 'chariot-wheels' and 'citadels' remind the reader of the Roman Empire or the Middle Ages with glorious knights and honest man-to-man battles, modern war rather resembles hell in both noise and sound. The reader is drawn into the speaker's dream-world, anticipating Eliot's *Waste Land*, during the first twelve lines of the poem only to learn that both protagonists are dead and all hope is thwarted. However, death is gradually presented in positive terms as the only possible release from suffering. While Geoffrey Thurley argues in *The Ironic Harvest* (1974) that all great literature must commit itself fully to its subject, and that no ironic vision can muster that commitment, I would argue that this is exactly the purpose of irony, to avoid total commitment to preserve one's sanity in the hellish world of modern war.

In the anti-world of war, the laws of nature are reversed and even the sun loses its creative power, as Owen's *Futility* demonstrates. The order 'move him into the sun' establishes the nature theme of stanza 1, which is then revealed as a futile and even childish idea in stanza 2. Significantly, the poem ends with a question mark, as a final answer to the speaker's questions cannot be provided. These questions in the last stanza also show the importance of syntax as they raise awareness, reproach and protest. The irony of the poem rests on the notion of the sun as a major element of the creation process undone by war. We are thus dealing with what I would like to call 'existential' irony, an irony that is no longer limited to pointing out situational absurdities, but affects mankind as a whole. With the sun failing to wake up the speaker's dead friend, any harmony of nature and humanity is inevitably destroyed by war. Life cannot be restored the way it is restored in the natural cycle of seasons. The subtle rhyme scheme of the poem reflects this ironical situation. It is marked by a mixture of true and half-rhymes paired with consonant clusters. Additionally the rhythm and simplicity of diction reinforce the effect of despair and futility. In the second stanza the vowels lengthen and the rhythm is slowed down. However, despair is not the final tone. The poem rather ends with an outcry of protest and disgust established by the use of 'fatuous' in the penultimate line and thus characterises the shift from elegy to satire.

Robert Graves's *A Dead Boche* is again of a totally different nature. Graves had enlisted in order to take part in the defence of Belgium and for a long time considered it to be a just war. Even though he finally condemned its prolongation as a war of attrition[14] only a few of his poems are overtly critical; rather, they attempt to trigger further thought. 'For Graves, dread, conflict, the simplest daily worries, disgusts, and irritations are experiences to be tamed in allegory, personification, happening; then civilized by irony, so that the evil is neutralized and we are left with its power to shake complacency, to stimulate' (Grubb, 1965, p. 121). However, this might also be due to the fact that Graves's technique of survival was to think as little as possible about the war and the circumstances it entailed: 'Graves (...) seldom faced up to the ugliness of battle; instead, his artistic reaction was reminiscent of that of a child who is forced to study the conditions of his disordered room: he looks but he does not want "to see."'[15] Thus Martin Stephen argues: 'It is as if Graves is desperate to comfort himself with a vision of nature as it was, yet he suffers from the Georgian failing of finding an inspiration in nature's beauty that is not always conveyed to the reader, but which it is expected the reader will understand' (Stephen, 1996, p. 209). As a result, Graves never directly confronts the war, nor does he manage to ignore it completely, so that the two enter a disturbing symbiosis.

A Dead Boche is exceptional among Graves's work for its overt critique of the bloodlust of war for the sake of glory in stanza 1, but the second stanza is typical for Graves's portrayal of a war-time 'idyll'. In its first stanza the poem addresses an audience distant in place and/or time before it thwarts the reader's presumed aesthetic expectations in stanza 2 by an alternative anti-rhetoric of pure description without metaphors or abstractions. The content of the poem centres on an incident (the vision of a solitary man leaning against a tree) in Mametz Wood during the Battle of the Somme. What would otherwise be a typical scene in nature poetry of the Romantic period here becomes a form of mockery: nature is still there, but war has added death to it. There are no more pleasant smells of flowers and the setting no longer provides an idyll for someone musing about the world. The only thing that is left of the tree after the shells have exploded nearby is its trunk – symbolic for the destructive force of war on both man and nature. War thus dehumanises nature, yet nature will survive whereas many soldiers will not.

The poem's focus consequently is not on the dead man, but on the issue of poetic style, questioned by the presence of corpses and shattered landscapes: war turns landscape into landscape-with-corpse. 'Like stones and trees, the dead became one of the materials of the earth, to be walked over or around, and even used, when necessary, in the construction projects of the war' (Hynes, 1997, p. 69). Thus Graves wrote to Sassoon on 13 September 1917: the ideal of writing 'is to use common and simple words which everyone can understand and yet not set up a complex by such vulgarities but to make the plain words do the work of the coloured ones...' (O'Prey, 1982, p. 83). The result is a new form of art, namely an art without tradition and without nature in which the countryside only features as a devastated anti-landscape.[16] 'The destruction devised by man has no counterpart in the world of nature' (Khan, 1988, p. 62). By way of its boundless violence, the world of war in the original sense of the word becomes supernatural.

2.2   Comradeship

2.2.1   Comrades and friends

The all-embracing power of comradeship features prominently in letters, diaries and poetry written by those serving at the front. Combined with the bravery of individual men it not only provided a frequent topic for the greater, middle-class poets like Owen or Sassoon, but also appears in minor verse published in the various trench newspapers. As a result of the large-scale rupture of individual prewar friendships, most poems concerned with the topic share the following characteristics: they tenderly describe short exchanges with strangers, they express heightened emotions in particular situations, and they talk of shared experiences of suffering. Whereas the poetry of the time rarely speaks of 'men', a neutral term, it often talks about 'boys' or 'lads', a term heavily charged with emotions.[17] Through a focus on the physical details of the young men, their vulnerability to modern weapons is emphasised, especially in the poetry of Owen and Sassoon.

Due to the division between front and home, comradeship even seems to have included the enemy as a fellow sufferer with whom one felt solidarity. These sentiments found their most famous expression in Owen's *Strange Meeting*: 'I am the enemy you killed, my friend' but they can also be found in other poems such as Sassoon's *Night Attack*. The notion of 'enemy' itself appears in many poems as an artificial creation of war propaganda without any correspondent in reality even at the beginning of war. Thus Sorley had written very early in his poem *To Germany*: 'You are blind like us' and 'The blind fight the blind.' This was added to by the general acoustic presence of the enemy with whom verbal communication was possible, even though forbidden, over no-man's-land on days without fire. At the same time, however, war implied the transgression of humanistic boundaries, a fact that increased war's incommunicability.

Despite this closeness in both space and emotion, there were also times when the enemy remained invisible and close contact was limited to prisoners. Especially during the later stages of war, personal contacts with the enemy were rare, except when they were dead or terribly wounded. Read's interior monologue poems *Only a Boche* and *Meditation of a Dying German Officer* provide perfect examples for this kind of contact. Furthermore, the enemy was rarely perceived as an individual, for death made the corpses appear alike (even more so than a common uniform). Owen's *Strange Meeting* only may serve as an exception here, in which the individuality of the enemy is the result of the speaker's responsibility for his death.

It seems as if comradeship not only replaced absent friends and family, but also served as the major motivation to keep on fighting. 'With a few exceptions, what mattered to the men who fought in the Great War was not whether that war, or indeed any war, was just or justifiable. What gripped their imagination was rather the camaraderie of the trenches and the courage and sheer tenacity in the art of survival of the men with whom they served' (Winter, 1987, p. 292). The figure of the bereaved male friend therefore plays an important role in the context of comradeship and the Great War. Sarah Cole distinguishes between the two terms of 'friendship', as referring to individual relationships, and 'comradeship', as denoting a 'corporate or a group commitment' (Cole, 2001, p. 474).[18] In most cases, this group to which the soldier committed himself was the regiment or the division, and, in the case of the Navy, the crew of a particular ship. Yet it is important to note here that members of the Flying Corps were lacking this experience of comradeship due to the solitariness of air warfare. As long as they were on the ground pilots felt as close to their fellow soldiers as members of any other part of the army, including the experience of loss of comrades and personal feelings of guilt, yet as soon as they rose into the air pilots were alone with their fate, even though the end of the war saw an increase in group tactics and plane formations. However, pilots in general perceived themselves as a group, or a higher caste, and even extended this notion towards the enemy. Cole also points out that it was the term 'comradeship' that was preferred over 'friendship' in the official rhetoric of the war propagated by the staff, the government, and the Churches. In accordance with the public school ethos developed during the prewar years with its emphasis on group loyalty this is not surprising. However, this preference ignores the particular character of individual friendships among soldiers and the consequent impact of the loss of a personal friend on the individual perception of war. And, in addition to the fact that friends were killed during the course of the war, the bureaucracy of war did nothing to support individual friendships, as friends were arbitrarily separated in the restructuring processes of regiments following attacks with heavy losses. In the following both terms will be used interchangeably in order to convey the idea that comrades often became life-long friends even though their first meeting might have been coincidental; friends, on the other hand, often enlisted together and thus became 'comrades' according to military jargon.

The lives of Owen and Sassoon particularly illustrate this power of comradeship/friendship: 'Wilfred Owen and Siegfried Sassoon represent two of the greatest enigmas of the war. Both wrote bitterly effective poetry condemning the war and, by implication, those who supported it. And both won the Military Cross in actions where there could be no compunction about taking German lives. Owen and Sassoon were walking dichotomies, contradictions defying logic' (Stephen, 1996, p. 92). Both soldier poets lost personal friends during the war but at the same time felt an emotional attachment towards the men who were their inferiors. Although both poets had joined due to feelings of inevitability, in Owen's case war had also offered him a chance to better his status in society as his family's financial resources did not allow him to go to university. What is more interesting than these two poets' reasons for enlistment, however, are their reasons for returning to the front after long periods of convalescence back in England. It was mainly a sense of duty towards their men, strongly enforced by a feeling of comradeship or even love which caused a strong desire to join them again. Together with their soldiers they shared an 'insider' perspective on the war which the population at home lacked for various reasons. With these sentiments, they were by no means alone. 'While they were in the trenches men longed for leave to escape their physical wretchedness, their fear and their misery, but at home they were unable to settle down and found themselves longing to return to France' (Spear, 1979, p. 90).

In Owen's case the idea of comradeship is transformed into what he calls the 'pity of war' in his famous preface for his first volume of war poems. 'By adopting the role of pleader for his suffering men, which would also involve the distinct possibility that he would be killed, he would fulfil what in terms of the sentiment of the time would give him a kind of Christian role, silencing any remaining scruples' (Pittock, 2001, p. 210f.). Sassoon expressed his idea of comradeship in a different way, namely in the hatred for all the wartime obstacles against it. From an insider perspective, however, there was nothing to be ironic about with regard to comrades and friends. For both men, the feeling of comradeship was stronger than their opposition to the war and it drove them back to the front after longer periods of absence. However, their desire to name the evils drove them, and many other poets, to experiment with various observer positions, of which the distinction between insider and outsider perspectives to be dealt with in the next section became the most prominent.

2.2.2 Outsider perspectives

Another influential factor was the soldiers' perception of wartime society. In their eyes the population of the time was divided into two – those safe behind the lines or at home and those suffering at the front. The self-indulgence of the civilian population back in England as presented in Owen's *The Calls* or Sassoon's *The Fathers* was set against the compassion for all the victims of war, most often identified as a large group of comrades. These comrades, as 'insiders' of war, gradually turn into 'outsiders' of civil society, an experience shared by many veterans of war to the present day. Owen's bitterly sarcastic poem *Smile, Smile, Smile* thus draws an ironic picture of comrades depending on the support of each other to prevent disintegration. While the poem primarily addresses the ignorance of the yellow press with regard to the war, its description of wounded men leaning together intimately to read the paper is striking for the simultaneous absence of eroticism and the presence of mutual attachment through their common secret which excludes the reader. And in this case, the exclusion is not gender-specific, but includes both male and female civilians, while nurses might even have found themselves on the side of the wounded. However, several soldiers even wished for German Zeppelins over England to teach those at home the reality of war and felt united in their deprivations and common experiences.

Accordingly, Owen's poem *Greater Love* not only refers to the Christian ideal of self-sacrifice, but also draws a comparison between the love of soldiers and that of traditional romantic discourse. For the speaker, soldierly love is preferable for its honesty as it fulfils the promises it makes. Because the concept of physical intimacy becomes shattered by the war, the poet needs to replace it with a different kind of love language – namely one that is closer to the reality of war by rejecting the standard hollow phrases.

While most poems tackling the theme of friendship are marked by a feeling of fellowship between the officer-speaker and his men, one of Sassoon's unusually long poems is rare for its irony, which targets the speaker himself for training young men for the war at Litherland, as a result of which the officer becomes an outsider. By doing so, *Conscripts* introduces a further use of irony in the context of comradeship, namely that of self-critique or even guilt. The absurdity of the whole situation described in the poem becomes obvious when we consider the role of the speaker. Although he loves his young recruits, he does not refrain from sending them to France in order to die there for their country. The irony becomes even stronger in the last stanza of the poem. While most of those he counted as friends fall victims to the war, the ones he despised for their softness and ordinariness succeed in returning home as heroes. Adrian Caesar therefore argues that the poem may serve as proof for the increasing sublimation of Sassoon's homoerotic feelings and class-consciousness for a shared sacrifice with his men (Caesar, 1993, p. 82). Yet, according to Wilson, the poem might also be seen as an attempt to describe his change of poetic technique, which was to mark his later war poetry, as the poem 'uses the metaphor of army conscripts to show how inadequate his former lush descriptiveness has proved in the face of War's harsh realities. In a striking opening to the poem, the narrator addresses his former poetic attitudes as though he were shouting at a bunch of clumsy conscripts on the barrack square' (Wilson, 1998, p. 310).

Interestingly, it was the officer-poets who felt most deeply attached to the men for whom they were responsible, while in both Isaac Rosenberg's and Ivor Gurney's work – both of them serving in the rank – there is a sense of detachment from the troops. In the first lines of Rosenberg's *Marching (As seen from the Left File)* the speaker observes the marching soldiers rather than being part of this mass and most of his other poems equally share the view of the outside spectator watching his comrades' battle against the lice or talking about the dead as 'they'. Gurney's position, on the other hand, is a slightly different one as he perceives himself not as an outsider, but rather as an individual in the ranks opposing war's uniformity. 'Gurney's sense of separateness or individuality in the ranks is one of the most important features of his war poems, for the recognition that "the men" are not a mere mass is a necessary critique of the mentality from which wars come' (Parfitt, 1990, p. 80). Thus, even though privates felt attached to their comrades, records of this sentiment from their perspective are rare.

While sentiments of comradeship are usually perceived as typical for the male experience of the First World War, a fact that is enforced by the various commemorations on Veteran's Day all over the world, many VADs felt a similar unity based on shared experience during wartime. May Cannan, for instance, dedicated her poem *France* to Carola Oman, listing the war impressions that bind them together: death, loneliness, stretcher bearers, railway stations etc. With their fellow nurses, women were able to share their thoughts without having to fear misapprehension, an idea that also bound their male counterparts together.

2.3   Pride and glory

Another way of evading the bleak reality of modern warfare was to focus on the positive attributes attached to certain areas of the military. The Navy and the Royal Flying Corps particularly lent themselves to portrayals highlighting the values of heroism and glory, with which they were traditionally associated. However, while the functions of irony will be shown to be different from other areas of the military, the phenomenon is by no means absent as a tool to express a certain attitude towards the poets' unit as well as other war-related issues.

2.3.1   War at sea

In this most traditional part of the British military forces, poetry writing was rare due to several reasons. First, members of the Navy usually came from families with a long naval tradition. Volunteers from other classes were rare, and, with writing being a predominantly middle-class activity, the number of potential poets was limited. Second, poetry about war at sea was strongly determined by a long tradition of heroic lyrics about the pride and glory of the British fleet. It is thus not surprising that critical poetry concerning the war was rare and that a general spirit of adventure among the crew dominated over other moods. And third, despite the rivalry between the German and British fleets at the beginning of the First World War, naval warfare only played a minor role compared with other areas of the war.[19] Only in the battle of Jutland on 31 May 1916 did British and German fleets meet at full strength, both losing more than 2,500 men. All of these factors may serve as reasons for the limited amount of poetry concerning war at sea.

While most of the strategies of naval warfare were lacking innovatory elements and manoeuvres had been practised in other wars for centuries, there was, however, one major novelty. The First World War was the first one in which submarines were used extensively, after the German declaration of unrestricted submarine warfare on 1 February 1917. However, their effect in the struggle to win the war was marginal. Like mines, they were mainly perceived as unfair and thus un-English, representative of the barbarous nature of the Germans, a pack of cowards refusing to meet the enemy in 'real battle'. The secrecy and lack of glamour of submarine warfare might also have been a reason for the minor impact of submarines and mines on poetry about war at sea. However, 'by eliminating the submarine threat and exercising a stranglehold on Germany's bid to dominate the seas, the Royal Navy was defeating the greatest threats that Britain faced during the war' (Wilson, 1986, p. 693).

Despite the prevailing attitude of pride in the British Navy, there are stylistic and topical exceptions. Thus E. Hilton Young's poem *Mine-Sweeping Trawlers* differs from other poetry about naval warfare in that it focuses on the non-heroic duties of some of the seamen, namely those who did the dangerous work of finding and destroying enemy mines. The poem, rather traditional with regard to rhythm and rhyme scheme, is notable for its choice of diction. The expression 'fishermen of death' in stanza 2 is heavily charged with irony as it evokes both the peaceful character of fishing and Jesus calling his disciples to become 'fishermen' of life. Here, the connection to fishing is of a practical nature as fishing vessels were and still are used today for patrol duties and minesweeping. Instead of preparing the way for life-enhancing or life-preserving activities, such as the delivery of food, the minesweepers clear the 'path of doom', so that the following battleships will be able to destroy their German counterparts.

This task of minesweeping was not only an important one, because the Royal Navy lost more than one ship to German mines, but also one of the most dangerous activities in the Navy. While real battles in which the Navy could prove its skill and efficiency were rare, the loss of a minesweeper did not imply any act of heroism or bravery and thus did not serve the prestige of the Navy, as *A Minesweeper Sunk (The Duty Chief Petty Officer to the Duty Writer)* by Edward L. Davison points out. The light-hearted tone established by the colloquialisms of the officer, as well as the officer's desire to be off to the canteen as quickly as possible, contradicts the serious content matter of the poem. As an instance of verbal irony the poem violates the maxim of manner according to Grice's version of Speech Act Theory. While the writer stares into the water where his dead comrades have found their grave, he is rebuked by his officer interested only in the resulting financial matters and his momentary struggle with his coat. On a metaphoric level, the incident will clearly leave unwanted stains on his white coat as officer. On the other hand, the first line makes clear that he expected higher losses, so that he is able to evaluate the mission in positive terms. The irony of the poem is mainly established by the presentation of the officer as a bureaucratic rather than a caring person, for whom the loss of the ship only requires unwanted additional effort. The poem's style thus resembles that of poetry by Sassoon and others expressing a critique of the military leaders among the infantry.

Although the Navy was Britain's most prestigious area of the military, it failed to develop along the lines most members expected. Britannia did not indeed rule the waves. The major part of the day on board a battleship was spent on patrol in the North Sea looking out for cargo vessels. The major perils for the crew were bad weather, mines and torpedoes, as well as a shortage of water and constant lack of sleep, rather than enemy contact (Wilson, 1986, p. 686f.).[20] In addition to the uneventful nature of sea warfare during the First World War, reports other than those by members of the Navy were largely prohibited. 'The press were allowed to visit the fleet on carefully organised tours when it was in port, and occasionally important individuals were allowed to go to sea with the fleet on manoeuvres for a short period, but there was no question of correspondents remaining aboard for a protracted term or of reporting naval engagements at first hand' (Sillars, 1987, p. 24). As a result, the Navy and its activities remained obscure to the majority of civilians.

One of the rare instances where home and the war at sea are connected in ways other than the expression of pride can be found in Henry Head's *Destroyers*. The poem begins with a peaceful vision of ordinary English life on a sunny day full of harmony, which is then ironically contrasted in the second stanza with the reality of war. While the population back at home seems untroubled by the war, a deadly shadow hovers above the scene and intrudes into the peaceful picture. Not only does the description of the ships as silent and grey clash with the lively atmosphere and gay colours of life on land, but the choice of cormorants also underlines the effect of imminent threat. The birds are known for their immense appetite for fish, which they search from the air and for which they rapidly dive into the sea. The 'submerged prey' for which the ships look out are of course German submarines daring to come too close to the English coast. However, the image of the destroyers is by no means a positive one. On the contrary, by presenting the German ships as prey, they become victims of their English hunters. Although their task is to preserve the security of the population by guarding the English coast, they are described in negative terms as 'angels of destruction'. The peace and safety they are supposed to guarantee are bought with death. By its combination of situational with verbal irony through a particular choice of diction which contradicts the general perception of the British Navy, the poem turns into bitter sarcasm when the poet focuses on the fragility and the price of peaceful dreams during times of war. However, this does not imply a general critique of war, as can be found in many of the famous poems from the Western Front,[21] which is also the case with the following poems concerning air warfare.

2.3.2 War in the air

Air warfare has never been at the centre of the First World War, nor its critical heritage. However, it was of particular importance as it added a third dimension to war, hitherto unknown. On the one hand, war in the air was the most innovative of all technical developments of the war. On the other, it was the most glorified and romanticised branch of the military in all European armies. At the beginning of the war, members of the Royal Flying Corps (RFC) mainly came from the upper classes and the aristocracy, and thus increased its charisma by spreading an anachronistic public school ethos of pride and honour. The lack of tradition was compensated for by medieval chivalric rhetoric to describe the heroic deeds of the RFC and the Royal Air Force. One has to note here that the Royal Flying Corps had been formed in 1912 whereas the Royal Air Force only came into existence on 1 April 1918 by the unification of the Royal Flying Corps with the Royal Naval Air Service. The abbreviation RAF up to this point stood for Royal Aircraft Factory and should not be confused with the Royal Air Force.

The rhetoric of chivalry found its basis in the military purposes for which the air forces were used at the beginning of war. The pilots' main task was to detect the position of enemy troops and to survey larger areas. As such, they slowly replaced the cavalry, the military branch most strongly dominated by the aristocracy. Manfred von Richthofen, the Red Baron, also began his military career in the cavalry before attending pilot training. It is thus not surprising that battles came to be called 'duels in the sky' and that the pilot's ideal was that of the honourable knight (courteous and considerate towards the enemy, but with limitless courage) being a member of a sacred elite. War in the air was not only the great adventure, but also the last stronghold of an anachronistic image of war as dependent on the heroic deeds and bravery of individuals. However, the legend of the chivalric hero enjoying the freedom of the air largely ignores the dangers of air warfare at the beginning of the twentieth century and the constant fear of many pilots.

An airman's prospects of survival were small due to various risks the pilots had to face, and as a result the average life expectancy for pilots over the Western Front was less than three weeks (Sillars, 1987, p. 96). The list of possible dangers is long and includes hostile aircraft, ground fire, mechanical failure (planes remained uncertain creatures with an experimental character until the end of the war), unreliable engines, 'human error', and adverse weather in the air. Altimeters only recorded the aeroplane's altitude above the point of departure. If the pilot was flying over land higher than his own aerodrome, the altimeter would not register the difference, a fact that led to many crashes in dense fog. Early morning was the most dangerous time for the Allied pilots because the sun, rising in the east, blinded them so that the German enemy was hardly visible, a fact that provided the topic for Jeffery Day's *Dawn*, in which romantic peacefulness associated with the early hours of the day is thwarted by the reality of war. Similarly to the 'nature' poetry of the first two sections of this chapter, dawn for the pilot in the poem signifies death rather than enjoyment. This seems to be due, however, not to the enemy, but to his officer's 'morbid sense of fun' (l. 9). By being sent up every day, the pilots were reduced to mere targets as their individual abilities had to give way to chance. Like a hunter for its prey, 'the sportive Hun' (l. 11) only had to wait until the English appeared and were blinded by the rising sun, a pretty un-sportive affair. The loneliness of the pilots should also be added to these factors, for they participated in the war as individuals rather than as part of larger divisions which would provide support in dangerous situations. In the case of crashes, it was therefore hard to blame someone else for the resulting injuries or death.

Nevertheless, the novelty of flying caused a feeling of delight among many pilots. In addition to the visual excitements offered by flying, they were able to get away from the destroyed earth and the noise of the battlefields.[22] Seen from the air, the front line and no-man's-land were reduced to labyrinths in which insects fought each other as in Plowman's *Going into the line* ('Poor craven little crowd of human mites') and Sorley's *A hundred thousand million mites we go*. The dehumanisation of mankind as the result of war gains its greatest expression here. At the same time, the interaction of sun and clouds often produced magnificent views and inspired feelings of admiration and awe which are expressed in Bewsher's *The Dawn Patrol,* and *A Song of the Air* (published under the pseudonym Observer, RFC), which describes these contradictory emotions of pilots, as does Jeffery Day's *The Call of the Air.*

Despite all the above feelings and the novelty of air warfare in general, the quantity of poetry composed on the topic is little compared with other areas of the war. Most poems have a humorous, song-like character and are of minor aesthetic quality. This might also be due to the lack of literary predecessors. At the same time, most poems neglect the fact that the planes were carrying bombs to take part in the killing of the enemy, and irony rarely targets air combat itself. War instead only provides the background for a critique of the minor quality of planes with their mechanical inadequacies due to the use of cheap material. The anonymous poem *They called them RAF 2C's* uses verbal irony to criticise these drawbacks. Yet, in order to analyse the ironic potential of the poem, it is necessary to consider the various linguistic approaches to verbal irony. Both pragmatics and discourse analysis perceive each form of language in use as (inter)action, which is supposed to follow certain rules. Irony violates these rules in order to achieve a certain effect, but, contrary to the phenomenon of the lie, verbal irony is supposed to be discovered despite its violation of the norm. Its interpretation is already implicated in the ironic utterance by the speaker, or, in the case of poetry, the author. All of the following linguistic approaches to irony distinguish two realities: a surface reality and a deeper reality, both of which are subject to individual judgement. To discover the irony of a text, the reader or listener must perceive a difference between these two layers of reality. If he or she fails to do so, irony remains undiscovered and thus unsuccessful.

A pragmatic model of irony required here should shed light on three major aspects: (1) the relationship between speaker and listener/reader;

(2) the possible functions of irony in different communicative situations; and (3) possible signals for irony in the context of the utterance. As the name already indicates, the focus is on the speech act rather than an ironic event or situation. Whereas ironic events are by nature unintentional, or rather it is only their interpretation in retrospect that renders them ironic (the event itself is value-free), ironic utterances are always intended by the speaker and thus of interest for speech act theoreticians.

The first aspect of interest is the relationship between sender (author) and recipient (reader), which, in the case of irony, can be threefold: Either both communication partners recognise the irony in the utterance, or one of the participants employs irony but the communication partner fails to discover it. A third case is often created by historical distance separating the communication partners, so that the reader today might perceive something as ironic which in fact was not intended as such by the author – a misunderstanding that may, however, also happen synchronically, such as in the case of over-attentive readers who claim to perceive ironies in utterances where none exist. Irony would then only appear in a secondary encoding or decoding process rather than in the original one.[23]

To analyse the functions of irony, speech act theory relies on the classification of utterances into different speech acts. In principle, every type of speech act can be marked by irony, with the exception of the performative speech act as it is impossible to 'ironise somebody'. However, this classification is defective in itself as it excludes many social and emotional functions of utterances that cannot be covered by the classification criteria. In order to be able to categorise speech acts, it is necessary to look for signals in the text that suggest a certain reading. Such signals might be found in the text itself, for example in a juxtaposition of contrary utterances, a combination of mutually contradictory terms, or a violation of an audience's expectations in the course of the text. In other cases, these signals might only become obvious in a comparison of various speech acts involving the same speaker or an analysis of the context of an utterance.

Accordingly, discourse analysts claim that the ironic speaker leaves indications of his counterfactual intentions, because 'he does not intend to fully deceive his audience, he merely desires to be ironic and thus wants his counterfactuality detected' (Amante, 1981, p. 84). These indications have to be differentiated from typographical 'irony-signals' such as question or exclamation marks, inverted commas or hyphens, and they need not necessarily be textual. Irony markers can also be of non-literary quality, such as information on the social role of the text, the psychic disposition of the author, the mimic expression of the sender or the historical situation of the war. As contextual elements, they are subject to the conventions of the respective culture of the author, which the recipient has to share for a successful decoding. Both literary scholars and linguists talk about overt irony if these signals strongly enforce an ironic reading, or covert irony if signals do not exist at all or try to disguise the irony. The decoding process in both cases, however, requires the linguistic competence of the recipient, i.e. cultural and ideological skills. However, the problem remains that all possible signals might also refer to other functions of language and the more signals the less effective is the irony.

Resulting from the above, any decoding process of an ironic utterance follows certain principles, though not necessarily in a linear order but more often simultaneously. (1) The reader perceives a linguistic devi- ation, for instance a violation of the cooperative principle Grice presup- poses for all utterances. (2) The ironic utterance is transferred back into normal language use. (3) At the same time the communicative situation is analysed with regard to speaker and listener, the mode of speech, or its historical context. (4) An analysis of the function of irony in the particular communicative context follows in a last step. Although this decoding process is similar for all readers, the results may differ from reader to reader as it is subject to individual background knowledge, the level of attention, personal antipathies and so on.

This decoding process is based on the assumption that when a maxim, in the case of irony, for example, that of quality/truth or manner, is flouted on the level of what is said, the interpretation of the utterance consequently has to be consistent with the maxims on the level of what might be implied. Irony is thus perceived as operating mainly by neg- ating one or even more conditions (or rules) that normally govern non- ironic speech acts.[24] Grice unfortunately does not analyse the specific processes of interpretation, but only in retrospect explains how certain interpretations might have been achieved.

As a result of the violation of Grice's cooperative principle, 'the illo- cutionary force of a speech act is retained but rather curiously blunted so that a perlocutionary-like effect is added' (Amante, 1981, p. 77). The effect created by this blending of perlocutionary and illocutionary force can be qualified as an affective one. It draws attention to language itself and therefore has a poetic function. Language in irony is not only a means of presenting information; it additionally conveys the attitude of the speaker about the content of the utterance. Irony may thus even 'add perlocutions to speech acts that normally do not have them' (Amante, 1981, p. 91). The affective quality is understandable especially when we consider the fact that the target of irony is, in most cases, the violation of a series of social, moral or other norms. Situational expectations are not fulfilled and irony is thus felt to be an appropriate means to pass judgement on someone or something. The social expectations or customs that are violated at the same time are part of the background knowledge the ironist ideally shares with the audience because they are closely linked to language itself. The context thus has to be added to a system that distinguishes between propositional, illocutionary and perlocutionary speech acts. The success of each of these acts is largely determined by this context, and only by taking it into account will it be possible to decode the purpose of verbal irony, especially when the irony is used in a subtle way.[25]

An additional problem of irony in literature is the identification of the ironist. Whereas in non-literary conversation the ironist is usually the speaker, in literature it can be a narrator, a fictional character, or the author himself. Speech Act Theory, however, hardly focused on literary speech acts, and if it did they were categorised as 'pseudo' speech acts (Plett, 1982, p. 80. See also Ohmann, 1971), regarding their literary 'use' of the speech act types set up by Austin (1962) and later developed by Searle (1969 and 1976). Scholars argued either that the literary speech act was merely taking place between an implied author and an implied reader instead of real author and real reader,[26] or that the speech act was only established between various fictional characters, the speakers in the poem. The distinction of three instances as developed by Booth and others – real author, implied author, and the various possibilities for the dramatisation of the narrator – will doubtless prove helpful for the close analysis of the poetic material. However, I will claim that it is precisely through irony that a real author is able to enter into direct communication with his/her readers, as irony always conveys a personal position and is thus able to create an emotional bond.[27] Rather than talking of 'pseudo' speech acts, poems need to be perceived as real or external speech acts linking the author and his/her readers over decades and cultural differences according to the communicative approach to literature developed in the introduction. This view, however, does not prevent the analysis of internal speech acts as established between different speakers in particular poems. In some cases, the ironic mood of a poem might even result from an active interplay between the two types – internal and external – of speech acts realised in one single text, as for instance in Sassoon's *The Hero*.

To sum up, speech act theory assumes that an ironic utterance does not mean what it says on the literal level. It presupposes a mechanism of inversion that has to be decoded in the conversational process. In contrast to this view, Mention Theory by Sperber and Wilson (1981) is based on the idea that the ironist mentions the literal meaning of the utterance in a way that shows his or her attitude towards it. However, this attitude need not be expressed explicitly but can be hidden behind an unemotional or casual tone. The notion on which the theory is based is a distinction between the usage of a meaning and its mentioning. Sperber and Wilson argue that 'the meaning expressed in an ironical utterance is the literal one and no other. However, this literal meaning is not *used* by speakers to convey their own thoughts. Rather, it is *mentioned* as an object of contempt, ridicule, or disapproval' (Jorgensen, Miller and Sperber, 1984, p. 112). Mention theory thus might become a useful tool when it comes to the analysis of the poets' attitude expressed in their poems. Consequently, the reader's task is to reconstruct both the literal meaning and the attitude of the speaker/writer towards that meaning. This might prove difficult as attitudes are mostly expressed implicitly rather than explicitly as they blend into the context. In oral situations, attitudes might be indicated by the tone of voice or a grimace, but not so in written texts. The authors of the theory try to solve this problem by proposing an echoic mentioning based on recognition. These echoes could either be immediate or remote echoes of past utterances and thoughts. In the case of poetry this implies the literary tradition in which the author finds him- or herself, but also newspaper articles and other written material of the time. To decode the ironic utterance, it is thus sufficient if the audience is able to recognise the material mentioned by the author.

Another theory based on psychological assumptions of the speaker's attitude towards an utterance is that of Clark and Gerrig (1984), who propose that the ironic speaker pretends to be an injudicious person speaking to an audience that is able to discover this pretence and thus to recognise the speaker's attitude towards the utterance. The scholars fall back on the original meaning of the greek *eironeia* despite the difficult etymology of the term, and argue that 'to be ironical is, among other things, to pretend (as one possible etymology suggests), and while one wants the pretense to be recognized as such, to announce it as a pretense would spoil the effect' (Clark and Gerrig, 1984, p. 121). Similarly to Sperber and Wilson, Clark and Gerrig argue that verbal irony is inevitably connected with the expression of feeling, attitude and evaluation. However, its discovery is not linked to the recognition of an already mentioned utterance. The pretending person, rather, takes on a new identity for the moment of the utterance. Clark and Gerrig argue that 'all ironic mentions (...) can be translated into ironic pretense' (Clark and Gerrig, 1984, p. 123) but not vice versa.

When looked at more closely, both theories are very similar to each other, as many of the analysed features (victims, deception, attitude of the speaker) play a role in both of them. As J. P. Williams puts it, 'linguistic judgements as to whether an utterance is better categorized as mention or as pretense obviously depend on whether the judge has a broad or a narrow view of the scope of echoic mention' (Williams, 1984, p. 129). As a matter of fact, both theories are based on the same traditional definition of irony as a situation of incongruity or meaning substitution, which has to be solved by the reader in order to grasp the ironic potential of an utterance. The interpretation of an utterance as ironic thus becomes difficult or even impossible if the topic is controversial, if we have no information about the author or the context, and if the author does not give any clues in the text.

All three of the above pragmatic approaches, however, fail to enlighten one aspect: why do authors use irony instead of saving their readers the effort of decoding? Irony seems to be more than just another way of expressing what could equally well be said literally. Similar to metaphors, irony adds a special meaning to *what* is communicated by *how* it is communicated. It is here that relevance theory becomes a useful tool of analysis. It argues that ironic utterances do not deviate from the norms of ordinary language use. The interpretation of an ironic utterance, relevance theorists claim, does not adhere to the standard pragmatic model of comprehension according to which readers first go through the stage of literal interpretation before solving the irony. Based on Wittgenstein's theory of family resemblance, relevance theory argues that the relationship between utterances and thoughts is one of interpretive resemblance.[28] Utterances are perceived as interpretations of thoughts, which, however, do not necessarily follow the structure of language. Irony, sarcasm or satire, in some cases, might thus be the most economical way of communicating a certain thought and/ or affect. Relevance theory consequently argues that 'it is sentences in the language of thought, rather than natural language sentences, that refer directly to states of affairs in the world' (Pilkington, 2000, p. 91). As for the process of decoding, the author relies on the reader's ability to filter the relevant information given by a certain context of a certain utterance in a flexible process in order to grasp the meaning of the utterance. The information used in this process 'includes the most readily accessible assumptions in the context that yield contextual effects' (Pilkington, 2000, p. 97), in our case an ironic one conveying affect (Sperber and Wilson, 1995, p. 224). However, we have to bear in mind that it is human beings (the author and the reader) who can convey emotions by sharing certain thoughts, not the utterance itself.

The anonymous poem *They called them RAF 2C's* ironically focuses on the cheap quality of the material used in the production of British planes by pointing out that pieces of discarded metal were riveted together:

> Oh! They found a bit of iron what
> Some bloke had thrown away,
> And the RAF said, 'This is just the thing
> We've sought for many a day,'
>
> They built a weird machine,
> The strangest engine ever seen,
> And they'd quite forgotten that the thing was rotten,
> And they shoved it in a flying machine.
>
> [...]

This fact in itself, however, does not explain the irony. Speech Act Theory fails to provide a convincing explanation here because the utterances of the speaker do not violate the norms of ordinary speech acts. However, Sperber and Wilson's Mention Theory becomes useful in the search for a solution. The speaker's complaint that those responsible for the production of planes used discarded metal might be based on a newspaper report or rumour at the time, which the poem echoes. Clark and Gerrig, on the other hand, would postulate that the speaker of the poem objectively reports what is going on in an exaggeratedly light-hearted tone, so that the reader is able to discover at once that the speaker is only pretending to depict the situation with humour. As the utterance does not violate any cooperative principle, even relevance theory proves useful here:

> [...]
>
> They were so darn' slow, they wouldn't go,
> And they called them RAF 2C's!

When the reader filters the context for information on the possible thoughts of the speaker, he or she will find out that plane BE2C was a slow and poorly armed two-seater. It was perceived by many pilots as an 'engineering and fighting death trap' (Stephen, 1998, p. 240).

Martin Stephen furthermore points out that the plane not only had an unreliable engine but also failed to allow pilots a proper forward and downward view. However, even after its uselessness became obvious, the planes were kept in service at the cost of many lives:

> [...]
>
> Then they ordered simply thousands more,
> And sent them out to fight.
> When the blokes who had to fly them swore,
> The RAF said, 'They're all right
> The 'bus is stable as can be;
> We invented every bit ourselves, you see!'
>
> [...]

On the basis of historical evidence the speaker must have intended his poem to be read ironically. The producers' consolation for the pilots in this stanza especially increases doubts about the machine as British inventions were often inferior to German aircraft. Furthermore, instead of aiming at better planes, the predominant interest according to Owen's *Smile, Smile, Smile* seems to have been in building aerodromes. The poem contains an ironical commentary on the Air Force by pretending that the male population prefers aerodromes over proper housing. It thus mocks the concept of heroic sacrifice not only propagated by the press but often considered as the ethos of the pilot.

The anonymous song *Every Little While* presents this dilemma of ambition and failure by juxtaposing the dangers of flying with the motivation of the pilot to 'fly a posh SE'. It was not unusual that planes did not reach their destination and crashed into the Channel, neither was it rare for pilots to land on fields, repair their plane and then rise up into the air again. Unfortunately, the British were reluctant to distribute parachutes among pilots because they feared this would limit their courage and take away their concentration, with the result that more pilots died due to the failure of their machines or bad weather, rather than enemy contact. The anonymous satire *The Pilot's Psalm* is based on these experiences in the form of a mockery of Psalm 23.

Another aspect of air warfare was that for the first time in centuries it brought the war to the British Isles rather than limiting it to the continent. Zeppelin air raids over London (51 in total between 1914 and 1918) generated outrage as evidence of German frightfulness and evil destroying the notion of home as a safety harbour. Yet war was also intruding into an otherwise peaceful world as in the non-ironic descriptions of air raids in Nancy Cunard's *Zeppelins* and Marian Allen's *The Raiders*. The result was texts by both male and female poets using the traditional method of satiric attack through degrading humour. At the same time, people were fascinated with the mechanical aspects of airships, as well as their beauty. W. H. Davies' poem *The Birds of Steel* thus catches the ambivalent effect of air raid noise on the population at home when death suddenly intrudes into the garden idyll with its apple tree and flying bees at night. The noise of the airships is so similar to that of the bees that the speaker at first confuses the two. However, while the bees fill their bags in the garden, the 'bags' of the steel birds will be emptied before they will rise up again 'nearer to God'. Ironically, the noise they make in doing so is even called a song. The poem shows the injustice of the attack on harmless and innocent children, while at the same time the notion of 'birds of steel' reveals an attempt to include them into an already existing concept of the natural world. The irony of the poem is thus established by oppositions and incongruencies on the levels of both diction and situation. As will be shown, the same ambivalent emotions of fascination, fear and anger feature prominently in poems concerning military technology.

2.4 Technology

As the first technological war in the history of mankind, the First World War entered the collective imagination as one massive 'Materialschlacht', a war of machines involving such new developments as smokeless gunpowder, machine guns, grenades, poison gas, tanks, aircraft and flamethrowers. The poetic treatment of weapons and war machinery consequently hovers between fascination and disgust. However, what unites all poems concerning the technology of modern war is the fact that they rely on traditional metaphors from all areas of natural life to describe the new phenomena. This results from the rapid development of the machinery, yet the rather slow adaptation of language. Another reason for the lack of technological terminology may lie in the background of the poets. Although many volunteers were highly educated young men, they were by no means professional soldiers or engineers, and as such had no previous experience with military technology.

Military technology, in general, implied a fragmentation of perception.[29] Similarly to the effect of the division of labour as a result of industrialisation, modern war technology required a high amount of specialisation of the soldier for its effective use. Furthermore, the immobility caused by heavy armour limited the men's freedom, as did the fact that troops had to spend most of their time under surface level. Consequently, troop movements and positions were only visible via periscopes or the help of aviation. Men became part of the machinery which hindered them in their mobility, rather than the other way round. Instead of perceiving the totality of war with its long-term results, the soldiers' view, as well as their knowledge and experience, was limited to their area of action and their particular duty. Thus military orders given in a clear hierarchy inevitably replaced individuality as the source of identity of the common soldier. At the same time, war even at the front remained distant and anonymous, as death came suddenly, like an accident or the plague, rather than in a personal battle of man against man. Mary Habeck (2000) distinguishes three ways in which technology was perceived: (1) as superhuman and thus demonic, (2) as subhuman and machine-like, or (3) as human or at least connected with the human world. In literary texts, however, the representation of technology hovers between these three possibilities.

2.4.1 The beauty of armour

While the perception of technology as demonic and beastly outweighs all other forms of description,[30] one of the earlier poems of war sees the guns as part of the ordinary human world. In *The Sower (Eastern France)* by Charles Hamilton Sorley war and ordinary life meet on a spring day. While the second stanza of the poem focuses on the work of a local farmer 'sowing his children's bread', the first one describes the movement of a battery on the nearby road. And while the sight of the horses and guns is described in objective terms with the harnesses even making a merry sound, they are nevertheless identified as killing instruments. The fact that they 'make orphans' entirely ridicules the sower's work as described in stanza 2. After the guns have served their purpose, there will be no children left to eat the bread once the wheat is harvested. Nevertheless, the speaker experiences a certain fascination for the slow movement of the battery on the road as it seems to be part of the ordinary. The irony of the poem is thus mainly established by the striking contrast between the peacefulness of the situation envisaged and the killing potential of the guns once they have reached their destination.

This killing potential reached its climax with the introduction of shells and machine guns. Nevertheless, the bayonet, which had become obsolete in a war that was fought over long distances rather than face to face, retains its prominent position in many war poems such as

Gibson's *The Bayonet* and Sassoon's *The Kiss* (see also Stanzel, 1993, pp. 83–98). On both sides of the front, offensives with close combat remained the ideal despite, or rather because of, the disastrous results of trench warfare. In general, modern military technology increased the feeling of vulnerability and helplessness among the soldiers as 'men no longer made war; war was made on men' (Eksteins, 1989, p. 183). Just as war dehumanised nature, technology dehumanised war. The resulting sentiments of alienation were further increased by the confusing noises of technology which new recruits were unable to distinguish. In an attempt to deal with these unfamiliar auditive impressions, poets compared the noise of flying shells to the sound of trains, or that of machine-gun fire to a storm of hail. Most frequently, however, technology was transformed into a personified force of nature with the tank becoming a beast (as in Sassoon's *Attack*, l. 5: 'Tanks creep and topple forward to the wire') and the airplane a bird, populating the devastated world of war.

However, the passivity of the men, resulting from the immense usage of technology during the First World War, also diminished their personal responsibility and thus their worries. At the same time this implied dehumanisation in that it reduced men to mere tools of war, incapable of but also prevented from thinking and acting individually, as in former wars of man against man. For Ivor Gurney, among others, the technology of war was the result of a century of general technological progress and the Western Front was 'the modern industrial world in miniature' (Bogacz, 1986, p. 644. See also Leed, 1979, pp. 95, 193–194). His evaluation of this development remains an ambivalent one, as can be seen in his two poems entitled *First Time In*. There is an ironic tension between the poem's archaic vocabulary, especially the word 'lore', and the mechanical facts of modern warfare. In another of his poems, *The Mother*, the biblical image of the turning of swords into ploughshares from Isaiah 2:4 is ironically reversed to underline the effects of industrialised war on mankind: 'We scar the earth with dreadful enginry.'

While most poems concerning technology are free of irony but focus rather on either the mechanical facts or the killing potential of the weapons, Owen's minor poem *Soldier's Dream* envisions an ironical dispute over the guns between God the Son and God the Father. He had begun the poem at Craiglockhart in October 1917, and on 27 November had passed it on to Siegfried Sassoon so that he could send it to either the *Nation* or Cambridge. Owen later revised the poem at Scarborough but never considered it to be of good quality. Nevertheless, the poem is interesting for its use of technical particularities. The 'Mausers and

Colts' of line 3 are German and American brands of revolvers and the 'flint-lock' in line 6 is an old-fashioned gun still in use during the First World War but rarely appropriate for situations in which survival depended on speed. The use of 'pikel' in line 6 is unusual, as the *OED* definition reads 'hay-fork or pitchfork', but Owen might refer again to the bayonet already mentioned in line 4, as Jon Stallworthy suggests in his critical edition (Stallworthy, 2003, p. 159).

While the irony of the poem is established via the ideological differences between Jesus and his father, the poem at the same time reveals a fascination for the variety of weapons used by the different armies. Although Jesus even bothers to spoil the bayonets, they hardly played a role at the Western Front, as they were outdated by bombs, shells and machine-guns. Finally Michael, the archangel who according to Revelations fights Satan at the end of times, is given all power to repair the weapons.[31] Thus the soldier's vision of Jesus as the prince of peace has to give way to the continuation of the war as a battle of good against evil, of the heavenly 'English' armies against the German 'devil'. Owen's own position concerning the continuation of the war, at least so in this poem, remains ambivalent.

Another of Owen's poems that reflects on the beauty of some of the weaponry is *On seeing a piece of our artillery brought into action*. It describes the weapon as an aesthetically beautiful, but at the same time humanely reprehensible object as the grandeur of the big gun clashes with the death and pain it brings. Again, the religious influence on Owen's diction is obvious, but it is turned into 'a rhetoric pregnant with irony and sadness' (Lane, 1972, p. 48). The target of this rhetoric of irony in this case is the author himself having a bad conscience about his fascination for the killing potential of the gun. Thus in the end he asks God to destroy the weapon, but only after it has served its purpose in the war.

2.4.2 'Thick green light'

Of striking importance with regard to the corpus of poems evolving from the conflict is the fact that gas, the psychologically though not militarily most effective new weapon of the war, only rarely occurs in combination with an ironic voice. The ironic potential of *Dulce et Decorum Est*, Owen's 'gas poem' (Owen, 1967, p. 499), as he called it in a letter to his mother, and the poem most often recalled when talking about gas warfare, is overshadowed by its polemic message. However, the poem clearly shows that gas warfare destroyed all illusions of a purification of society through war.[32]

The poem's form consists of two sonnets, of which the first follows the Shakespearian rhyme scheme though the last two lines deliberately fail to provide the concluding couplet. The content of this first sonnet, however, resembles the Italian variant with its strong focus on physical detail. Yet while the sonnet originally celebrates love, war overwhelms the senses and hinders any emotion. As a result of constant exhaustion, the soldiers are 'all blind;/drunk with fatigue; deaf even to the hoots/of tired, outstripped Five-Nines that dropped behind' (ll. 6–8). In accordance with the structure of the Italian sonnet, line 9 establishes a change of tone and perspective and thus creates a difference between the speaking man – most likely an officer like Owen – and the rest of the weary men. From this group of soldiers, however, one man is further separated by his late reaction to the gas warning and the dreadful consequences of breathing in the gas. Although he is surrounded by his fellow soldiers, they can only watch him 'drowning' through the misty panes of their gas masks. They cannot, but of course they also do not want to, share this experience. Even 'the officer can only see, remember, and retell the event.'[33]

The second sonnet then begins with a couplet and continues as a 'reversed sonnet' representing the dead man on the wagon with his 'hanging face' in line 20 of the poem. According to Hipp, lines 15–16 are indicative of the poet's situation in Craiglockhart war hospital, the place of composition of the poem. The dying soldier haunts him in his dreams as 'Owen identifies with the sufferer on the basis of their common isolation from the collective body' (Hipp, 2000, p. 36). This identification is particularly underlined by the shift from past tense in the descriptive first sonnet to present tense in these lines. In both form and content *Dulce et Decorum Est* thus ironically negates Brooke's sonnets of 1914. Heroic death becomes an anachronism: modern trench warfare has nothing to do with dying in battle during the ancient times of Horace. Instead of directing his anger against the realities of war, however, Owen attacks the ignorant population at home. The realistic description of a gas attack serves to make them aware of the bitter truth of modern warfare with its haunting effects, but the poem itself is too overt in its rhetorical use of anger to tap the full potential of its ironic elements. It rather accuses other poets for their evasive, if not patriotic, lyrics.[34] Owen himself preferred to take a more critical position on the war in the tradition of Sorley and others, even more so after he had met and befriended Siegfried Sassoon in Craiglockhart War Hospital.

3
Confrontation

Although there had been a demonstration of loyalty especially among the older generation of writers pledging themselves to England's cause, many of the younger authors felt the necessity to raise their voice against this war. Even though opposition to the war in its early stages is now almost forgotten because common myth links it to the experience of the trenches and thus to a later stage of war, the war had its opponents right from the start and not only among serving soldiers, but also among those who never fought. However, any opposition of the First World War writers to the situation of modern war was a difficult endeavour. Official censors suppressed all specifics in reports from the front and open criticism was treated as a crime according to the Defence of the Realm Act (DORA). This legislation gave the state 'unlimited power to control the instruments of communication and transmission of information, and to define what was meant by those terms' (Hynes, 1990, p. 79).

To counteract the threat of pursuit, poets only had two possibilities. The first was to create colourful fantasies emphasising the glorious work of the Allies or the barbarism of the enemy and thus to violate the truth. The second was to resort to various means of disguise, one of which has been identified in the first chapter of this book as irony. How the poets used the possibilities provided by irony not to evade war's horrors but this time to oppose them critically – and also the establishment, women, military leaders and the press whom they saw as culprits – is the topic of this chapter.

Confrontation in this respect largely signifies critical opposition towards the human targets of irony, those who were perceived to be responsible for the outbreak of war, its prolongation and the continuous suffering on all fronts, including at home. Government and politicians were not the only targets of attack. As the poetry discussed in this chapter will show, criticism was also directed against the institution of the churches, especially the Church of England, for taking sides with the government instead of telling the truth about war. Another part of the poetry is directed against the incompetence and arrogance of the war leaders far away from the actual battlefields at the relative safety of the base behind the lines. As the population at home was systematically denied insight into the real nature of warfare by the government, and soldiers found it hard or inappropriate to speak about their experiences when home on leave, a large part of the poetry directly confronts the ignorance of civilians regarding the nature of modern warfare.

Women in particular were accused of unthinkingly repeating the government's position, of persuading their sons or husbands to enlist without knowing the nature of this war, or even of being responsible for the slaughter by producing weapons and ammunition. However, one has to bear in mind that many women directly experienced the effects of war through bombardment, as nurses on hospital ships or behind the lines of the Western Front, or through the loss of loved ones. A general accusation of women for their ignorance will thus be revealed in the third section of this chapter to be unjust and only half the picture. The last section of this chapter will deal with the poetry attacking the so-called yellow press for spreading lies about the war and denying the public access to the 'truth', as many soldiers saw it, and thus prolonging the war by suppressing calls for peace.

In addition to this open critique, confrontation furthermore implies the ironic confrontation of the poets' emotions, fears and desires. Irony in this respect served as an outlet for feelings that would otherwise have been suppressed or at least neglected and it is thus not necessarily of a critical nature. It can rather be qualified as the poet's attempt to achieve a higher consciousness surpassing the basic, everyday functions of language, in order to gain psychological insight and to find his or her own balance again, while at the same time increasing awareness of the conditions of war among his or her readers. This alternative rhetoric, however, inevitably separated soldiers from civilians, front from home, and men from women. It increased the gap between the two parallel worlds of civilian and military existence.

As 'one of the most powerful of all forms of public disapproval is ridicule' (Elliott, 1970, p. 67),[1] satire gains particular importance for the critique of war. Throughout literary history satire confronted various ills in both society and politics. In order to do so, the genre may, but does not necessarily, use verbal or situational irony. The satirical poems of the First World War attack various targets, ranging from politicians and military leaders to female civilians and the clergy of the different churches. As only few of them are satires proper in the sense of a distinct genre, it is often more appropriate to speak of a satirical voice as the author's prominent mode of expression in these works.[2] According to Mahler (1992), satire can be seen as a type of 'non-straight' communication, which makes use of conventional schemes of communication but only so in order to express a certain critique on reality. Satire can therefore be considered as a form of false speech, yet, in contrast to the lie, satire always wants to be discovered by the reader.

However, Samuel Hynes points out that 'very little satire came from the anti-war dissenters, the pacifists, and the conscientious objectors; their opposition was of the more sober and persuading kind. But satire does not set out to persuade: it emerges when the feeling of opposition is strong, but the chances of changing circumstances are weak – it is the anger and the bitterness of the helpless' (Hynes, 1990, p. 243). Thus the medium of satire is that of bitter and tragic laughter rather than of objective voice. The satires of the First World War do not aim to stop the war with their arguments, but they are rather the expressions of anger, bitterness and frustration of many fighting men – among them the famous war poets Sassoon, Owen and Graves – seeking an outlet.[3] These poets were not pacifists in their thinking, but they critically opposed the way this war was fought and the goals it was supposed to achieve. Only in the aftermath of war and popular memory was this critique of individual details perceived as questioning the whole war. Satirical war poetry, however, mainly rejected the prewar ideas of nationalism and its emotional form of patriotism, and it questioned English moral superiority by attacking those associated with these ideas: the older generation,[4] women, generals, the Anglican clergy, politicians and the press.

Satire may use irony, but does not necessarily need it as its striking weapon.[5] Other than irony or sarcasm it is not a particular form of speaking but rather a genre[6] distinct from other – for a long time considered nobler – types of literature, and it is one which eschews conventions and clichés in order to express the opinion of its author. In order to do so, satire uses the language of its time in a free, easy and direct manner for a description of reality that provides the basis for a subsequent critical analysis of society. Thus the characteristic features of satire are its topicality, its shocking potential, its informality and, most importantly, its sometimes bitter but nevertheless funny elements, enhanced by a certain universality.[7] Even if satire usually exaggerates or distorts the situations or events it describes, it nevertheless claims to be realistic in its exposure of wrongs. However, satire's main problem is that it usually draws a black and white picture[8] which is often too simplistic, as we will see in some of the following examples.

One of the main problems satire has to face is its inherent link with the time of its production.[9] The author's aim is to tell the truth about actual events or persons, so when the historical personalities mentioned in it are dead or the situation has changed, satire might easily be misunderstood and then forgotten. However, even at a later time, the specific style and technique of satires may prove attractive, as we know from personal reading experiences. An important feature in this respect is the use of contemporary language in a tightly concentrated way. The vocabulary of satire, and especially so the ones dealing with the First World War , often includes cruel and dirty words, trivial and comic words and colloquial expressions. The main technique of satire, however, can be seen in its provision of the unexpected to achieve its aim of shocking the reader with ever new aspects of the argument. At this point, irony plays an important role as a weapon to achieve this aim in combination with other devices such as 'paradox, antithesis, parody, colloquialism, anticlimax, topicality, obscenity, violence, vividness and exaggeration.'[10]

Satire as a genre is inevitably a distancing mode, separating the satirist from those he attacks: the soldier from the population at home, men from women, rank from General, young from old.[11] It was therefore chosen by many poets as an appropriate mode for the expression of the soldier's general feeling of alienation. Additionally, satire does not rely on individuals, but the central target figure becomes universalised and, as a result, representative of a whole group of people such as the institution of the Church of England (as for instance the bishop in Sassoon's *They*) or the military leaders (see for example Sassoon, *The General*). On the other hand, the satirist is and has always been in a fragile position. He might easily become the object of both public hatred and fear and thus threatened by censorship or punishment.[12]

By blending a satirical voice with other stylistic devices and poetic genres, the borders between satire, parody, joke and humour are blurred.[13] In the course of the following paragraphs I will therefore speak of satire as a genre and the satirical voice as a mode of expression in rather general terms. With regard to satire's use of parody, it is enough to say that it depends on the reader's recognition of the source of the parody, in most cases a literary one. Parody works by applying the style of one context, such as the Bible, to another in which it serves to mock or to criticise on the basis of some common element.[14] It contrasts the values of earlier texts with those of a world at war. Though not all of the poems to be discussed here are satires or contain satirical elements, war with its clash of classes, strict rules and high losses provided the context for a revival of the genre unknown to former times, as will be demonstrated in the following paragraphs.

3.1   The establishment

On 2 September 1914, 25 authors who wanted to contribute to the war effort met in Wellington House in Buckingham Gate, London. Head of the commission was C. F. G. Masterman, a cabinet minister who had recently been appointed chief of Britain's war propaganda bureau. The immediate positive response to the government's call by so many influential authors of the time showed that English writers were quick to support the war *as* writers.[15] Although most of the pro-war writers later reconsidered their work, the consequences of literary support of the war were irrevocable: the younger generation of authors especially lost confidence in the authority of the written word as their older colleagues were seen to have sacrificed the traditional detachment and integrity of the writer. And, as Masterman's authors were almost all too old for military service (the average age was about 50), they seemed to the fighting soldiers not to be in a position to make moral judgements as they were not taking an active part in the struggle. Many younger writers of all European armies were thus united in their belief that the real enemy was to be found at home and behind one's own lines.[16] Consequently, hostilities against the older generation at home – especially against politicians and clergymen, but also against older authors supporting and defending the war – increased the longer the war lasted and the critique of the establishment became a common element in war writing. It was mainly directed against the false optimism and deliberate ignorance, but also against the prolongation of a war that was perceived as a 'just' one to defend Belgian neutrality, but which was then turned into a war of conquest in the eyes of many authors. The following two sections will concentrate on the role and position of both politicians and church officials, but will also deal with the organisation and relevance of the two most important institutions in society, the government and the various Churches, as triggers for ironical opposition.

3.1.1   Politicians

Despite the frequent critique of the government in poetry dealing with the war, irony is surprisingly rare. One major point of confrontation was the government's propaganda of war as a just and necessary one.

However, the war in Edward Thomas's words was 'no case of petty right or wrong/That politicians or philosophers/Can judge' (*This is no case of petty Right or Wrong*). At least not so from their distant position far away from the scene of action. Therefore politicians are equally implied in Owen's critique of the older generation; they are the warmongers who are so keen on wasting the lives of young men that they will not hear of peace negotiations. They are the plotting 'greybirds' in Harold Monro's last two stanzas of *Youths in Arms I* who are busy planning the proceedings of the war 'at their tables with their maps' and by doing so feel very wise. However, their wisdom is presented in the following to be based on self-deceit. Even though many young men voluntarily joined the forces, this does not imply that they 'died ungrudgingly', nor did the majority of them do so 'with delight' (l. 10), but out of financial or social necessity. The irony of the poem is thus based on the difference of perception between those at the planning table and those in the trenches. It is not only a question of age, but also one of intellect and empathy. By denying this empathy, the poem not only questions the self-imposed wisdom of the politicians, but also their qualification as representatives of the English people.

A similar point is made by Chesterton in his *Elegy in a Country Churchyard*. Again the critique centres on the fact that those who plan the war do so from a distance and thus do not suffer the consequences. Instead, politicians are the survivors and possible profiteers of the war they wage at the cost of the young generation. Other than the soldiers, the poem concludes, they have not yet done anything 'for England' worth mentioning but are nevertheless better off than both soldiers and workers, as is also mentioned in Sassoon's *Memorial Tablet*. The Squire in this poem is not necessarily politically involved, but definitely in a position of considerable power when he urges the young speaker to join up in stanza 1. The poem then goes on to mock the setting up of memorials for the dead as a cheap means of easing one's conscience. While the tablet reads *'in proud and glorious memory'*, the young man's death was anything else than glorious, but that is a fact the Squire is ignorant of as he never saw and experienced the conditions of trench warfare.

A totally different element regarding political practices enters the discourse with Emily Orr's *A Recruit from the Slums*. The poem is directed against a government that embodies middle-class values, but in doing so it disregards the interests of the other classes. The hypocrisy of the government is contrasted sharply with a working-class soldier's heroic sacrifice. Like other poets, with Owen's *Greater Love* as the prominent example, Orr makes use of the biblical verse from John 15:13 'Greater love has no man than this/That a man should die for his friend' as the intertextual basis for her irony in the last stanza. However, while expressing some moderate critique on the recruiting practice of the government, Orr's rhetoric could equally be read as supporting nationalism. This potential ambiguity originates in the fact that the poem emphasises the nobility of the soldiers remaining loyal to one another even though they are betrayed by their country.

It is the bitterness over this betrayal that finally dominates much of the poetry concerned with the government and its attempts to honour the dead. Seen from a personal situation of loss, any wreaths, memorial services or processions fail to console because they remain impersonal and thus dishonest, as indicated in stanza three of St John Adcock, *The Silence*. The mother in the poem, having lost a son, rather prefers private remembrance over politically dominated commemoration ceremonies. When considering the cost of the war, even irony no longer seems to be an appropriate means for the expression of critique. Instead, people seek a place 'where silence reigns, / Not for brief minutes, but through all the year'(ll. 31f.). With regard to religious affairs, however, the situation is a different one, as the following section will show.

3.1.2   The Church

Christian religion,[17] especially in its institutionalised (and national) forms of the Church of England and the Roman Catholic Church, played a crucial role during the war, despite its frequent underestimation by both military and social historians.[18] This underestimation is partly due to the difficult definition of what 'religion' implied for the individual at the beginning of the twentieth century, and partly results from the largely negative representation of both religious practices and the clergy in the famous war memoirs of the 1920s and 1930s, such as Graves's *Good-Bye To All That*. Yet Christianity was by far the most dominant religious belief among the British troops despite spiritualist, fatalist or humanist tendencies and the participation of many young men from the colonies with their various religions. Religious responses during war, as well as during peaceful times, ranged from absolute faith in an all-powerful God to strict atheism.[19] None of these variants, however, seriously challenged the Christian doctrine as they were of an eclectic and pragmatic nature and thus remained marginal.

To begin with, both churches considered it appropriate for Christians to take part in the war. Thus Article 37 of the *Articles of Religion* reads: 'It is lawful for Christian men, at the commandment of the Magistrate, to wear weapons, and serve in the wars.' This was especially so if fellow

Christians, in the case of the First World War the Belgian Catholics, needed help in their struggle against barbarous Germany.[20] Furthermore, Christian life was perceived by many as a continuous war against evil, this time embodied in the German Kaiserreich. The reactions of the free churches were more varied, but corresponded largely to those of the Anglican Church. However, conscientious objection to the war was proportionately more frequent among members of the free churches. Nevertheless, only the Quakers corporately remained pacifists. Other Christian Societies such as the S.P.C.K. and the various Bible societies published tracts for German prisoners of war and produced translations of devotional books in African and Maori languages for colonial troops. The Salvation and the Church Army provided tents for canteens and recreation centres, as well as ambulances for the wounded. As a reward for their effort, these groups never became targets of critique like the Anglican or Catholic Church.

It was an irony in itself that England suddenly became an ally to orthodox Russia, while English Protestants had always felt close ties to Germany as the home of the Reformation. Germany had been the source of biblical criticism and theological liberalism widely accepted and taught at English universities. While these ties were inevitably cut by the war, interdenominational links grew stronger (reformed Judaism in parts included), if not for theological at least for practical reasons. So pulpits were occasionally exchanged, non-Anglicans were admitted to Communion, or YMCA huts were used for services by all groups. Yet only when the war was over were international religious organisations able to resume their work.

One can speak of the mutual influence of both churches and state during the First World War, as the support of the churches was considered desirable by politicians with regard to several war-related topics, especially the recruiting of volunteers. Within English society at the beginning of the twentieth century, the churches still held a position of influence that could not be neglected by the state despite falling rates of church attendance. For the fighting generation of public school boys Christianity was deeply connected to their education and social fabric. Not only was the Christian service a major element of school life, but many public schools' headmasters were members of the clergy and thus enforced a Christian school ethos on the basis of duty, fair play, and sacrifice. This form of 'muscular Christianity' (Schweitzer, 2003, p. 4) attempted to fuse religious and civilian obligations by emphasising comradeship, loyalty and self-denial as preparation for the way to eternal life.

The clergy of all churches often voluntarily engaged themselves in the war for various reasons. Their predominantly rhetorical engagement, however, caused some contradictions, especially with regard to conscription from which the clergy was exempt. While praying for victory and arguing for the good cause of the war, most chaplains refused to take part in the killing itself, causing many to accuse the clergy of cowardice. Some chaplains, however, worked for ammunition factories, in agriculture, hospitals or other war-related services. The role of the churches and their clergy was thus a difficult one as they were criticised either for being too pacifistic or for not being pacifistic enough. Most bishops furthermore shared their social background with politicians and military leaders and thus close relationships traditionally existed between them. Their argumentation closely resembled that of government propaganda, namely that if England's war was just because it was a struggle of good against evil, it was the duty of all Christians to fight God's war as his chosen people.[21] Following this thought, Germany was the very incarnation of evil and Kaiser Wilhelm II the Anti-Christ who had to be destroyed. The just war thus soon became a 'holy war' (see Wilkinson, 1978, p. 252ff.) in terms of Christian propaganda. Consequently, the term 'holy war' was frequently used in sermons and implied that England was fighting on the right side with Christ supporting the British war effort.[22] On 6 September 1914 Winnington-Ingram, Bishop of London, preached a sermon entitled 'The Holy War', and on the same day H. C. Beeching, Dean of Norwich, proclaimed that Germany was no longer a Christian nation and that therefore this war was a war of Christ against anti-Christ, a battle for the cross. Of course, this brought God into a dilemma, as was ironically expressed by J. C. Squire among others. However, with increasing casualties it became increasingly difficult to portray the war as just. It was a matter of speculation both at the front and at home as to why God sometimes exercised his power to control events and sometimes seemed to refuse to do so. The interpretation of war had to change and so it gradually became a divine punishment for the sinfulness and decadence of the nation or, in other words, God's method of rousing England from its selfishness and complacency. This sinfulness included, of course, the refusal of wholehearted support for the war as a just cause. Yet there was a general hope that a better Church and a better society would be the outcome of war, especially as it seemed to unite Christianity again. Accordingly, the Churches propagated the traditional images of womanhood and motherhood as they proved particularly useful for recruiting. Furthermore, the churches provided the general biblical imagery that lent itself easily to propaganda purposes. Even if this propaganda only reached a minority of the British population, its ideas were rooted in the moral and spiritual universe of the majority of British citizens at the time and created a common ground between the different denominations and classes despite their varying religious practices and beliefs.

The various concepts of suffering, sacrifice, redemption and renewal were most readily applied to a war in which the English soldier was the 'Christian soldier' following the example of Christ as declared in John 15:13: 'Greater love hath no man than this, that a man lay down his life for his friends.'[23] It is therefore not surprising that the Church Lad Brigade, a Youth organisation within the Church of England, provided over 120,000 recruits to the British Army (Schweitzer, 2003, p. 8). Thus, despite the fact that before the war secularism had flourished in England (see Bruce, 1992 and Cox, 1982), the early months of war saw an increase in Church attendance and the numbers even fuelled hopes of a religious revival.

Among the soldiers, faith in a good God was a welcome means of dissipating stress, especially before offensives. In prayer, the ranks prepared themselves for the possibility of their own death while at the same time asking for protection against enemy bullets or gas. During battle itself, however, God was often perceived to be absent. Few soldiers had the time to think of God in the middle of combat. Furthermore, the idea of God in combination with battle always proved to be a difficult one as it inevitably raised questions of personal guilt for the violation of the fifth commandment (Exodus 20:13; Deuteronomy 5:17). Many Christian volunteers therefore asked for non-violent forms of active service, serving, for example, as stretcher bearers. In the reconstitution process after battle, religion furthermore functioned as a diverse means of honouring the dead, praising God for having saved one's own life and avowing one's sinfulness. It involved a special form of survivor's guilt, namely the question 'Why did I survive when my friend, brother or cousin had to die?'[24]

With regard to historical evidence for the role of faith during the war, it is important to note that it is unequally distributed among the various groups of participants. Among the upper classes, documentation of religious beliefs and practices was rare because Christianity was part of their social fabric and as such taken for granted. Junior officers, on the other hand, mostly came from upper-middle-class backgrounds in which religion had always played an important role in both education and family life.[25] Their religious response to the war is the most widely documented as many of these officers used to keep war diaries, wrote about religious issues in their letters to family and friends, or left behind other written documents such as poetry or prose texts. Thus the most difficult evaluation of religion proves to be that of the working classes, due to a lack of documents. Even before the war the British clergy were frustrated by their failure to spread Christianity among the working poor. On the one hand, the pew system and the air of elitism had repelled the working classes from the Anglican Church. On the other, their lifestyle was perceived by members of the middle and upper classes to be largely immoral or even blasphemous. Yet 'although the documentary record is sketchier on the men's religious beliefs it is possible to conclude that many soldiers (...) held highly idiosyncratic religious beliefs. These beliefs were held deeply, despite the fact that many men did not usually participate in the public social dimension of organized religion. It can also be concluded that those men who (...) were religious (...) were more inclined to be Evangelical Christians' (Schweitzer, 2003, p. 117).

Yet once more, we have to differentiate between the population at home, who still found consolation in traditional religious rites, and the men at the front where the Church no longer enjoyed a strong position of power and respect, as 'pure Christianity [...] [does] not fit in with pure patriotism' (Owen and Bell, 1967, p. 461). For many serving soldiers, 'the windy spokesmen of the Established Church emitted a gas nearly as toxic as the substance more hideously encountered on the battlefield' (Gilbert, 1999, p. 187). Most serving soldiers therefore went on a religious journey from traditional Christian faith through scepticism or even atheism back to a highly individual concept of Christianity, distinct from the institution of the Church.

The poet and novelist Robert Graves might serve as a good example here. From his mother he had received a strict religious upbringing, but in 1914 he claimed that he was losing his religious faith. When Graves joined the Royal Welsh Fusiliers, however, his faith rekindled and he even claimed in letters home that religious services had more meaning to him in wartime. With the death of friends and Lieutenant David Thomas in particular on 18 March 1916, his religious faith seems to have been broken, judging from the poetry of the period. Despite the fact that he refused to attend religious services after Easter 1916, his letter to his brother on 14 October 1918 ends with the valediction 'bless you'. Religious faith thus mixes with periods of doubt and even anger.[26]

On the other side of the Channel, the stress of war with its air raids, food shortages and constant sorrow rather increased the appeal of religion. As the same set of problems was shared with their parish members, the relationship between ministers and believers grew closer. Furthermore, most parish clergy were unaware of the statements of their Bishops, but rather expressed their own ideas about war in their teaching. Christianity's doctrine of resurrection here proved to be most useful as it suggested a possible reunion with loved ones after death in the near or far future. However, the long expected and hoped-for religious revival never set in. On the contrary, 'the war experience contributed to the decline of organized religion' (Schweitzer, 2003, p. 206)[27] that became characteristic of the twentieth century.

All of these factors have consequences for the literary legacy of war. The following analysis of irony in poems dealing with religious issues will largely be based on the poetry of middle-class writers, due to a lack of other documents, and will therefore portray a very specific and sometimes limited attitude towards institutional Christianity. Yet it is also possible to deduce the importance of religious elements for the common soldier, from anonymous poems or songs and the imitation of colloquialisms. It is debatable whether the spontaneous invocation of God's name may qualify as sincere prayer, but it shows the misery and fear among those facing immediate danger or death as in Hodgson's *Before Action*. Phrases like 'Oh God!' or 'Christ!' occur frequently throughout the poetry, in particular in combination with the verb 'to stop'. These invocations gain particular ironic potential when used without piety in conjunction with criticism of a distinctly Christian diction or even in blasphemous curses such as in Sassoon's *Redeemer*. At the same time they reinforce the motif of Christ as the prince of peace, rather than war. However, one of Sassoon's other poems, *Christ and the Soldier*, starts with a reproaching question: 'Lord Jesus, ain't you got no more to say?' and continues with an ironic interplay between the suffering of Christ and that of the soldiers only to show that Christ's death was irrelevant and does not prevent further suffering.

On the other hand, his deliberately transformed sonnet[28] *Attack* epitomises this faith, or rather faint hope in a divine intervention when nothing else can stop the killing. The poem presents war as collective suicide, after the mud of Flanders has drowned all hope. That the invocation of Jesus in the last line is an ironic one becomes clear earlier in the poem with the description of the destructive potential of modern weapons such as tanks and bombs, in front of which men – and God with them – are left entirely impotent.[29] This impression is reinforced by the form of the poem, an incomplete sonnet ending abruptly after the thirteenth line.[30] The poem's focus is the most desperate of all battle procedures, namely the beginning of an attack, the 'going over the top' of the men, which might equally stand for their transition from life to death. The final cry of desperation is thus at once a blasphemous oath and a plea to a God who seems absent from what is actually happening. *To Any Dead Officer* uses the same cry, this time transformed into a question, thus reinforcing the scepticism inherent in the question itself.

A similar device in this respect is the quotation of hymns for the sake of both consolation and outcry. On the one hand, these hymns constituted a link with home and nearly every soldier knew some of them by heart. On the other hand, they easily lend themselves to satire by the composition of mockery verses to well-known tunes.[31] The humour of these verses was less directed against the faith expressed in the original hymns – although some of them were rejected for their heroism and romantic imagery – but was rather intended to mock both military and clerical authorities.

While the individual soldier could easily identify with the suffering of Christ, as Wilfred Owen's poem *Greater Love*[32] indicates, the Church itself was accused of spreading a wrong, i.e. non-biblical, image of Jesus. Only a God who was suffering with the men made sense to most soldiers – and comforted many women, as Eva Dobell's *Advent 1916* shows – and, through the strong love for their comrades, soldiers were re-enacting Christ's sacrifice for mankind, knowing that their own was to no purpose as it required ever more sacrifices. Yet it should also not be forgotten that in doing so they took life as well, and that their sacrifice was thus by no means a passive one. To avoid the criticism of misinterpretation, the nationalist clergy mostly referred to the Old Testament as better suited for pro-war propaganda with its passages on the vengeance of God, his jealousy and his power over Israel's enemies. This image of an angry God was difficult to combine with the peaceful Jesus of the Gospels and Paul's letters. From the New Testament only the Book of Revelation with its depictions of the coming of Christ, the last battle against evil and the renewal of God's kingdom after the furnace, was as frequently quoted in propagandist sermons.

Whereas the ancient stories of the Old Testament thus became a source of militaristic imagery and language in the hands of the war's supporters, many soldiers once in a while sought refuge in the Bible, especially in the book of Psalms and the gospel of John. However, even these most favourite passages sometimes served a satirical purpose. The destruction of biblical myths became a frequent technique of both professional and amateur poets. Reversals of psalms, biblical stories or Jesus's words are thus common elements of many trench poems.

Thus *The Pilot's Psalm*, an anonymous poem, effectively (mis)uses Psalm 23:

> The BE2C is my 'bus; therefore I shall want.
> He maketh me to come down in green pastures.
> He leadeth me where I will not go.
> He maketh me to be sick; he leadeth me astray on all cross-country
>   flights.
> Yea, though I fly over No-Man's Land where mine
>   enemies would compass me about, I fear much evil
>   for thou art with me; thy joystick and thy prop discomfort me.
> Thou preparest a crash before me in the presence
>   of thy enemies; thy RAF anointeth my hair with oil, thy tank
>   leaketh badly.
> Surely to goodness thou shalt not follow me all
>   the days of my life, else I shall dwell in the house of Colney
>   Hatch forever.

Both the poem's archaic language and its form reveal it to be a parody of psalm 23, probably the most well-known psalm of the Bible and thus easily recognisable as the basis of the poem's irony by the author's contemporaries. In the poem biblical language is fused with pilot slang to create an effective blend. Yet, although the speaker expects the reader's knowledge of the Psalm's original form and content, contradictions of the biblical verses in every line of the poem and the constant negation of the psalm's positive content reveal the irony to such an extent that large parts of it might even be detected without background knowledge. However, as religious knowledge is constantly decreasing, a time might come in which readers will no longer perceive the intertextual irony of the poem.

The target of the poem's irony differs from other poems in this chapter as it is not directed at the clergy or the interpretation of the Bible by the Church. Instead, the irony focuses on the experimental character of the machinery and the lack of care of the mechanics resulting in the bad condition of the plane. Against the biblical negative, aviation is portrayed as a risky business: navigation was hardly possible, especially in bad weather, and crashes were frequent. In the context of war, it seems, God loses his omnipotence and fails to protect the pilots. At the same time, however, the poem questions man's right to transgress God-given boundaries.

While the psalms in other cases helped the soldiers to praise God's providence – for which the non-demolished crucifixes at roadsides and

Bibles protecting from bullets were often considered proof – the men also prayed for other causes, especially the welfare of their families back at home. The main obstacle, however, to prayer and to religion in general was neither a feeling of self-reliance, nor one of humility or guilt, but the idea that the Germans were praying for the same cause (Squire, *The Dilemma*), which turned the idea of God taking sides with the Allies into absurdity. At the same time, it was impossible to adhere to the Christian commandment to love one's enemy while war's main aim was to destroy him. Humanism in this respect also offered no real alternative because its principles equally encompassed all human beings and could not be limited to one's own side of the trenches.

Despite the poets' frequent identification with Christ – and accordingly France and Flanders with Gethsemane as in Kipling's *Gethsemane* – and thus their concentration on the New Testament, they also made use of the Old Testament, either to criticise the war for murdering innocent young men and thus creating the myth of the slaughter of youth still prominent today, or to revert the image of God fighting on the side of the Allies, as Robert Graves does in his poem *Goliath and David*. The David of Graves's poem strongly relies on the assumption that 'God will save' in a situation of unequal power, just as he supported David in the biblical story. In the poem, however, God's eyes do not see the boy's struggles and God's ears do not hear his cries, so that finally David is killed by the stronger Goliath, portrayed in the last two lines as a German soldier. The reversal of the names in the title is significant in this respect as it puts the emphasis on the victorious Goliath yet still names David as his brave opponent. Thus, despite the general pessimism and hopelessness of the poem, the English David dies as a hero, which sets Graves's poem apart from the ones to follow in this section.

Wilfred Owen equally uses Old Testament material, but for a more critical purpose with regard to heroism and England's military engagement.[33] In the case of his *Parable of the Old Man and the Young*, the story of Abraham's sacrifice of Isaac provides the basis for the intertextual irony. Unlike in Graves's poem, it is not God who is accused of failure, but the older generation of warmongers[34] represented by the biblical figure of Abraham. These old men, according to Owen, prevent the divine will from being fulfilled and are thus an easy target for the irony of the poem. Owen's version of the biblical source is a non-rhymed sonnet to which a fully rhymed couplet is added as a conclusion, changing the biblical ending into one more appropriate for the description of war experience. In addition to the content, the form of the poem thus serves to underline the focus of the irony. As a parody, Owen retains the logical structure of the original biblical story in order to reinterpret the material symbolically. Abraham insists on offering his own sacrifice of pride despite other alternatives. The irony of the poem thus 'emanates from the contrast between the relieved humanity of Abraham and the wilful homicide of the leaders of Europe' (O'Keefe, 1972, p. 79). Yet Owen emphasises his point by using intertextual allusions also on the level of language. Isaac's question on the 'fire and wood' in the original story in Genesis 22:7 is parallel to the 'fire and iron' of the battlefield in the poem, and, while the biblical Abraham only binds Isaac, Owen's Abraham 'bound the youth with belts and straps,/And builded parapets and trenches there' (ll. 7f.). With the appearance of the ram at the end of the biblical story, the blessing given to Abraham in Genesis 12:17 is fulfilled, and God will multiply his seed through Isaac. *The Parable of the Old Man and the Young*, however, prophesies the opposite, namely sterility and destruction effected by the 'old man' in the last two lines of the poem.

Both form and content of the poem clearly show the influence of Sassoon's satires, with the author's critique being implicitly mentioned in the last lines. However, in the eyes of Owen's critics, the poem represents the view of the childless, single young man lacking insight into the feelings of parents who often felt that something of themselves died with their sons. Yet another less well-known example of a war poem dealing with the same material, Osbert Sitwell's *The Modern Abraham*, draws a similar wartime moral. Here Abraham is presented as a profiteer who takes as much as he can from the war by sacrificing others.

Siegfried Sassoon concentrates on Old Testament versions of useless slaughter, such as the story of Abel and Cain in which the young man loved by God is slain by his brother, which Sassoon interprets as God's (unjust) punishment rather than fratricide in *Ancient History*. The young men both fall victim to the desires and interests of others against which they are powerless. 'The idea of laying down their lives was accompanied in the minds of the soldier-victims by the idea of there being someone to perform the sacrifice who was not personally laying down his own life. The sacrificer was always older, always more powerful, always in a position of some authority' (Spear, 1979, p. 104). Accordingly, G. A. Studdert Kennedy ridicules or at least questions the idea of sacrifice by calling it a folly in stanza 2 of *Woodbine Willie*.

Unlike Christ's sacrifice of love, the soldiers' sacrifice is a foolish one representative of the churches' divergence from what Christ had originally taught his disciples, namely to love one's enemy. Wilfred Owen, who had grown up in an evangelical Christian household with a strongly religious mother, and who had even considered becoming an Anglican priest, particularly focused on this point in his poetry. His position as assistant to an Anglican vicar at Dunsden had altered his view of organised religion and during the course of war Owen rejected official theology in favour of a deinstitutionalised 'primitive' form of Christianity (Owen and Bell, 1967, pp. 467, 534). In a letter to his mother in May 1917 he thus states: 'I am more and more Christian as I walk the unchristian ways of Christendom. Already I have comprehended a light which never will filter into the dogma of any national church: namely that of passivity at any price! Suffer dishonour and disgrace; but never resort to arms. Be bullied, be outraged, be killed; but do not kill. (...) I think pulpit professionals are ignoring it very skilfully and successfully indeed' (Owen and Bell, 1967, p. 461f.). While himself an officer carrying arms and suffering from a 'seared conscience',[35] his war poetry often portrays Christ as a pacifist, the prince of peace.[36] While Jesus, the Son, was aligned with the soldiers in suffering, God the Father was to be found on the other side together with the staff, the government and the older generation in general. Father and Son were no longer one, but distinct entities with different interests.

Again his friend Osbert Sitwell's poetry shares the same ideas. *Rhapsode* focuses on the horrors of the crucifixion with words that could also be describing death in France. Jesus's cry 'why hast Thou forsaken me?' can easily be imagined as that of a dying soldier. However, the cry is renounced as unheroic by the Pharisees and Sadducees, the warmongers back at home arguing about a soldier's 'appropriate' last words. In Sitwell's second crucifixion poem, the bystanders do not therefore pity Jesus on the cross, but rather Joseph, his father, while Christ himself is criticised for his bitterness and despair.

While some of Owen's poems such as *Greater Love, At a Calvary near the Ancre* or his poem about the Virgin of Quivières admire Christ's sacrifice, they question its relevance in the context of war. These poems renounce any militant interpretation of the Bible as nothing less than 'selective ignorance'. However, it was only as a combatant that he felt he was able to ease and make public the sufferings of the men because he, too, 'saw God through mud' (*Apologia pro Poemate Meo*).[37] At the same time, he compared his work as a soldier to that of Christ's sacrifice. In *At a Calvary near the Ancre* Owen presents the soldier as a Christ figure: Christ died but rose again, so hopefully will the soldier. This concept of patriotic sacrifice in Owen's eyes, however, is none that the soldier accepts voluntarily, but rather one that is prescribed by official Christianity. The equation exposes the disparity between the ethics of the Sermon on the Mount and the doctrines of hatred for the Germans (the Hun) as propagated by bellicose clergymen who only 'brawl allegiance to the state'.[38] As a result of his argumentation he denies the clerical nationalists the status of Christians: '[T]here are no more Christians at the present moment than there were at the end of the first century' (Owen and Bell, 1967, p. 483). Owen's attitude towards religion, however, despite the occasional bitterness in his poetry, is dominated by despair rather than rejection, as captured in the last line of the penultimate stanza of *Exposure*: 'For love of God seems dying.'

The resulting ironical view on organised religion reflects his experiences[39] but fails to provide answers to the most pressing questions, as it does not offer anything to replace it. Thus the subversive critique of hollow rituals in *Anthem for Doomed Youth* is indicative of Owen's opposition to religious traditions which he dismisses as mockeries.[40] Written in September or October 1917, *Anthem for Doomed Youth* is one of Owen's earliest poems showing the influence of Sassoon: Owen already felt that the war was destroying the world and began to question the validity of old rituals and traditional aesthetic norms. However, he had no ready answer at this point. Instead, he only felt that the mechanical sounds of the battlefield[41] were more appropriate for the funeral of the slaughtered soldiers than the harmonic melodies of hymns or bells. 'The hymn, a song of praise, has been swallowed into the discourse of elegy, a song of mourning' (Kerr, 1993, p. 298). As such, the poem questions the genre of the religious hymn as well as the consoling function of Christian faith.

Despite its ironic overtones, the sonnet was often criticised for relapsing into Owen's youthful Romanticism and unintentionally glorifying death at war (Silkin, 1972, pp. 210–211).[42] It continues the topic of *Greater Love*, namely the soldier's sacrifice. Owen chose the word 'anthem' for the title as it reminds the reader of 'The National Anthem' and thus suggests the close link between Church and State at the time. Additionally, the word underlines the seriousness of the poem's content by stressing the structural organisation of a choir piece. The ironic potential is underlined by the fact that, as a religious song, an anthem often expresses joy, for example about Christ's birth or resurrection. Here, however, it ironically refers to the celebration of mass 'sacrifice' in accordance with which the poem is dedicated to 'doomed youth'. When we consider Owen's draft of a Preface for his first volume of poetry, it becomes clear that the term does not only imply the dead young soldiers he mourns in the poem. Rather, it includes all young men of coming generations who might be endangered by wars. The purpose of the poem is thus already established in the title: to warn against the horrors and consequences of war.

The poem starts off with a question about how to mourn the dead. By using 'these', the author deliberately creates an impersonal atmosphere. There are so many dead that it is impossible to care for the individual. Structurally, the second line gives the answer to the question of the first and thus establishes the unconsolatory direction of the poem by keeping the reader's attention on the condition of the death process. Ironically, the only mourning voices on the battlefield are the guns that at the same time create the cause for the mourning by killing the men in masses. This irony is continued in lines 4 and 10/11 of the poem. By uttering their 'prayers', the rifles constantly increase the number of those they will have to mourn and the light in the boys' eyes will soon die with them on the battlefield once they are old enough to go to war.

Owen suggests that the only appropriate response to death is awareness of it. The 'bugles'[43] halfway through the poem mark the transition of focus from the battlefield to home. Thus Part 2 of the poem concentrates on the traditional rites of mourning back in England, such as the 'drawing-down of blinds'.[44] Yet the difference between the octave and the sestet is not only one of content (front vs home), but also one of tone. Whereas the first part reproduces the aggressive sounds of battle as symbolic of the poet's anger, the second part is dominated by an ethereal atmosphere. While acknowledging the poetic effect, Jon Silkin sees an ambiguity here: 'The consolatory and decorous ceremonies of the religious and institutional mourning contrast with the brutal nature of their deaths. Yet there is ambiguity in the poem in that Owen seems to be caught in the very act of consolatory mourning he condemns in "What passing-bells for these who die as cattle?" – a consolation that permits the war's continuation by civil assent, and which is found ambiguously in the last line of the octet: "And bugles calling for them from sad shires"' (Silkin, 1972, p. 211). Geoffrey Hill has also argued that the sestet fails to provide an appropriate response to the war by trying to demonstrate an internal contradiction: 'The fact that Owen employs irony in this poem cannot alter the fact that he takes thirteen lines to retreat from the position maintained by one. If these men really do die as cattle, then all human mourning for them is a mockery, the private and the public, the inarticulate and true as much as the ostentatiously false' (Bloom, 2002, p. 37f.). But even if the poem stresses the uselessness of mourning, it does not deny its existence as a human reaction.[45]

Earlier drafts of the poem had contained more patriotic and sanctifying language, which Owen had removed under the influence of Sassoon in order to render religion as impotent and meaningless as possible when faced with war and its consequences. By doing so the remaining diction of the poem reinforces the opposition between the indignity of death at war and traditional, inappropriate ways of dignifying it. Even religion itself seems to become a mockery. The poem thus confirms our modern vision of warfare as a pointless slaughter. However, many soldiers did not want to perceive themselves as cattle going to slaughter, nor did they wish to be told that their effort was a waste of life.

As already expressed in the above poems, protest was directed not only against the churches' involvement in British war propaganda, but also against the ineffectiveness and cowardliness of the clergy. While at the outbreak of war there were 117 Anglican chaplains serving in the British Army, this number had dramatically increased to 3,475 when the war ended in 1918 (see Schweitzer, 2003, p. 63). Most of these men entered service without real preparation and only in 1916 was an initiation course established. Furthermore, at the beginning of war no provision had been made in the mobilisation plans concerning transportation, accommodation, payment or rations of chaplains and this situation only gradually changed. Whilst the majority of ordinary soldiers came from working-class backgrounds and thus knew hunger and hardship, the clergy were almost entirely of middle or even upper-class origin, a fact which separated them from the men right from the start.

Once they were at the front, the chaplains had to fulfil both secular and religious functions in the Army: superior officers often used them for running errands, for construction work, for censoring letters or as stretcher bearers. They also functioned as mediators between rank and officers in disputes, and between the battlefield and home. As such, they were often asked to notify families of soldiers' deaths. Furthermore, as a counterpart to the military parades, the clergy at the front were responsible for the so-called Church Parades, mandatory religious services behind the front lines, which were often described as hollow by both clergy and soldiers (see Schweitzer, 2003, p. 200).

Thus only little time was left for their 'proper' job, namely providing consolation, giving moral counsel, conducting burials or offering services. With regard to their religious duties, many chaplains were more concerned with preaching against gambling, alcohol and sexual immorality than with lifting the soldiers up spiritually. The clergy failed to provide answers to moral dilemmas, such as the distinction between right and wrong with regard to the treatment of prisoners or reprisals for attacks, or that of Sunday work. As a result, respect for the clergy soon gave way to frustration and contempt as official religion did not meet the reality of war.

The combination of Christianity and nationalist propaganda in particular provoked some of Sassoon's most satirical poetry. Although Sassoon's poetry is by no means representative of the general mood, his criticism was shared by many soldiers. The poet had been raised as an Anglican by his mother despite the fact that his father was Jewish, and before the war he had been to Church occasionally and was on good terms with a number of parsons. With the prolongation of war, however, he became more and more disillusioned with organised religion. The most prominent example of Sassoon's critique of nationalist propaganda inside the Church of England can be found in his bitter anti-clerical poem *They*, in which the satiric effect is mainly created through exaggeration: it is a satire targeting the limitations of institutionalised religion, especially its impersonality. As such, the poem expresses the poet's despair over the lack of the Church's humanitarian responsibility. As a satire, *They* combines amusement and contempt: on the one hand, the reader shares the poet's hatred for the ignorant bishop; on the other he inevitably has to laugh at the absurdity of the communication. The title of the poem already conveys this division between the clergy and the soldiers, representative of the general perspective of home as opposed to that of the front. The bishop refers to the soldiers as 'they' (four times), which indicates his lack of attachment and empathy. The soldiers remain anonymous and impersonal for him, as does their fate. In contrast, however, the reader finds himself as part of the group of soldiers by way of the pronoun 'us' in the first line. As such, one is aligned with the boys in the rejection of institutionalised Christianity.[46] This division between the two groups is further underlined by a division in the structure of the poem, which consists of two simple stanzas of six lines each. In both of them the initial quatrain is followed by a couplet which allows Sassoon to highlight his irony with the help of the rhyme scheme.

This structure of the poem is exemplary of the general structure of satires, which have largely remained unchanged throughout the long history of the genre. In most cases it follows a division into two parts, of which the first depicts the situation the satirist wants to criticise. The second part then presents things as they should be and it is usually shorter than the first. Satire thus served the purpose of contrasting two versions of society, a real and an ideal one. This division can be seen as the result of the idealistic aesthetics of the classicists, such as Schiller and his contemporaries. In his essay 'Über naive und sentimentalische Dichtung' of 1795 he comes up with the following description of the satirical:

> 'Satyrisch ist der Dichter, wenn er die Entfernung von der Natur und den Widerspruch der Wirklichkeit mit dem Ideale (...) zu seinem Gegenstande macht (...)' And:
> 'In der Satire wird die Wirklichkeit als Mangel dem Ideal als höchster Realität gegenübergestellt' (Schiller, 2002, 39f.).

Though not applied rigorously, this scheme can still be discovered in many satiric works of the nineteenth and twentieth centuries. In the case of the poem, the first part of the satire presents the reader with the words of the bishop, a representative of the nationalist clergy. By using pompous language, the poet maintains an impersonal air and thus further adds to the formality of the bishop's speech. The second part, one line shorter than the first in accordance with the traditional scheme, reveals the reality of war by focusing on its individual consequences. The contrast with part 1, i.e. the bishop's words, is further underlined by the word *some* in italics. The boys do not talk about what things should or might be like, but what they really are like in this war, and by doing so they reveal the inappropriateness of the bishop's ideas about war. Changes are taking place, but not for good. This contrast between the bishop's speech in part 1 and the reality of part 2 supports the satirical interpretation of the poem.

Sassoon then deviates from the traditional form by giving the bishop's answer in the last line. Instead of changing his notion of war on the basis of what he has just heard, the bishop chooses to withdraw into hollow Christian phrases. 'Confronted with these stark physical changes rather than the spiritual change he had anticipated, the Bishop replies with a hollow and wholly inadequate injunction that "the ways of God are strange!"' (Schweitzer, 2003, p. 164). However, the blindness, mutilation and insanity of the boys render the attitude of the bishop's patriotism outfaced by reality. At the same time, the Bishop's last sentence stresses God's helplessness and indifference with regard to the war, a conclusion which he ironically shares with the boys.

In addition to the division into two parts, the bishop's answer may again indicate a satirical interpretation based on the use of the unexpected as one of the main techniques of satire (Highet, 1962). As Patrick Campbell argues, 'the key to the poem's power resides in the ironic force of "they will not be the same." Intended by the Bishop as a comment on the ennobling effect of war, the pronouncement acquires a different significance in the terrifyingly candid rejoinder of the boy soldiers. It is only when "they" recite a litany of personal disasters that the nature of the change is made starkly clear' (Campbell, 1999, p. 125). The Bishop's final sentence creates a surprise effect: the boys at first seem to accept the bishop's message, but the poem reveals that war did not transform them into heroes, but into maimed and pitiable objects. The Bishop's words are no real answer to the boys' needs. Thus the implications of the poem go beyond the ironic: there is nothing that can really console or heal, neither words nor counter-actions like good deeds to the disabled. As such, the irony is mixed with feelings of melancholy and compassion for the boys.

The poem effectively fires against religious hypocrisy, especially inside the Church of England, the largest denomination among the English soldiers. The war did not lay the foundation for an 'honourable race', nor did it 'buy new right'. In the jargon of the trenches, the expression ironically signified being blown to bits. Whether or not Sassoon's Bishop is aware of this connotation remains outside the focus of the poem. However, the shallowness of patriotic vocabulary is further emphasised by the fact that no-one wants to 'dare' death. Rather, the soldiers' main aim is to stay alive despite the mortal dangers of the front. And, even if they dared to face the enemy, modern warfare did not allow this. Instead of fighting noble bayonet fights, soldiers were confronted with long-distance weapons and the even more impersonal gas.

Whereas Owen often uses a sequence of images to build up tension, Sassoon successfully creates a dramatic interplay of voices for the same effect. It is this tension – culminating in the Bishop's final sentence – that renders the poem so successful. It was and still is, among Sassoon's poems, the 'most quoted by reviewers, both adverse and favourable' (Sassoon, 1973, p. 29). However, Sassoon's critique of the clergy did not imply a rejection of Christian faith. For Sassoon, especially in *The Redeemer*, Christ was constantly with the men in the trenches, as the son of man suffering the same tribulations of war.

Most pastors and priests had orders to remain behind the lines, mainly with the field ambulances, and it was this spatial separation of the clergy from the fighting soldier that caused the strongest resentments. The Anglican clergy especially were accused of constant absence from the fighting areas, whereas Roman Catholic chaplains often stayed with their troops in the most dangerous areas against official orders and sometimes even assumed military command after the deaths of officers during battle. Additionally, and unlike their Anglican colleagues, most Catholic chaplains were of working-class background and thus closer to the majority of soldiers in both thinking and lifestyle. This seeming difference between Roman Catholic and Anglican clergy was furthered by Graves's account of Anglican chaplains in his autobiographical novel *Goodbye to All That*, which first appeared in 1929 and for a long time has shaped the historical perspective of the First World War chaplaincy. However, as Schweitzer (2003, p. 172) points out, statistics differ from the general perception: 'the relatively higher fatality of Anglican chaplains serving overseas should once and for all clear the reputation of the Anglican chaplains in the historical record'. The numbers suggest that at least those Anglican chaplains who stayed at the front with their men even seemed to have been more inclined to expose themselves to fire than their Catholic colleagues. The frequent conversion of soldiers might thus not only have been a result of Anglican 'cowardliness', but also of the Catholic concept of mystery that was perceived as more useful in explaining the tragedies of war than evangelical Anglicanism. Additionally, Roman Catholic churches were more accessible in France than Protestant ones and consequently had a special appeal for the soldiers as places of worship, the rosary had a special appeal for its simplicity, and the strict organisation of the Catholic Church rendered it more efficient in times of war (Allitt, 1997).

In addition to criticism of the clergy by the serving soldiers, there was a widespread sense of failure among the chaplains themselves,[47] so that many chaplains did not renew their contracts. Many chaplains had enlisted because they saw an opportunity to carry out missionary work among soldiers who would otherwise not have set foot into a Christian church but were now exposed to religious influence. However, not only was it difficult to create a 'churchy' atmosphere in the trenches, but the diffusive character of popular religion among the soldiers did not necessarily require clerical guidance. Thus, although the general primitivism of Christian army services often had a special appeal to many soldiers, the clergy suffered from what they considered to be obstacles to professionalism. Their contempt for constant improvisation was also accompanied by homesickness and poor wages. This again led to an increasing estrangement between chaplains and soldiers, who had no choice other than to stay once they had arrived at the front. The war furthermore exposed the need for Church reforms as it revealed and increased the several schisms among the clergy, especially between traditionalists and reformers and between the different generations, but also between denominations.

However, it would be unjust to call the soldiers godless. They continued to pray to the Christian God for protection before an attack, and, despite their fatalist creed with regard to God's distance and helplessness, the belief in life after death was widespread. Most of the time religious sentiments ceased after the immediate danger of attack was over and turned into anger for the loss of friends, who were nevertheless considered lucky to have exchanged this hell on earth for heaven. Thus the representation of prayer could equally well be used as a means of irony, as in Richard Aldington's *Battlefield*. While the first part of the poem describes a desolate landscape with the typical barbed wire and the rotting corpses, the focus then shifts to the only object that grows there in abundance, namely the crosses of the dead. The poem finally ends with the prayer of a French soldier for a German corpse presented by an English poet. Rather than expressing a mere critique of war, the irony of the poem helps to evoke new hope that religion and prayer will finally transgress the boundaries of nationalism in favour of community.

The longer the war lasted, the louder the voice of scepticism became. How could a humane God allow the war to go on like this? Criticism of the church more than once turned into that of the Christian God of love. Edward Thomas in his poem *February Afternoon* sarcastically suggests the possibility of an uncaring God: 'And God still sits aloft in the array/That we have wrought him, stone deaf and stone-blind.' Wilfred Owen's poem *Greater Love* similarly describes the front as a place 'Where God seems not to care'. God was rejected as wrathful, weak, non-caring, or even insane by large parts of the wartime population, who fled into various forms of doubt such as fatalism, atheism, agnosticism, or spiritualism.[48] In the most extreme of cases, God was even declared dead, as in Harold Monro's *The Poets are Waiting*, in which Lord is no longer spelled with a capital letter as in texts of devotion. While God only seems to be drowsing, in fact he is dead and will no longer listen to the soldiers' songs of battle. At least he was 'not exerting Himself to save the victims of war' (Spear, 1979, p. 104), nor was he offering any guidance, as Ivor Gurney lightly pointed out in *The Target*. On the other hand, the Church itself was perceived as preventing God from intervening by its distance from the reality of the soldiers, as Owen ironically points out in *Le Christianisme*.

Contrary to their male counterparts, most women did not question Christianity but rather identified with the ideas of sacrifice and suffering as presented by the churches. They found comfort in the faith that God would heal the wounds without being aware that institutionalised religion largely sanctioned the slaughter. A further source of comfort for mothers in particular was their identification with Mary under the cross. Among the female responses to the relationship between war and Christianity, however, M. Sackville's poem *Sacrament* is notable for its direct mockery of official religion, especially so in stanza 3. Like Owen, the author focuses on a pacifist Christian agenda, embedded in the symbolism of Holy Communion. The enjambment between lines 2 and 3 creates a link between the lengthening casualty lists in the daily papers and the wine press as a container for the dead soldiers' blood. Yet this blood, unlike that of Christ, does not cleanse but rather pollutes and destroys. The poem finally even rejects Christianity as such because it provides too strong a support for militarist nationalism. Although 'Britain's historic Christian identity continued to console and support the nation' (Snape, 2005, p. 242), the war not only challenged religious ideas by setting up an array of moral problems, but also undermined the traditional Christian rhetoric that had dominated much of the literature of the eighteenth and nineteenth centuries. Phrases and metaphors became hollow when confronted with the horrors of the war; and especially during the later years of war authors struggled either to replace this Christian diction or to use it as a source of irony, as has been revealed in this section. The works to be discussed in the next section will again challenge wartime authority, this time that of the military leaders.

3.2   War leaders

A large portion of the poetry to be dealt with in this section expresses a critical position with regard to the military competence of the war leaders, especially the generals, and thus led to the creation of the image of the absent general unthinkingly sending his men to death. The generals were seen as having the ultimate responsibility, but using it inappropriately by planning campaigns on the drawing board instead of on the field. However, they were not only accused for their absence from the front lines but also for their lack of sympathy for, and interest in, the common soldier. Furthermore, medical treatment according to military ranks did not help to decrease feelings of betrayal among common soldiers as ironically presented by Siegfried Sassoon in *Arms and the Man*.

 Probably to ease his own bad conscience as an officer, Sassoon critically confronts the elitist underpinnings of military life in this poem. 'The poem, written soon after the event [his visit to the Medical Board at Caxton Hall, Westminster, to hear whether he would be able to return to France], makes full use of the macabre humour of a notice in the desolate waiting-room, advising amputees on how to get government replacement limbs free of charge, though the irony is a little laboured' (Wilson, 1998, p. 308).[49] The telling names of the protagonists, Croesus and Colonel Sawbones, in this case serve to distance the subject from the poem in order to guarantee an objective perspective. Additionally, the reference to the biblical Croesus suggests wealth and status which not only enables the rich to become officers but entitles them to free limbs despite their upper-class origins and higher pay, while the ordinary soldiers had to pay for them. Furthermore, the name might imply that Croesus is 'rich in health' as he is still in possession of all his limbs. Thus, on the one hand, the poem is interested in the major and minor injustices of war. On the other hand, however, the poem emphasised that the gift of free limbs hardly compensates for what is irretrievably lost.

Despite these class differences and other severe reproaches of military leaders, their main problem was one of training and technology. Not only did they have to operate with troops who only went through a short training period before being sent to the front, but this training was not aiming at offensive warfare. Furthermore, with the creation of Kitchener's New Armies, a lack of instructors and officers emerged as most professionals had already been sent to France with the BEF and were by then dead. An appeal for junior officers – unmarried men between seventeen and thirty with a university education – produced massive applications, but none of these men had enough experience to be ready for the job as efficient officers. Many of them came from the Officers' Training Corps and were of public school background, as both the commanders and those responsible for recruitment were keen on preserving the gentleman officer tradition. As a result, many who had the military potential to become good officers were excluded right from the start for reasons of class.

As a solution to this major problem, officers who had already retired were called back to duty, but many found 'that they could not adapt to the changes wrought in drill, tactics and equipment in the decade before the war, and particularly since the introduction of the new Field Service Regulations in 1909' (Simkins, 1988, p. 217). Furthermore, the new recruits were often better educated than the old soldiers and consequently were not willing to tolerate the intellectual as well as military shortcomings of their 'elderly' officers. Despite every effort, 'very few New Army units ever had enough competent re-enlisted soldiers to fill all their non commissioned officer ranks and, consequently, the majority of battalion commanders had to make up the required number simply by choosing promising recruits' (Simkins, 1988, p. 227).

In addition to this officer shortage and the resulting problems with regard to military training, all innovatory arms, the rifle and the machine gun, barbed wire, shells and even gas could well be used for defensive purposes, but they were not suitable for military breakthroughs. Only the tanks were particularly developed for that purpose, but they were still too slow, overmanned and mechanically unreliable to achieve the expected results during the First World War. The same was true for war in the air. Most planes could not carry enough bombs, and communication with the infantry was largely impossible, which hindered successful cooperation during an attack. Even the Navy faced similar difficulties. The ships were able to reach the enemy out of visible range, but did not have the technology to spot ships in the distance or verify hits. Thus, due to a lack of alternatives, the army generals mainly stuck to the use of cavalry[50] and mass attacks despite high losses. However, tactics changed considerably throughout the war, a fact often ignored by both the literature itself and its later critics.

Nevertheless, the view that the location of headquarters miles behind the front line was the main reason for the failure of military campaigns has dominated the imagination of the First World War ever since the publication of *Base Details*. The title of the poem already suggests that it deals with details about the war that are significant for the whole affair. In its 'simplicity and singleness of effect' the poem resembles 'the clever, hard-hitting political cartoon' (Johnston, 1964, p. 105) by way of condensation. This effect is reinforced by the fact that the poem's targets are types rather than individuals. The content of *Base Details* results from Sassoon's experiences in a hotel at Rouen while waiting for directions concerning his return to the front. Despite the horrors which were awaiting him there, he preferred, according to his wartime diaries, the front to England. As Quinn points out: 'But ironically, once Sassoon had left Rouen and moved back to the front, he reverted to his "happy warrior" mentality. Caught up in the machinery of the war, he was even to claim that if he had to choose between being in England or being at the front, he would choose the front because of the "quiet elation and absolute confidence" he felt in preparing for battle' (Quinn, 1994, p. 183 and Hart-Davies, 1983, p. 151).

The poem explicitly attacks the spatial gap between the staff and the world of the troops as the main reason for the scarlet majors' incompetence. The speaker of the poem mockingly identifies with the commanders in order to present their perspective as ignorant, superficial but also easy-going as the opening conditional 'if' implies 'but luckily I am not'. The pun on the word 'scarlet' plays with the red uniform of the majors and their alleged port-soaked, choleric disposition evident in their red faces due to overindulgence. At the same time, it evokes the redness of the blood of the dying soldiers. While the majors are presented as 'fierce', this harsh, rigid outer demeanour of the base officers is revealed only to be superficial. In reality they all lack courage and bravery to be at the front themselves with their men. According to Wilson, 'the fact that the Scarlet Major plans to die "in bed", rather than at the Front with the men he has sent there, underlines the discrepancy between his sybaritic lifestyle and their sufferings' (Wilson, 1998, p. 327). The understatement present in the choice of the word 'scrap' for the mass slaughter of the Somme, Loos or Passchendaele underlines the ignorance of the staff, whereas the verb 'toddle' suggests senility. Only 'when the war is done and youth stone dead' will these self-satisfied old men 'toddle' home to die in their own beds. The previous hyphens mark this sarcastically as a final pathetic act.

The main ironic contrast within the poem is that between the self-inflicted gluttony and ignorance of the majors and the unavoidable prospect of death or mutilation in the trenches. It is precisely the speaker's identification with the majors that leads to a sense of ironic detachment.[51] While Sassoon's other satires usually confront two contradicting positions in accordance with the traditional form of the genre, this time he chooses the monologue form, making it more appropriate to speak of a satirical tone rather than a satire proper. The poem even shows a tendency towards sarcasm due to its bitterness. In the final irony 'there is a suggestion that these men [the base officers] considered themselves to be in control of events, as though, being officers, the threads of destiny ran through their hands' (Silkin, 1972, p. 159f.). In reality, however, things were by no means under control.

In its satirical critique of military superiors the poem prepared the way for *The General*, composed only two months later, the bitter humour of which comes close to that of other poems like *Base Details* or *The March-Past* in which the general is a marionette-like figure who sends his soldiers to death without spending a second thought on their fate. *The General*, Sassoon's shortest published war poem, only consists of seven lines in tetrameters, but it is highly effective in its brevity. The frequent shifts of tone and rhythm enforce the final coup de grace while at the same time imitating the rhythm of colloquial speech. Thus the initial jaunty 'good-morning' stands in striking contrast to the grim mood of the last line[52]; and together with 'He's a cheery old card' the sentence frames a moment of bitter disillusion. The general's cheerfulness is contradicted by the terrible results of his incompetence. Harry and Jack faithfully, maybe even unthinkingly, trust their General, a trust which is horribly betrayed by the outcome of events. The use of colloquial speech in this case ('did for them both') reinforces the sarcastic effect as it sharply clashes with the horrific results of the general's plan. Furthermore, Sassoon widens the scope of the poem by making two soldiers comment on the general rather than one individual victim.

The general referred to in the poem was probably Sir John French, commander of the British Expeditionary Force at the start of the war (Stephen, 1996, p. 44) and although 'most satirists (...) *claim* one purpose for satire, that of high-minded and usually socially oriented moral and intellectual reform, (...), they *engage* in something quite different, namely, mercilessly savage attack on some person or thing that, frequently for private reasons, displeases them' (Connery and Combe, 1995, p. 2). The poem shifts responsibility for the disaster onto the staff and sarcastically condemns their plans of attack as doomed to failure when confronted with reality, yet this judgement is influenced by Sassoon's personal dislike for his superior. The focus of the poem, however, is not the development of personality but rather the action itself.[53] Arras, site of a disastrous battle, stands, like so many other names, for yet another example of incompetence and wrong-headed strategy due to the generals' absence from the front.

An anonymous song successfully combines the absence of military leaders and the failure of their plans by asking for the whereabouts of a sergeant and his battalion. The stress on the personal pronouns emphasises the contrast between the two while the verb 'to see' in italics underlines the poet's authority as eye-witness to this obvious injustice, but also his horror in seeing his fellow men dying:

> If you want to find the Sergeant,
> I know where he is, I know where he is,
> I know where *he* is.
> If you want to find the Sergeant
> I know where he is –
> He's lying on the Canteen floor.
> I've seen him, I've *seen* him,
> Lying on the Canteen floor.
>
> If you want to find the old battalion,
> I know where they are, I know where they are,

> I know where *they* are,
> If you want to find the old battalion,
> I know where they are –
> They are hanging on the old barbed wire.
> I've seen 'em, I've *seen* 'em,
> Hanging on the old barbed wire.

However, not all military historians condemn the staff so vigorously as the poets or Paul Fussell in *The Great War and Modern Memory* (1975, p. 13). Both John Keegan (1998) and Martin Stephen (1996) suggest that the exigencies of the situation left the army generals little room for manoeuvre. In many cases their only option was between equally dreadful evils: winning an attack without regard for the human costs, or losing it with an equally high number but gaining nothing. No one at the time really knew how to break out of the static and costly trench warfare. The insecure outcome of battle even provoked the otherwise enthusiastic Julian Grenfell to compose an ironic prayer to God for safety in battle. However, this safety is seen to be dependent not on God's goodwill, but on the hardly trustworthy plans of the staff (stanzas 2 and 3). A. P. Herbert in *After the Battle* describes the opposite scenario to that evoked by Sassoon, a successful battle. However, although the generals' plans work out in this case, the results for the soldiers are not so different from those implied in Sassoon's *The General*.

Despite the satisfactory end of the campaign, the poem is highly dominated by the bitterness of the speaker in the first four stanzas. Not only are the acknowledgements by the general perceived as empty, but they are a burden to those who want nothing more than a retreat to some peaceful village where they would be able to ease their wounds. Once again, the only profiteer of the action is the general who, without having faced danger himself, will be promoted from commander of a division to commander of a corps (stanza 3) while the men who gave their lives gain nothing in the end.

While the myth of the absent officer has been revealed as inaccurate by both historians and war diaries, what is equally forgotten is that soldiers usually were not very keen on visits by their commanders as this usually either meant extra cleaning of arms and trenches in advance, or reprimands afterwards. In the worst case, such a visit was paid before an attack. Whereas Sassoon directly blames the general staff, Owen uses abstraction and generalisation to show the ridiculous nature of such visits and army rules in *Inspection*. The first stanza of the poem, as in Sassoon's *Base Details*, sets off with an identification of the speaker with an officer. The imitation of colloquial speech has already been discussed as a traditional method of both irony and satire. But here it serves to create a double irony by way of the fact that the common soldier uses the best language. This implies that he would probably have been better qualified as an officer but was hindered by his class background. The voices heard in Owen's poems are usually those of the ranks joined by the ironising (officer-class) speaker,[54] but this time the situation is reversed to create the special effect of the poem. At the beginning, the reader becomes witness to an ordinary situation of military life in which the officer's reaction towards the dirty soldier seems justified. Only in lines 7 and 8 is the application of military rules revealed as an unjust punishment. The result is a changed evaluation of the officer as someone outside humanity, based on the idea that a different reaction could have been expected of an empathic human being.

The identification of blood with dirt, however, does not need irony to suggest the final transformation of the soldiers' blood into clay with the trenches being continually flooded with both rain and blood. On the other hand, if blood is identified with dirt, it loses its sacrificial power and is thus different from Jesus's blood which attempts to cleanse people and renew the bond of love between them. During war, the blood-shedding rather has the contrary effect of separating enemy from friend and increasing hatred.

Here Owen uses traditional religious imagery of purity and cleansing to establish a sharp contrast against the reality of war, where any cleaning can only be superficial. As war is always dirty cleaning might be possible – as suggested in Rupert Brooke's sonnet cycle *1914* – yet cleansing of the sins committed as a soldier never. The washing away of blood strongly recalls both Lady Macbeth's – this allusion to Shakespeare is reinforced by the acute mark in "damnéd" – and Pontius Pilate's desire to remove the real or symbolic blood from their hands as betrayal of their guilt. In Owen's poem, however, the spot of blood not only reveals the soldier as murderer, but it 'is also symbolic of the guilt of those who send soldiers to be killed'.[55] This imagery of washing away one's guilt reaches its climax in line 12, in which the phrase 'the world is washing out its stains' is used as a euphemism for the dreadful bloodletting. Again the question of responsibility is asked but solved differently. Whereas Sassoon directly blames the staff for the disaster, in Owen's poem it is 'the world' that is 'washing out its stains'. The sentence denies any sense of political or military responsibility. Instead, the irony of the epithet 'Field-Marshal' applied to God in the last line of the poem questions divine providence and omnipotence.[56] The only possible exception to Owen's usual refrain from direct accusations can be found in

Smile, Smile, Smile, which implicitly connects the suffering of the soldiers to human agents.

Yet despite the injustice of the officer's reaction felt by the modern reader, we have to bear in mind that, while individuality and initiative were highly valued and appreciated features, they could only be established in the second phase of military training, for which there was hardly any time left. First of all, the recruits had to be taught how to aim, fire and clean a rifle, or how to handle grenades. Maintaining standards – also with regard to personal hygiene – inevitably required strict rules and army drill enforced by superiors even if they were not welcome among the men, as A. P. Herbert's untitled humorous poem about a general inspecting the trenches attempts to show.

As there was no mutiny among British troops during the First World War, one may conclude that the generals were not as stupid and incapable as much of the poetry wants to make us believe. Otherwise, the men would have refused to follow their commands. Even the charge of a lack of empathy for their men cannot hold, as officers often felt like fathers towards them, as does the speaker in Mackintosh, *In Memoriam Private D. Sutherland killed in Action in the German Trench, May 16, 1916, and the Others who Died* (l. 17). Most soldiers did consider their training to be relevant. It was to make them fit for active service and this inevitably included some pain. Due to the lack of alternatives most military decisions were perceived to be sound at the time, and it is only in retrospect that they have been evaluated differently. In most diaries and records there is not even any evidence to show that soldiers hated their generals, above all Sir Douglas Haig. On the contrary, the troops remained loyal to their leaders to the very end. The main reasons for the corpus of critical poetry have therefore to be sought in individual bad experiences, such as the loss of friends resulting from unsuccessful campaigns, and the misbehaviour of a few military leaders who by no means represented the majority of the staff.

3.3   Women

As the First World War was for Britain no total war, women, by reason of their sex, were exempt from war service. As Samuel Hynes puts it, 'a nation at war is a male nation' (Hynes, 1990, p. 88). Women consequently felt excluded from most war-related activities and mainly supported the war effort at the periphery, whereas men found themselves at the centre of war both as fighting soldiers and as decision-makers.[57] It is certainly true that the battlefield was a forbidden zone for women[58] as they were not permitted within the firing lines, and for this reason both anthologies and critical studies of war poetry completely excluded women's literary responses for a long time.[59] The assumption behind this was that, without sharing the male experience of physical combat, women were not able to write about war nor did they have the right to enter the male-dominated discourse of war. The First World War, in affirming the gender dichotomies by reducing women to men's help-mates, at least partly silenced women as it destroyed a distinctly female culture that had developed during the decades before the war. However, women equally suffered during the First World War and many actively served near the various front lines. For this reason this section will not only deal with poetry written by male authors about women, but it will also critically consider female literary responses to war and their ironic potential. This entails questions concerning the influence of poetry by men. With regard to the irony of women's poetry one has to ask whether it results from male reports of battlefield experience or whether it has distinctively female origins. Furthermore, are the targets of the irony the same or do they differ from those of war poetry by men?

3.3.1 Women at work

When the war broke out, the women's suffragist movement[60] entered its third decade and had finally produced some results, namely in the education sector. With the war, however, the movement as such was threatened by interior disputes. The fight for the female vote in parts turned into nationalist militarism, a 'fight for king and country' (Byles, 1995, p. 25), and the movement split into pro- and antiwar groups. Those women inclined to peace, such as Silvia Pankhurst, Emily Hobhouse and Olive Schreiner as the most famous representatives of the pacifist wing, saw militarism as yet another version of patriarchy and argued for the vote for women to stop the war. It was perceived as a typically male method of solving conflict which women would not choose if they were in a position of power. Unfortunately, the majority of women were not prepared to take any action against the war despite the efforts of the Women's International Peace Conference that took place in April 1915 (see Byles, 1995, p. 30). The conference participants had insisted that militarism was antithetical to women's interests and even their very nature. S. Gertrude Ford's *A Fight to the Finish* (1917), *The Soldier's Mother* and *The Tenth Armistice Day*[61] provide good examples for this set of arguments, angrily rebuking the jingoistic patriotism of nationalist poets.[62]

By their militant fellows like Emmeline Pankhurst, her daughter Christabel, and Millicent Fawcett, who supported the war effort and nationalism although she rejected militarism,[63] the pacifist suffragettes were criticised as unpatriotic and even traitorous. They helped to organise recruitment meetings and handed out white feathers to men not wearing uniforms without caring for their reasons.[64] Most militant suffragists perceived their war effort as necessary to finally obtain the vote, while the pacifists argued for the vote as a means of preventing the war. Female militarism was mainly represented by authors of jingoistic poetry such as Jessie Pope asking for 'unselfish devotion' (*Profiteers*). She was accused of spreading lies about war not only by male soldiers like Owen, who dedicated the first draft of his *Dulce et Decorum Est* to her, but also by other women. However, one should not forget that women experienced a great deal of pressure from both the government (for instance with the help of recruitment posters) and each other to send their men to fight.

Yet the desire of some women to take an active part in the war was rarely based only on patriotic reasons. Cicely Hamilton's *Non-Combatant* expresses the misery of female passivity and boredom while the men are engaged in action. Rose Macauley's poem *Picnic*, written in July 1917, similarly shows the frustration, anguish and guilt of staying at home while the soldiers risk their lives and endure unimaginable pain. While the poem starts off by reporting the careless attitude of those taking part in the picnic when they hear the sound of the guns, the poem's following parts reveal this nonchalance to be a means of self-protection. On the one hand women are excluded from the war by way of their gender and are thus able to lead a life of pleasure safe at home. On the other hand, the symbolic walls around them by no means imply indifference on their behalf. The war continues to haunt their imagination in 'dreams of naked fear' as the walls can only shut out some of the worst impressions. On the whole it remains an ever-present reality despite the distance from the front.

In another of Macauley's poems, the ironic *Many Sisters to Many Brothers*, we can find the following lines: 'Oh, it's you that have the luck, out there in blood and muck:/But for me…a war is poor fun'. It is the 'blood and muck' that contradict the word 'fun', as the self-erected walls of ignorance contradict the lively imagination of what war was like. However, it is not entirely clear how ironic this poem is intended to be. Like Sassoon's *The Kiss* it lends itself to both readings and it is up to the reader to choose between the different interpretations. Once more, this decision has been and will ever be determined by the social, cultural, political and personal context of the reading process.

Although many women were engaged in war-related activities and thus contributed immensely to the war effort, one has to bear in mind that everything they did was on a voluntary basis. They chose to contribute for various reasons, of which the first two also attracted their male counterparts: patriotism, money matters, the desire to ease the fate of loved ones, and the distinctively female aim of trying to improve the status of their own sex. In the years before the outbreak of war, an independent existence had hardly been possible for women as they were not supposed to take paid employment, especially not so as wives or mothers. Paid work was considered indecent, so that, if women worked at all, their area of activity was severely restricted due to prejudices and preconceptions. The most desirable types of employment in the early twentieth century were social work, nursing, teaching, weaving, dress-making and domestic service. All of these areas met with women's expected role as mother and keeper of a household. For the working classes, factory work was another area of employment, whereas the middle classes preferred secretarial work to pass the time until marriage, after which they were expected to quit their position. As women's contribution to the workforce was therefore only considered to be of a temporary nature, the majority of jobs offered to women were poorly paid and offered no career possibilities, so that women remained unable to support themselves (Wilson, 1986, p. 717).

War, however, did not necessarily change the conditions of female work or increase the possibilities of women in the workforce at once.[65] On the contrary, unemployment among women became more frequent as the upper classes started to economise. Furthermore, there were enough men remaining in England at the beginning of war to fill vacancies. Thus women were not yet needed to replace them in factories and in the service sector. Women working in the textile industries in particular suffered from unemployment, as the war, especially in its early months, interrupted the pattern of supply and demand for cotton, linen and silk. Only when the supply of alternative male workers began to run out did employers extensively resort to female labour. Yet they only did so reluctantly as 'a threat to the special position of women was a threat to the values they stood for'. It was feared that women's new liberty would hinder them from providing a safe haven at home for returning soldiers. However, as the war continued, women's role changed and was no longer considered to be that of homemakers[66] and childbearers only. War brought a liberating social change, offering relief from a largely meaningless existence, and women adjusted themselves quickly to their new positions. Nevertheless, recent scholarship agrees that war represented an isolated moment in women's history, and, even if it momentarily resulted in greater mobility and independence, this liberation was not to survive after the war.

Officially, the role of women was to ease the decision of men to enlist by making sure that concern for the family did not hinder their husbands and sons in giving their lives for their country. There was, indeed, considerable pressure put on women poets to represent national honour as women.[67] In this role, women participated in the public recruiting campaigns, something which attracted harsh criticism from poets like Sassoon. However, 'this cheerfulness, which men attributed to women's keenness to get rid of their husbands, was regarded by women as a necessity' (Khan, 1988, p. 160). As the war took its toll, women were even allowed to join the military. However, their fields of activity remained behind the lines, replacing men as typists, cooks, cleaners, mechanics or chauffeurs. In order to get closer to the front lines, in 1917 and 1918 more than 100,000 women enlisted in the Women's Army Auxiliary Corps (WAAC), the Women's Royal Naval Service (WRNS) and the Women's Royal Air Force (WRAF) (Wilson, 1986, p. 712).

Despite the restrictions on female labour mentioned above, war had created one sector in which women were desperately needed, namely the production of ammunition. Especially after the introduction of conscription in 1916, many working-class women replaced men in the munitions factories in order to guarantee constant supply. This latter form of employment in particular led many women into a moral dilemma, as they enjoyed their new financial independence and freedom on the one hand, whereas on the other they felt that by producing lethal weapons they were not only contributing to the prolongation of the war but also maybe even responsible for the death of their husbands, sons or friends. For many women, self-respect and independence thus had a high price.

Yet most of women's war-related activities were still of a private nature or were rooted in the social sector. Women were engaged in seeking homes and employment for Belgian refugees, in providing First Aid, or in knitting socks for the soldiers in France. And, of course, they were bearing and educating the future generation of soldiers. In this position especially women's influence was decisive in shaping the next generation's position towards war by either encouraging or forbidding war games with toy soldiers and guns (Claire Ingledew, *The Song of the Children,* and Pauline Barrington, *Education*). Middle and upper-class women trained as doctors and nurses in order to care for the maimed, or as policewomen to uphold the social order. Others became ambulance drivers either in France or back in England. Before the war, female doctors had been restricted to caring for women and children, whereas policewomen had been totally unknown before the war, but their numbers in both branches rose quickly with the increasing demand.

Although some women had trained as nurses and doctors before the war, the wounds they had to face were a novelty inspiring a large variety of responses, from awe to fear and disgust. These emotions, however, found their parallel among their patients, who both feared and admired them for their work. The anonymous poem *Little Sister* humorously reflects this ambivalence from the perspective of a wounded soldier:

> Have you seen our Little Sister?
> Officers can ne'er resist her.
> She will flay and burn and blister
> Someone every day.
> Does she tend poor wounded wretches?
> No! Their wounds she probes and stretches
> Till the brandy flask she fetches
> When they faint away.
>
> Not for them the gentle touches
> Of a Matron or a Duchess –
> Little Sister simply BUTCHERS
> Everyone she gets.
> Rubber gloves her hands adorning
> Give to us a daily warning
> That the bone she cleans each morning
> Never, never sets.
>
> Though our misery's unending,
> Though with pain our wounds she's tending,
> Yet with courage still unbending
> We can bear the strain.
> But if once we woke and missed her
> We should cry with tears that blister,
> 'Have you seen our Little Sister?
> Send her back again!'

While this male evaluation of nursing focuses on the wounds and the pain, it also reveals the nurse's seeming cruelty as a necessity. Even though she 'butchers' (l. 11) the men – a logical continuation of the slaughter taking place on the battlefield – gentleness would hinder her from successfully dealing with the masses of wounded soldiers. The courage mentioned in the last stanza (l. 19) as a prerequisite of the wounded is thus also greatly needed among nurses and doctors as an antidote against despair.

In contrast to the description of nursing procedures by male authors, female poetry on the nursing profession strikes a different and far more serious note, as it reveals the fear for loved ones away from home as the main motivation, as for instance in Mitchell's *The Nurse*. Eva Dobell's *Night Duty* on the one hand realistically describes the situation in a field hospital at night with the silence of sleep interrupted by terrible dreams, revealing the psychological damage the front line service had inflicted on the men. On the other hand, the last stanza begins with the image of joyful laughter only to be revealed as a memory of a peaceful past now destroyed forever. 'The transition from the menacing and traumatic dreams of battle to the wish fulfilment dreams of the last stanza give the poem its ironic last line' (Byles, 1995, p. 58).

Furthermore, women's poetry largely focuses on the results of war for the individual (sorrow, wounds, disability, blindness, widowhood etc.) rather than on themes such as comradeship, nature, religion, sexual desires or the violence of fighting itself, as reserved for male authors. More than once a romantic note is added, though not always without self-irony, as for instance in the case of Stella Sharpley's *Mariana in Wartime*. The title of the poem refers to Alfred Lord Tennyson's *Mariana*, the romanticism of which provides the intertextual basis of the irony employed in the poem.

Notwithstanding the fact that most women were engaged in the background of both economic and war-related activities, some women became immensely successful public figures: the music hall stars and actresses. They were even regarded by government and military leaders as indispensable for the war effort as they were responsible for the nation's favour. Sassoon's *'Blighters'* can be read as a harsh critique of this entertainment culture of the time, which for many of the serving soldiers was the epitome of the superficiality and deliberate ignorance of the population at home, especially because the working women were now able to afford this sort of public enjoyment with their husbands away at the front. Although the poem's two quatrains mirror the structure of *They* as discussed in the last chapter, with the first stanza focusing on the nation at home and the second on the front, it lacks the element of satirical humour. *Blighters* seems to be entirely dominated by the speaker's own bitterness over the thoughtless self-indulgence (see also Gibson's *Ragtime*) as described in stanza 1 and his distaste for women evident in the description of the chorus girls as 'harlots' (l. 3). While 'tier beyond tier' in the first line reminds the reader of the disciplined ranks of soldiers marching forward into death (i.e. the 'show'), here they refer to a vulgar audience that 'grins', 'cackles' and is 'drunk with din'. The choice of vocabulary harshly rebukes the ignorance of the audience with regard to the reality of war. 'They respond by indulging in the sentimental claptrap of some vapid music hall number' (Campbell, 1999, p. 135). On the other hand, words with military connotations – show, ranks, shrill – strongly enforce the inappropriateness of this behaviour in times of war. The title of the poem 'blighters' is significant here as it simultaneously denotes what blights, and those who stay in 'blighty' and profit from the misfortunes of others. This clearly refers to civilians for whom others give their lives in places like Bapaume, Haig's objective on the first day of the battle of the Somme. Rather than ending in a glorious victory for the English, the result of this day was that 20,000 men were killed and 40,000 wounded. It is worth noting that the place name ironically rhymes with 'home'. With the tanks 'lurching', the poet wishes the audience a nightmare vision of war to cure their complacency.

However, the critique of popular entertainment culture was not only a male point. Edith Sitwell's *The Dancers. During a Great Battle, 1916* sarcastically rebukes the civilian population for dancing while soldiers are dying. Their dance is a dance of death, an unusually strong image in female antiwar discourse. The image of women in this poem is a thoroughly negative one. They are 'the dull blind carrion-fly' (l. 11), vermin living on the dead. But who are they? Female patriots sending their loved ones to death? Or the female population in general trying to forget for a short while the sorrow and grief of wartime? The poem expresses both critique and despair (God dies at the sight of the horror), as well as a certain relief about the relative safety at home that still allows the continuation of a prewar entertainment culture ('God is good'). Surprisingly, the poem mirrors the typical division established in 'male' poetry between those who stayed at home and those who went to fight and suffer on the continent.

3.3.2 Anger and grief

As we have already seen in the above paragraph, women's literary response largely consists of mourning – the devastation of war and the loss and grief it implies. May Wedderburn Cannan's *Lamplight*, for instance, accuses war and the desire for heroism and glory of being a destructive force. The crossed swords against the name of the soldier in the first stanza would have indicated bravery in battle and service under fire, but it is only a torn cross for his death that he receives. The female speaker's heart 'was broken by the war' when she lost her fiancé and the only thing that remains for her are bitter memories of some youthful plans that were suddenly disrupted. However, although May Cannan, like Vera Brittain, had lost the young man she loved, her fiancé, she believed that despite her loss she had kept much. According to her father's Clarendon Press publications of propaganda series, the poem does not question the war as such but rather reinforces the idea of British Imperialism.

For statements such as these, many trench poets perceived an increasing gulf between their front-line experience and the absence of such in the population at home.[68] The longer the war lasted, the more serving soldiers were annoyed by the outcry about the discomfort imposed on civilians by air raids and food shortages as they seemed to ignore the far worse privations at the front. Thus Rose Macaulay, *The Shadow,* gives an apocalyptic vision of a zeppelin air raid in an attempt to link this civilian fear of the raids with the soldier's fear at the front. Both civilians and serving soldiers are presented as victims of the same man-made horror, yet the population at home was accused of showing an increasing indifference to the experiences of the soldiers. However, despite the harsh criticism of women by many serving soldiers, women were not unaware of the barrier between genders. Thus Margaret Sackville, *Home Again,* Edith Sitwell, *The Dancers*, or Helen Hamilton, *The Ghouls*, portray and accuse the insensibility or indifference the soldiers had to face when returning home on leave or wounded. Neither was the female population spared acute suffering. Despite the censorship system they were able to perceive and comprehend many aspects of the war. However, in order to be able to speak of trench warfare, women largely had to rely on their imagination based on what they saw and heard in the hospitals. Thus Ruth Comfort Mitchell, *He Went for a Soldier,* focuses on the horrors of trench warfare in a rather general and abstract way due to the lack of experience, but inspired by a real compassion for the dying man. Only from the end of March 1917 onwards did women replace soldiers in the communication lines and thus came closer to the actual fighting so that poems like *The Hill* or *The Song of the Mud* by Mary Borden are based on a close observance of the conditions at the Western Front.

With their husbands away at war, married women had to cope with problems for which they were ill-prepared, such as dealing with accounts, managing businesses, caring for the education and welfare of children. Unmarried women were deprived of male company during the war and later of any hope of a future marriage with its connotations of security, motherhood and the social status attached to it. Furthermore, all women had to live with the daily fear that their sons, brothers, fiancés or friends would be killed or missing, or return home severely maimed by war. Most women were thus outraged by what they saw as a pointless waste of a generation while at the same time feeling politically powerless. May Herschel-Clarke's *For Valour* therefore rejects posthumous medals as inadequate payment for a life, while questioning women's patriotic duty: why should she bear and nurture children if they are then slain for nothing?

This distinctly female experience of grief, fear and anger is reflected in much of the poetry written by women at the time,[69] which is in parts as ironical, satirical or sarcastic as that of their male counterparts, but based on a different experience and perception of the war. Irony and satire, however, are often used to a different end. Thus Byles points out: 'Satire was for the men poets who could ridicule the war in all its preposterous ramifications; women, by and large, did not make fun of the war – to them it would have seemed like making fun of their menfolk. When they did use irony, it was mostly for tragic or elegiac effect rather than satiric ends (...)' (Byles, 1995, p. 57).[70] For this tragic effect, Rose Macauley's and Alice Meynell's poetry provides perfect examples.

War's incommunicability, on the one hand, resulted from the difficulties many soldiers experienced in articulating their traumas of war, and who therefore sought refuge in neurotic reactions. Women's resulting inability to understand the physical facts of war due to the lack of communication, on the other hand, increased the constraint on what men felt they could reveal about their experiences. Therefore we have to distinguish clearly between the deliberate ignorance of some civilians and the charge of ignorance articulated by such major authors as Sassoon and Owen. Some women might really have enjoyed the glamour of men in uniform and the idea of war as a great adventure, but it was women's general reaction to war's consequences that repelled many soldiers. Many women did not consider wounds as degrading, but as signs of heroism that simply had to be nursed. This idea provides the background for Owen's ironic comment in *S.I.W.*: 'Perhaps his mother whimpered how she'd fret/ Until he got a nice safe wound to nurse.' The main accusation was that it was a pleasure for women if they managed to nurse a soldier back to health so that he was able to return to the front – perhaps to be killed there. At the same time, 'to nurse back to health a deserter who was to be court-martialled and shot, "truly that seemed a dead-end occupation" ' (Tylee, 2000, p. 97). However, two points are important here. First, the position of women should rather be qualified as one of resigned acceptance rather than patriotism. Second, there is an overt misogyny in many of the famous war poems for various reasons. Owen, Sassoon, Rosenberg, Graves and many of the other young war poets did not have children themselves, nor were they married at the time of the war. As a result, it was an easy though not entirely convincing idea to put the blame on parents, and mothers in particular, or as Martin Stephen put it: 'All too often women are merely a convenient punch-bag' (Stephen, 1996, p. 191).[71] Sassoon, for instance, bitterly accused women's chivalric ideas and their self-deceit in *Glory of Women* as he had already done in poems like *The Hero*, *Their Frailty* and *Supreme Sacrifice*, but this time it is 'more satirically charged than these earlier efforts' (Campbell, 1999, p. 169). The sonnet consists of an octave and a sestet both following the regular Italian rhyming pattern, while many of Sassoon's other sonnets rely on final couplets with epigrammatic character. With regard to the content, however, the argumentative volta takes place in the middle of the sestet so that the last three lines can be seen as a similar epigrammatic ending. As for the poem's form, the poet himself considered it to be a 'very good sonnet' (Hart-Davies, 1983, p. 188). Its charge, however, is highly unfair as it is based on unrealistic generalisations.

While strongly opposing women, the poem shows compassion for all male victims of the war. Its argumentative effect is largely based on alliterations (e.g. 'blind with blood'), its concision and the accusatory 'you'. By combining opposing images, Sassoon achieves a sardonic perspective, such as when 'laurelled' is connected with 'memories': they are anything other than pleasant. According to the speaker, all glorious reports are patriotic inventions of the press, and, as a result of this propaganda press, women do not realise what kind of hell they are sending their boys or husbands to die in. As Patrick J. Quinn points out: 'In "Glory of Women" and "Their Frailty", he [Sassoon] ambushes the blind nobility of the female population who refuse to see behind the façade of war and continue to send their "glum heroes" out to die' (Quinn, 2001, p. 191).

It is the image of the German mother that finally takes the reader by surprise and thus reinforces the content of the poem. Her ignorant optimism that her son is still alive is revealed to be misplaced when faced with reality, but her knitting of socks[72] is less condemned than the English women's love for decorations and heroism. However, this last part also reveals the pointlessness and absurdity of any female war effort, be it making shells or knitting socks. This pointlessness further-more is universal as it affects both the allied nations and the German enemy and can therefore be extended to refer to the whole war as an absurd undertaking.

In *Their Frailty* we find a similar message but one that is less effect-ively conveyed. The poem mocks those women who still urge a conven-tionally benevolent God to send their sons back home again. Another aspect expressed and ridiculed here is the rivalry between mothers and sweethearts for the affections of the soldier, who, ironically, might never come back to them anyway. While Sassoon limited his hatred and ridicule for women to a few poignant poems, in Owen's work this bit-terness is more widespread and influences a large number of his poems, for example *Disabled*; *Anthem for Doomed Youth*; or *Dulce et Decorum Est*, without being the dominant charge.

Yet many female authors have not only vitiated this male prejudice of female ignorance and flippancy, but they have proved capable of imagining and expressing war's horrors right from the start. Even as early as 1914, the Georgian images of pastoral England, gentleness, fer-tility and growth are turned into images of rage and pain. The typical English rain proves particularly useful here: it suggests more blood-soaked mud in Flanders and France. Anna Akhmatova's poem *July 1914* ironically transforms the peaceful image of summer rain into a vision of hell. In the last stanza 'warm red rain soaks the trampled fields'. The rain thus no longer stands for renewal, but for death. Furthermore, the bloody rain is fused with the image of mud prominent in male war poems. Yet, while rain first of all implied wet boots, trench foot and slimy decaying bodies for the soldier, the female image is more abstract for lack of combat experience, though no less realistic.

Sara Teasdale in *Spring in War-Time* equally protests the coming of spring with its suggestions of hope and regeneration by confronting the conventional imagery of spring with the effects of war in each stanza. The repetitive structure of the stanzas mimics the ever-returning sea-sons as opposed to the nature of war which prevents the soldiers from returning home. This ironical twist reinforces the elegiac effect of the poem. England, again and again, is presented as a blossoming or fertile garden in ironical opposition to the war on the continent, destroying not only Europe's landscape, but humanity itself. The flowers and fruits even turn into a mockery of mankind, as Alice Meynell suggests in her poem *Summer in England 1914*. And, even if it is rare, some women did use satire, such as Ruth Mitchell in her poem *He went for a Soldier*, which parallels Owen's *Disabled* as a young boy leaves for war under the cheers of some girls. The boy does not know what will await him in the trenches or what the war is all about until his painful death on the field. War turns from a joke and adventure into bitter reality summed up in the sarcastic questions of the last stanza.

Though traditional demarcations cannot hold any longer in modern criticism, especially the gendered dichotomy between male soldiers and female civilians safe at home, women's poetry about the war has for a long time been considered backward-looking in style and subject, as it was seen only to enforce women's home front experiences of waiting and mourning, of which Margaret Sackville's poem *A memory* is representative. The poem's last lines express women's typical experience of war, namely the loss of relatives and friends rather than the sights and sounds of battle. Its main focus is on the so-called side effects of war, its civilian victims, yet at the same time it portrays the sorrows of the survivors of the attack. Not only are they haunted by the memory of the dead, but they have to struggle for their existence; hence the line from the Lord's Prayer gains special importance. Furthermore, the poem differs from official discourse in that it rejects the language of sacrifice: there can be no pride of conquest for those who remain (l. 9). Sackville protests the idealisation of heroism and glory by focusing on the scene from a distinctively female perspective in which soldiers, both English and German, do not play a role. However, this distinctly female view led to a marginalisation of women's literary responses to the war as they did not qualify as 'war poets' in the strict sense of the term. 'We have fallen into the trap of believing too often that the only valid experience of war is that of those who fought it' (Stephen, 1996, p. 184).

Female poetry on the First World War, as we have seen, largely excludes the violence of war, yet this does not render it less valuable.[73] 'They [women poets] did not seek to adopt either the masculine traditional vocabulary or the realism of the soldier poets. (...) The soldier poets saw the violence done to nature and to man as it was happening through the vile machinery of war; the women saw this violence as it affected them as nurses, mothers, wives, sisters, lovers, and activists. Both accounts are necessary for a full understanding of the significance of war for men and women' (Byles, 1995, p. 49f.). By questioning gender stereotypes, women's poetry pinpoints how these preconceptions helped to support the war policies of the time. Many of the works discussed here tried to imaginatively overcome the gulf between those who fought and those who could not for reasons of gender. And, more than their male colleagues, female authors focused on the difficult task of surviving the survival and the question of guilt. As we have seen, much of women's poetry focuses on the social consequences of war, in the portrayal of which irony played a major role. At the same time it values female achievements during the war which otherwise would have remained unnoticed. Feminist criticism on the literature of the Great War has done much to bridge the gap between male and female responses to war, as did Catherine Reilly's (1981) important anthology of female poetry of the First World War.

3.4 Journalism

One of the main aims of newspapers and journals is to bridge the gap between the place of immediate action and the readers back at home. As the First World War was mainly taking place on the continent rather than on the British Isles there was a constant need of this sort of mediation. However, instead of bridging the gap between those at the front and those back at home, the effect was in many cases counterproductive. The First World War was a conflict in which propaganda played an important role at the home front.[74] In the first place it served to convince the British population that the war was a just one, and in the war's later stages it attempted to secure both moral and financial support for the troops. On an extended level it countered the large-scale propaganda campaigns of the Germans in neutral countries. One must distinguish between official propaganda launched by the National War Aims Committee and the Department of Information, and the non-officially inspired forms of propaganda mainly emanating from the newspaper press. The latter often reduced war to a struggle between a good and a bad side with no regard for the cost. As such, the press did not attempt to give a faithful account of the situation at the front. Instead, it published anecdotes stressing the heroism of the soldiers and the glory of their deaths. Yet, even if journalists aspired to tell the truth about war, they were prevented from visiting the front lines by war officials. Reporters and photographers were regarded as threats to national security and therefore banned from the front. Similarly excluded from the area of battle were cinema cameramen and non-official war painters. Only official army photographers (officers without photography training) were allowed to approach the action. Photographing the dead was strictly forbidden, as well as actual scenes of combat. Yet these photographs still showed the conditions of fighting, the ruined landscape and the wounded, especially after control loosened in the second half of the war.

In contrast to the simplification and disinformation of the press, many poets saw their work to be a journalistic alternative. However, as poets they did not strive at an analysis or counter-programme which could have put an end to the slaughter. Siegfried Sassoon's famous letter of protest in this respect reveals his impression of the ineffectiveness of his poetry as a means of stopping the war. Their major motivation becomes particularly clear with regard to the press: it was not about making peace, but about telling the truth. Their poetry was directed against empty words and a rhetoric considered shallow, not against the war itself, which was still perceived by many to be a necessary one despite its horrors. But these horrors of modern warfare had to be told rather than withheld, in order to prevent further wars, so that First World War would really be the 'war to end all wars'. This desire for 'telling the truth' was not a male-only affair, as various satires by female authors show. Thus Margaret Leigh's *The Journalist* or Helen Hamilton's *The Knowing Watch-Dog* both accuse reporters of deliberately spreading a misleading picture of war and thus preventing peace.

However, despite wanting to confront the 'lies' of the press, many soldiers found it impossible to communicate certain facts about war. Significant in this respect is Sassoon's poem *Remorse*: 'there's things in war one dare not tell/Poor father sitting safe at home, who reads/ Of dying heroes and their deathless deeds.' Consequently, newspaper reports often remained the only source of information civilians would get. English society thus for a long time thought about war in the traditional terms of heroism, artillery battles and care of arms, despite personal losses. As a result, some soldiers felt closer to their enemies, who shared the same horrors, than to their relatives and other civilians at home. To hate the Germans was considerably easier for the population at home as a result of the propaganda spreading anti-German material than for the soldiers at the front who were paid to fight them but did not believe the stories about atrocities so frequently spread by the press.

Yet 'even press magnates were inhibited in what they could write by what their customers were prepared to read' and 'newspapermen are the reflectors, rather than the creators, of their readers' opinions' (Wilson, 1986, p. 678). For a long time in the critical analysis of journalism during the First World War this commercial argument has been neglected. Furthermore, even though the traditional language of war continued throughout the war, the war correspondents gradually altered their rhetoric in accordance with events. However, as most of the following poems will show, these alterations were either perceived as insignificant or seen to appear too late.

On the other hand, British propaganda ultimately depended on Allied success. As Trevor Wilson (1986, p. 747) argued: 'To treat propaganda as

a significant element in the achievement of victories, rather than victories as the major element in the success of propaganda, is to engage
in a serious reversal of cause and effect.' It is therefore only understandable that newspapers highlighted even minor victories for the sake of
presenting them as major breakthroughs and thus dictating the popular opinion, as Sassoon rebuked in *Editorial Impressions*. It is this slight
misrepresentation of facts and the neglect of those who gave their lives
in these minor victories which frequently provoked harsh criticism
of the press, as in Sassoon's *The Effect*, which starts by quoting a war
correspondent. The beginning of the poem reveals Sassoon's anger at
reading one of the typical newspaper reports ignoring the terrible personal losses of a campaign. Throughout the course of the poem, he
uses this inept phrase as an ironic refrain and comment on the war.
His technique of treating the correspondent's words like a slogan leads
to a ballad-like effect. Unlike the correspondent safe behind the lines,
the reader is forced to contemplate death on the Hindenburg line in its
finality and irreversibility (see Campbell, 1999, p. 159). *The Effect* aims
not only to destroy the myth of death as a heroic deed, but also to condemn the notion of death as desirable for the enemy.

In this poem, it is the technique of montage which particularly
reinforces an ironic interpretation and turns the poem into an exemplary case for the application of Sperber and Wilson's Mention Theory
on irony (1981). While the quotation as a whole at the beginning of
the poem serves as an introduction, the last part is used by the poet
twice throughout the poem as an ironic comment on the war and
on newspaper reports in particular. As the poet quotes it literally but
questions its content, the phrase – and the press reporters with it – not
only becomes an object of contempt or ridicule, but also serves as an
ironic evaluation of the whole war. To increase the reader's understanding, Sassoon even marks the quote with the help of a different style of
lettering which he also uses for his final comment. In between these
quotes, the reader becomes aware of the reality of war in the form of
an interior monologue. We can thus speak of a mixture of voices in
which the words in italics, apart from the last three lines, represent the
direct speech of the correspondent. In contrast to this, the plain text
mirrors the experience of the soldier as a stream of consciousness, and
the narrator finally reveals his own thoughts in direct speech at the
end of the poem. The hollow words of the War Correspondent are thus
directly confronted with 'the truth' as presented in the last lines of the
poem.[75] While representing the press's and thus the public's ideas about
the war, the narrator at the same time distances himself from them – a

process by which the author achieves the ironic effect recognisable by the reader on the basis of both content and linguistic form.

Further critique of journalistic practices is expressed in J. C. Squire's satirical attack of the aim of popular newspapers to whip up mass hysteria against the Germans in his poem *Homoeopathy*, in which some men in a pub decide to steal from German shops with the excuse that they are thereby attacking 'Prussian *Kultur*': they 'did not confuse moral protest with stealing' The poem shows a strong distaste for the hypocrisy caused and inspired by the war. Another poem by E. A. Mackintosh, *Recruiting*, ironically criticises the relationship between journalism and recruitment in stanza 5. Yet it was mainly for the casualty lists that people were buying the daily papers, which profited immensely from this fact. Even those who had not been avid readers in times of peace were now interested in the fate of their relatives and friends at the front.

All of these factors together might explain why soldiers on a victory parade through London suddenly fix their bayonets on the crowd of yellow-pressmen in Sassoon's *Fight to a Finish*. The title-phrase of the poem is an allusion to a speech by Lloyd George arguing against peace negotiations. The poem thus not only criticises the press for misrepresenting the war but makes the point that by doing so it helps to prolong the war and is therefore responsible for the deaths of the soldiers. The poem's 'initial impact is considerable, the scene is deftly portrayed and the language subtly modulated, ranging from simple colloquialism to heavy irony' (Wilson, 1998, p. 405). This irony is strongest in the third line where the soldiers 'refrained from dying'. However, to refrain from something implies a wilful decision, one that was denied the soldiers during an attack as well as in hospital. Some of the terribly wounded would probably even have preferred to die rather than spend the rest of their lives locked away in sanatoriums dependent on constant care. At the same time, the term 'refrain' suggests that the survival of these soldiers is not entirely welcome. Had they died, the newspaper pages would have been even fuller as the casualty lists would have been longer and thus increased the sales of the paper.

While the first stanza gives a rather panoramic view of the parade from the outside, the focus shifts in the second stanza to the action of the returning soldiers. Their attack on the cheering mob at first seems uninspired. However, the last line of this stanza is indicative of their reasons. These civilians have lived a 'cushy' existence while the soldiers were giving their lives for them. Now it is time for revenge and total change, which even requires a new government, as implied in the last stanza of the poem. However, it is this radicalism that weakens the poem's success and reduces the irony to a mere tool of the speaker's anger.

The alliance between government and press also provides the topic of the final stanza of Wilfred Owen's *At a Calvary Near the Ancre*, the success of which as an ironical critique of this alliance is based on the disparity between the ethics of Jesus's Sermon on the Mount and the doctrines of hatred of the Hun propagated by both government and church.[76] Rather than enforcing this hatred by spreading lies about the enemy, Owen argues, the press should aim at supporting the call for peace according to Jesus's commandment to love one another.

Smile, Smile, Smile, another of Owen's poems, again focuses on the inadequacies of the press, which is accused of following propaganda purposes by producing biased reports. According to Owen and others, this favour of propaganda was even evident in the layout of the paper with the casualty lists in small print and assaults/minor victories in large print. Even photos did not reveal the nature of war but were misleading as they showed soldiers posing happily in front of the camera rather than worn out, wounded or dead after more or less successful attacks. The title of the poem thus already hints at an ironic reading of the poem. While the soldiers still smile from the newspaper page they might already be dead. Thus Stuart Sillars argues: 'The title itself is a heavily ironic reference to the refrain of the song which soldiers were frequently described as singing. The insensitivity of the press, and its sheer ignorance of the true effects of the fighting on the soldiers, is shown in the first lines' (Sillars, 1987, p. 83). But the title also stands for the knowing smile of the war veterans and soldiers home on leave or in English hospitals. It is not a happy smile, but one of knowledge that expresses the relief of being safe for the moment, as well as ridicule for the ignorant population.

Owen's first draft of the poem used 'news' instead of 'Mail' in line 2. However, by mentioning a particular paper, he reinforces the effect and also hints towards the evaluation of the *Daily Mail* by the troops as misleading and callous with regard to the real nature of the fighting. Accordingly, the poem further ridicules the content of the paper, which promises better housing after the war, but stresses that the immediate primary need is aerodromes.

On a wider scale, the poem ironically confronts the idea of glorious sacrifice, as the paper presents the soldiers as upholding the nation's 'integrity', namely its moral purity and physical wholeness. As Owen knew from his own experiences in France, it was impossible for the soldiers to achieve this. Thus by questioning the notion of 'nation' the readers of the paper express their disbelief and in doing so function as interpretative guides for the readers of the poem. The scope of irony thus widens and readers both at the beginning of the twentieth and twenty-first centuries are confronted with the ever-valid question of what is left of a nation when its people are dead. Accordingly, the following chapter will mainly be dedicated to the inevitable experiences of injuries and death and their aesthetic transformation into ironic war poetry.

4
Resignation

When reading the poetry of the First World War is struck by the entire lack of reference to victories or defeats. For most poets, neither were of interest. If soldiers celebrated, they celebrated their survival; and when they were sad it was for the loss of friends rather than ground. Instead of focusing on the facts of battle, the poets were interested in how war *felt* at a particular moment in time. This implies reflections on the unpleasant realities of wounds and death, but also on the less life-threatening conditions of food and weather. These aspects all have in common the fact that the ordinary soldier had no influence over them and thus experienced a certain helplessness which slowly gave way to the resignation characteristic of the poetry to be discussed in this chapter. Again, as we will see, the poets referred to irony to compensate for this helplessness, yet this time they did not evade the side effects of war, but faced them directly and faced them ironically. As Muecke argued in *The Compass of Irony* (1969, 238): 'Self-protective irony may be an expression of prudence or wisdom in the face of a world full of snares or a world in which nothing is certain.' And this nothing even included death. Wounded soldiers, due to medical progress, no longer died of their wounds as they would have done in previous wars, which, in some cases, might have been better for them. These men now had no choice other than to live the life of cripples locked away in sanatoriums[1] without a share in the pride and glory of having won the war. Furthermore, modern military technology caused injuries which led to slow and painful deaths in the casualty stations, not at all consistent with the notion of heroic death on the battlefield (see, for instance, Owen, *A Terre*, l. 5f.). Thus irony sometimes even takes the shape of a prophylactic self-irony for fear of what might happen in future attacks.

While readers at the time largely preferred literature with 'positive' messages to that about the horrors of war, many war poets focused on the negative aspects of military experience. However, this does not turn them into antiwar poets. Despite growing resignation among the troops during the war, most soldiers (including the soldier-poets) remained proud of their regiments and personal achievements as soldiers of a victorious British army. Additionally, they were grateful for the experience of comradeship despite their anger about certain aspects of war. However, this did not ease their sufferings nor did it limit the desire to tell the 'truth' about modern warfare. Even more so, 'pain was a way of proving the truth on the pulses and of learning how to be a spokesman for "speechless sufferers", an idea expressed first in "On my Songs" (1913) and eventually in Owen's famous statement in 1918 that he wanted to "plead" for his voiceless soldiers' (Hibberd, 1998, p. 62). Only by sharing in the soldiers' misery were the poets able to give a valuable report of front-line conditions. Insight, however, was always limited. While civilians lacked knowledge of the front, soldiers away from home were deprived of information on the suffering and danger at the home front. The most striking portrayals of the situation in hospitals were therefore written by nurses, just as the atmosphere during air raids was best documented by those who experienced it directly rather than relying on oral or written reports. As a result, the poems to be discussed in the following paragraphs not only centre on private issues, such as the fear of mental breakdown, but also represent their authors' most individual views of the war as a life-threatening, badly organised and futile affair.

Most volunteers of 1914 and 1915 were unprepared for what was awaiting them at their destination. Britain had not known a major war for nearly a century, as the British involvement in the Crimean War and the Boer Wars had only been a minor one and these wars had taken place far away from the British Isles. Most men had enlisted out of a spirit of adventure without knowing what modern war would be like and were thus severely shocked by the constant threats to their lives. Soldiering, they had expected, would be similar to playing a part in a bigger game in which death only featured marginally, if at all. The vocabulary of early First World War writing gives clear evidence of this spirit of chivalry: the soldier is still a 'warrior' in the traditional sense fighting a 'foe' rather than an enemy. Accordingly, obedient soldiers are 'the brave' and the dead 'the fallen'. In addition, those who arrived at the front after their short periods of training were unprepared for outdoor life and the total lack of privacy, nor did they anticipate the brutality of attacks alternating with the boring passivity of waiting. Furthermore, the world of war was largely a world without women, despite the efforts of nurses, singers and prostitutes. Consequently, soldiers at the front not only were deprived of their loved ones, but also greatly suffered from loneliness, for which comradeship was only a weak substitute. The result was a general feeling of powerlessness, which was not helped by the constant lack of food and sleep. On the one hand, there was a clear rota in trench duty of one week of rest after three days in each of the three trench lines (front, support, and reserve line). On the other hand, this rota was often inhibited by night attacks or immense losses. Whereas the days were usually passed in relative quietness, cleaning weapons, repairing the trenches and hunting rats, the nights were used for more dangerous and nerve-wracking duties, such as repairing the wires, night patrols, raiding parties in No-man's-land or carrying rations, mail and engineering material from the rear to the front lines.

As the following sections will show, personal experiences of suffering or success largely shaped the perception of war in its entirety. Among these individual experiences, minor issues such as the quality of food, the weather, injuries and their treatments came to play a more major role the longer the war lasted, as they had a great impact on the soldiers' chance of survival, as the following sections on the conditions of war will reveal. Of similar importance were the various wounds of the soldiers, which have so far been neglected. Not only do they constitute the topic of the many hospital poems of the First World War, but their evaluation differs between soldiers and nurses. Furthermore, while physical wounds were often perceived as marks of bravery, the mentally afflicted were blamed for their lack of courage. In the portrayal of both, however, irony became an important tool as it allowed a fragile balance between mockery and despair while at the same time expressing contempt for the conditions that were responsible for these injuries. A third paragraph will then focus on the ultimate result of the most fatal of war wounds, namely death. Yet, although it was dreaded among both soldiers and civilians, it was more than once believed to be a release from the horrors of war or a crippled half-life. With regard to death, irony became particularly suitable as it allowed the necessary detachment for the preservation of one's sanity. Yet, even if war had fulfilled expectations, if there had been constant sunshine and an abundance of food, this would not have prevented soldiers from finally evaluating the war as futile on all fronts. The final section of this chapter will therefore concentrate on poems that ironically capture this mood in order to show their authors' contempt for the war as well as the failure of poetry to educate its readers.

4.1   The conditions of war

4.1.1   Weather

Suffering under particular weather conditions was part of the soldier's experience in all areas of war. For those fighting in the East the heat was a fairly new experience and one which they had not expected to such a great extent. The same was true for sand storms blurring their view and destroying their guns.[2] In the West, heavy rain often filled both trenches and shell holes. Though the English were used to rain, they largely associated it with glistening flowers and meadows, of which Gibson's *Retreat* is a perfect example among many others. In Flanders, however, everything became muddy and it was hardly possible to keep clothes and food dry. Yet the rain not only led to soaked trenches and seriously hindered air warfare but also caused so-called trench foot, an archaic and medically inappropriate term for an infection nowadays called 'immersion foot'. During the first stages of infection, the feet become numb and change colour to either red or blue. The feet begin to swell and develop open sores which may lead to fungal infections. When the infection was not treated, which meant that the soldier had to be removed from the front with its wet and damp conditions, it could turn gangrenous and thus require amputation. To prevent the disease, soldiers were advised to change socks at least three times a day and were provided with whale grease to make the feet 'waterproof'. Once the threat was discovered, officers went on 'foot inspections' in order to make sure instructions were being followed. Additionally, the rain prevented the dead from being buried and many found their grave in the mud of Flanders.

On rainy nights, a strange silence set in as neither enemy nor friend were able to see anything, let alone use their wet weapons. Major H. D. A. B. captured this mood in *Givenchy Field*, in which the irony is an entirely situational one. Whilst the rain is perceived as embarrassing on both sides because it hinders the usual routine of attacks and counter-attacks as well as worsening conditions in the trenches, it also provides a rare moment of quiet. Guns are being hooded to prevent their destruction, an image that strongly evokes thoughts of peace, as do the slumbering soldiers. The resulting silence is thus not a deadly one, despite the similarity between the dead and the sleepers, but is a silence which preserves life by stopping the killing. However, the rotting dead in no-man's land still speak of the former violence and also remind the reader that the rainy interlude is only a short one.

When it did not rain, in winter it became freezing cold in the trenches, especially because open fires could not be lit as they would attract the enemy. A non-ironic description of trench life in winter can be found in Owen's *Exposure*, which clearly sees nature as a hostile force in opposition to mankind, as expressed in the first line of the poem: 'Our brains ache, in the merciless iced east winds that knife us...'. Accordingly, the weather also plays an important role in the dramatic monologue of *The Veteran* (especially stanzas 7 and 8) by Sergeant Frank S. Brown. Throughout this dramatic monologue, the speaker answers the questions of a young volunteer about life in the trenches. Due to his wounds, the veteran is no longer fit to return to the front himself, but he envies his conversational partner for the excitement that is awaiting him there. However, the light-hearted tone of the poem – emphasised through the use of the ballad-stanza – fails to veil the hardships and miseries of trench warfare, the wounds, the gas and the cold. Instead, the reality of winter under open skies strikes with full force as the imagery clashes with both diction and rhythm. However, even though the speaker has lost more than one limb in the war, the experience of trench reality did not have a lasting effect on his evaluation of war as such. In the end, he even urges his conversational partner, a young volunteer, not to mind these hardships but to go off to the front for 'the thrill it carries!' (l. 5).

Though all areas of warfare had their evils with regard to the weather, many soldiers preferred the sand and heat of the East to the mud and cold of the West, as did T. Hodgkinson in *The Sand of Palestine* after careful comparison. Ironically, the decision for the East in the poem was not based on the quality of the fighting or the dangerous nature of the enemy, but rather on the weather as it affected the soldiers more immediately than the occasional battle. The light-hearted tone with which the speaker compares the two war zones supports this ironic interpretation, as the reader recognises it as unfitting in the context of war on the basis of his or her own previous experiences with the subject. Yet, similarly to the following poems on the quality of wartime food, war is rarely mentioned explicitly. It rather enters the poetry by way of alluding to places of battle, propaganda phrases or intertextual references, which require a large amount of background knowledge from the reader in order for them to be interpreted ironically.

4.1.2   Food

It is often forgotten how good army conditions were for many who joined up in comparison to their previous civilian lives. Working-class families especially suffered from severe privations before the war. While conditions in the trenches were certainly not pleasant, rural poverty before the war had been even worse. For many working-class privates, war was the first time they received three meals a day, a rum ration and the money to buy cigarettes. Thus, 'the horror of the middle-class officer on facing them [the conditions of war] was sometimes not matched by his men, used to prewar conditions that by middle-class standards were already hellish' (Stephen, 1996, p. 109). Nowhere is the prewar background of the men more important for the perception of wartime conditions than with regard to the food question. However, while the weather was something one could not help, many thought that rations could and should be improved as a reward for their sufferings.

At the beginning of war, Field Kitchens were set up to provide soldiers with one hot meal a day, but, as the availability of food declined during the winters, soldiers soon had to rely only on their rations. These field rations consisted of dry biscuits and tins of corned beef, the so-called bully-beef, in addition to rations of jam and tea. Furthermore, there was a daily allowance of rum for those on the frontline and regular cigarette rations, for smoking made the soldiers forget their hunger for a while. From time to time, the Red Cross sent food parcels, the quality of which was better than the usual rations. The biggest problem, however, was to guarantee a constant supply of fresh water. Usually it was brought to the front in big tanks that provided perfect living conditions for germs and bacteria.

Due to its elementary importance, the food question, together with the weather, remained a frequent topic of discussion among all classes, although it features most prominently in poems by less well-known authors and the anonymous rewritings of popular songs, such as *When this Blasted War is Over*:

> [...]
>
> When this blasted war is over,
> Oh, how happy I shall be.
> When I get my civvy clothes on,
> No more soldiering for me.
> I shall sound my own revally,
> I shall make my own tattoo.
> No more N.C.O.'s to curse me,
> No more bleeding Army stew.
>
> N.C.O.'s will all be navvies,
> Privates ride in motor cars.
> N.C.O.'s will smoke their Woodbines,
> Privates puff their big cigars.

> No more standing-to in trenches,
> Only one more church parade.
> No more shivering on the firestep,
> No more Tickler's marmalade.

Not only do stanzas 2 and 3 of this song portray the speaker's reveries of a life after war, they also reveal the small injustices between officers and privates with regard to rations. Although the tone is humorous, the poor quality of army food becomes obvious, as the soldier is looking forward to never having it again. This evaluation of rations as disgusting and insufficient is similar in the East, and it even affects the horses, as shown in the anonymous *Mesopotamian Alphabet* (see letters G, J, N, R, and S/T in particular).

As we have seen, inequalities existed not only between the different ranks, but also between Infantry and Navy. Furthermore, rations were the same for all areas of war regardless of the different weather conditions, meaning that the water shortages affected those fighting in the desert climates even more than at the Western Front, while biscuits were easier to keep dry in the hot areas. Despite careful planning, it also seems that nobody had thought of either the impossibility of grazing horses in the desert or their additional need for water, so that shortages not only threatened the lives of soldiers and animals alike but also the successful outcome of campaigns (see also A. P. Herbert, *The Cookers*: 'Tommy is best when Tommy has dined'). Though both examples of 'food poetry' directly and realistically confront these mistakes, their poetic effect is strongly based on a clash of regular rhyme and rhythm with the seriousness of the content concerning irregularities in the food supplies.

While the limitation of food was self-imposed at the beginning of war, for fear of later shortages, the situation for the population at home also gradually became worse, as Germany was attacking not only military, but also merchant vessels in their attempt to starve the island. Although this plan never entirely worked, the need to save, as well as a shortage of certain supplies such as sugar, increased the general inconvenience both at home and at the front, especially during the second half of the war.[3] Rationing was finally introduced in January 1918, starting with sugar only, but during the following weeks more products were added to the list, including meat, butter, cheese and margarine.

Authors mockingly express their contempt for the situation in England, while at the same time dreaming of a better past. Catherine Durning Whetham's *The Poet and the Butcher*, dating from May 1918, even calls for the help of Milton to ease the desire for better food. The poem in the style and diction of Milton parodies Wordsworth's sonnet of 1802 to Milton. Just like the original, it is not without a certain bitterness, this time for the unjust distribution of provisions – they are only for 'the good' (l. 10). The lack of delicious food for the author implies that obviously she and those around her do not belong to this group and so even Milton cannot ease their situation as they are unworthy of him. But who are 'the good'? It remains unclear whether the expression is meant ironically, and thus denotes the profiteers of war for whom it does not imply suffering and limitations, or whether it refers to the peaceful. In this case, nature would punish mankind for waging this war by not providing enough food to sustain the troops. While on the surface level the poem only talks about food, the topic is closely linked with the notion of culture. According to its author, a nation at war is unworthy of claiming a cultural heritage. On the contrary, artistic traditions abruptly find their end during wartimes; they no longer have any value or uplifting potential for those who struggle for survival. Irony in this case clearly serves to encode a deeper message behind humorous language and a straightforward topic. In order to do so, the author refers to her own cultural heritage, which she expects her readers to share.[4] War as such, however, is not mentioned explicitly but can only be deduced from the term 'provisions' (l. 10) and the reference to sugar cards and meat coupons. Although this necessitates contextual knowledge for the interpretation of the poem, the author also achieves a widening of scope. Her critique of war becomes universal.

A more overt kind of irony is used in a poem by Aelfrida Tillyard, *Invitation au Festin*, expressing contempt and disgust for the new eating habits resulting from the war. The poem's irony is mainly based on exaggerations and a choice of animals that, in peaceful times, would never occur in the context of food. Thus the absurdity of the menu serves as indicator for the irony of the poem. The author constantly plays with the reader's individual borderline between fascination, taste and disgust and by doing so engages him in a sensual dialogue. The underlying message, however, is expressed in the second stanza of the poem where the author doubts whether all this saving will actually help to win the war. This idea is further elaborated on by the peculiar combination of vocabulary in the following stanza: only in wartimes can joints become 'unpatriotic' (l. 13). And, while the poet uses a lighthearted tone throughout the whole poem, the idea of bright dreams at the end directly opposes wartime reality. While husbands, sons, or friends are away at the front, nobody's dreams are bright, regardless of the quality of the food. In addition to hunger, it is constant sorrow that prevents sleep, as well as the noise and danger of air raids in the southern areas of the country.

4.2   Wounds

While representations of war deaths feature prominently in the First World War poetry, other sorts of casualties rarely enter the poetic discourse. At the same time, the poetry of the First World War contains a thematic novelty in that it deals with the psychological consequences of war. First World War was the first war in which psychologists played a major role in the treatment of wounded soldiers. As a result, individual trauma and its therapy for the first time in literary history enter the catalogue of topics together with fear of death and the resulting mechanisms of self-protection which range from insensibility (see Owen's poem of the same name) to madness (as represented in *Mental Cases*) and suicide as the last possible escape (as in Sassoon, *Suicide in the Trenches*). The following two sections will therefore deal with the particular functions of irony in the poetic discourse on the physical and mental consequences of the First World War. In both cases, the tradition of romantic irony[5] lent itself to poets questioning the fate of the soldier. Romantic irony grew out of the scepticism resulting from historical situations of turbulence such as the French Revolution or the American War of Independence. 'It posits a universe founded in chaos and incomprehensibility rather than in a divinely ordained teleology' (Mellor, 1980, p. vii). However, while modernity and progress were generally greeted with enthusiasm by the romantic ironists of the eighteenth and nineteenth centuries, the results they produced in the form of weapons and the effects these had on the individual soldier during the First World War gave way to fear and feelings of guilt and shame.[6] The outcome of this shift of perception is the bitterness that dominates most of the ironic war poetry of the time. During the high times of English romantic irony in the nineteenth century, the world was perceived as chaotic but the chaos itself as highly fertile. Now, at the beginning of the twentieth century, this fertility seemed to have turned into its opposite, namely ultimate destruction.[7]

What remained, however, was the search for an aesthetic mode to come to terms with a reality that included death as well as survival. The belief in a positive outcome of the chaos of war, even if it was only a faint hope, was the only way not to despair with the present situation, and detachment the only means to flee its destructive impact.[8] The wartime poet has no other option than to acknowledge ironically the inevitable limitations of his own being, but he must also affirm the process of life by creating new images and ideas. The difficulties arising out of this experiment have already been acknowledged by Schlegel, arguing that finite human perceptions can never completely capture infinite chaos.[9] This is due to language being a structured rational system and thus by nature unsuitable for the representation of chaos. Only with the help of irony does it become possible to encompass two ideas at the same time, to affirm life while simultaneously lamenting its destruction.[10] For the artist this means that he must create an ordered world with the help of language as an ordered system, while at the same time acknowledging the limitations of his or her perceptions of the chaotic world of war. 'In form as well as content, then, the ironic work of art must join together chaos and order' (Mellor, 1980, p. 18).

This theory, of course, has consequences for the reader as well. In order to fully understand the resulting piece of art one must be aware of this duality inherent not only in the poet, but also in the world described.

4.2.1 Physical

As a result of the development of medical technology and hygiene, men who would have died from their wounds in previous wars now survived with horrible injuries. Most of them were maimed for the rest of their lives and thus constantly depended on professional care. The poetry to describe both the actual wounds as well as the fear of becoming disabled as a result of the war usually focuses on two major settings, the hospital and the trenches. Consequently, women poets have a major share in the poetic discourse because of their being eyewitnesses as nurses, relatives or friends of the wounded. However, while the men 'have learned to laugh at pain/ [...] / And suffering has not spoiled their ready wit' (Alys Fane Trotter, *The Hospital Visitor*, ll. 15, 24), women's voice is usually less humorous and also less ironic. This most likely results from the different experiences of sufferers and carers.

The bitterness of having lost one's limbs and thus one's prospects of leading a happy life after the war was most famously expressed in Wilfred Owen's *Disabled*. The poem possibly grew from several experiences Owen had in 1916 and 1917, although Owen himself never suffered from severe physical wounds. In a fashion characteristic of many of Owen's poems, the poet blends irony and compassion for the victims of war in order to drive home once again his message of war as a waste of youth (see also Lane, 1972, p. 151). The cripple's fate, however, is worse than death in battle because 'now he will never feel how slim/girls' waists are, ...' His youth is over and he is now doomed to live without any sensual excitements that would compensate for this loss. Thus Lane argues that 'although he has not lost his life, he has lost the ability to live it' (Lane, 1972, p. 151). This point is particularly reinforced by the last two lines of the poem, which shift from a description of the young man to his consciousness, which clashes markedly with the image of the sporty teenager presented in stanzas 2 to 4 of the poem. As such the poet draws an ironic parallel between the soldier's past and present states which, according to Hibberd, is 'directly taken from Housman's "To an Athlete Dying Young"' (Hibberd, 1998, p. 113). Apart from this intertextual reference, the cripple's outcry 'Why don't they come?' iron-ically sounds like an echo of a poster which showed soldiers in need of reinforcements under the slogan 'Will they *never* come?'.[11] In this case, only cultural and historical background knowledge reveals the irony inherent in the phrase.

While the poem is usually cited for its description of the cripple, it can also be read as one of Owen's frequent comments on the role of women during the war. Not only are they made responsible for the young man's desire to enlist (as in *Dulce et Decorum Est*), but when he returns as a cripple they ignore him and instead focus on 'the strong men that were whole'. By doing so they deny him the reward or at least the thanks he was expecting for his efforts and sufferings. By referring to the classical legend of Adonis, the poet presents the war victim as both physically and sexually maimed, a fact which turned out to be a major problem for British society in the aftermath of war.

Eva Dobell's *In A Soldiers' Hospital I: Pluck* equally represents a crippled youth; this time still in hospital. By focusing on an individual case, the poet, like Owen, exposes the ideology of war as hollow due to its disas-trous results. However, whereas Owen's poem centres on the thoughts of the veteran as a result of his wounds, Dobell describes the physical pain of the soldier. Although the idea of gallantry is ridiculed with a sarcastic voice, the young man maintains this ideal by hiding his fear and pain. At the end, he even coolly smokes a cigarette despite the tears in his eyes. The position of the poet thus retains a certain ambiguity, for she seems to value the soldier's attitude despite her contempt for the cruelty of war as such.

This female awe for the brave soldier, which has so often been the subject of male contempt, does not, however, hinder either their insight into the suffering or their empathy for the male victims of war. Margaret Postgate's *The Veteran* is one of the many poems by female poets show-ing remarkable understanding for wartime reality. The poem focuses on a wounded soldier who seems to be reduced to a pure object by his wounds. Thus the young soldiers asking for advice treat the veteran as a crystal ball, a source of advice, but not as a real human being. As a passive victim of an inhuman society, he is left on a bench in the sun like a forgotten book to be opened at any page to give the required information. However, it becomes clear that the information the veteran can give surpasses the understanding of the questioners. War remains indescribable even when the official propaganda rules are neglected.

While the first part objectively describes an encounter between the veteran and some young soldiers coming out of a pub, the irony of the poem is mainly based on the invalid's answer to the question about his age in the last line. All of a sudden reality seems to enter the scene again as the veteran's answer clashes abruptly with the notion of the 'war hero' the young men want to see in the cripple. All their excitement about going to war is abruptly demolished in this last sentence of the poem. Not only does this final dialogue between the veteran and 'us' restore some personality to the veteran, but it also drives home the poet's notion of war as destroying youth. Who poses the final question, though? Most likely, the author implies the nurses or carers of the young man; in any case, a female group. Thus, unlike the male part of the population, women are not only interested in the essentials of life, but are also perceived by the veteran as belonging to those who know what war is like when he addresses them in line 8. Their work in hospitals and sanatoriums provides them with a knowledge and insight that the young soldiers from the pub are still lacking.

In this popular sub-genre of the hospital poem we find a variety of ironical poems, ranging from the anonymous *To Little Sister* to the artistic *Conscious* by Wilfred Owen. Both poems represent the thoughts of individual victims, although, while the speaker of *To Little Sister* lightheartedly mocks the cruelty of the nurse while at the same time valuing her work, Owen's soldier hardly perceives her in his short interval of consciousness. However, the nurse in the latter poem is a sight that reassures the wounded soldier of being safe behind the lines, though she is hardly more than a mere object in the casualty station, like the rug or the mayflowers. Norgate (1989, p. 524f.) thus sees a parallel to Gilbert Waterhouse, *The Casualty Clearing Station*: ' "The Casualty Clearing Station" contrives an image, virtually, of paradise regained, whether read as the prelude to safe awakening on the morrow, and the road to recovery; or, possibly, as the moment of happy release into serene death.' However, the conscious soldier feels alienation rather than comfort, as memories of slaughter infiltrate his mind rather than pleasant visions of 'red-roofed farms' as in Waterhouse's poem. The poem furthermore has a parallel in Sassoon's *The Death-Bed*[12] in which the soldier must die in order to achieve the moralising polemic effect of the poem. By showing the soldier in one of his rare conscious moments, which Owen represents as worse than death,[13] he exposes the limitations of Sassoon's poem. The irony of the poem mainly rests on its title: Consciousness as the first step towards recovery does not have any positive connotations for the soldier but rather forces upon him the bleak reality of war. Thus, at the end of the poem, he gladly drifts off again into the sleep of oblivion.

A similarly ironic title is chosen by Sassoon for his mockery of the cold-hearted arguments of politicians and civilians. For this purpose *Does it matter?* uses a straightforward language and a ballad-like directness. The composition of the poem was probably triggered by two major events Sassoon witnessed. The first was Ralph Greaves's loss of an arm and the second the mental breakdown of Julian Dadd, both of them friends of the author. Additionally, Sassoon was most likely thinking of the haunted patients of Craiglockhart in stanza 3 of the poem. The simple structure of the poem – each of the three stanzas starts with a similar question followed by equally unsatisfactory answers – ironically clashes with the poem's serious subject matter. Yet this content is mirrored in the poem's form where the masculine ended lines of the quatrain are always contrasted with an unrhymed fourth line with a feminine ending questioning the certainty and insensibility of the speaker.[14] According to Wilson, 'the effect is to alienate the reader, who is nevertheless unwillingly drawn into the poem by those same rhetorical questions. The reader's shock at the speaker's callous and inadequate response in the second line of each verse provokes the outraged indignation Sassoon aims to elicit from complacent civilians. A similar effect is achieved by the irony of the final line which, though said ostensibly to reassure the man who has gone mad, underlines a general lack of concern for the victims' (Wilson, 1998, p. 407).

As in many others of Sassoon's poems, the two locations of home and front are contrasted. Again, the soldiers are forced to endure not only their own mutilation, but also the platitudes of those that remained at home, namely women and politicians. However, the poem not only demolishes the idealised vision of a noble war wound but reveals the madness of individuals as resulting from the madness of war itself. With this idea, the irony of the poem strikes at full blow[15] in the last stanza, in which nobody will rebuke a veteran for his mad behaviour. Yet this refrain from comment is more than a lack of understanding; it is a sign of indifference as 'no one will worry a bit'. Against this indifference, the victims' world of 'amputation, darkness and shell-shock is mute but eloquent testimony to the fact that these horrors really *do* matter to the ever-growing ranks of "shattered heroes"' (Campbell, 1999, p. 163).

It should not be forgotten that wounds were not only life-threatening and painful; they were for many soldiers a welcome means to be sent back home and quit the bloody war scene without having to commit the war crime of deserting. Thus the veteran in Sassoon's *The One-Legged Man* is grateful for the wound he received as it ironically has saved his life. The poem had been one of Sassoon's earliest exercises in his new epigrammatic mode and it comments ironically on both home and military values. What begins as a peaceful pastoral piece ends as a poem about a crippled amputee in which the last line puts the rest of the poem into a new perspective. On the one hand the veteran has lost his leg, but on the other this was the only possible way to escape death at the front. His 'thank God' is thus an honest one and the fact that he is able to contemplate his luck from a distance makes clear that the anger is Sassoon's, not the victim's![16]

The use of direct speech and the careful choice of diction here stress the satiric effect, but it is the merit attached to the wholeness of the human body in Western civilisation[17] that increases the absurdity of the scene, as it constitutes a clash of values. The veteran does not seem to mind the loss of a limb but is rather grateful for his wound which most likely saved him from a lonely death in a muddy shell hole. Yet, for the reader, the idea of amputation evokes images of danger, pain, bereavement and continuous suffering. By opposing these different connotations, the poem not only questions the fate of the individual soldier, but confronts the reader with a subtle critique of war as a destructive world which in the worst case annihilates any civil value system on both individual and cultural levels.

This clash of values in war became – and still remains – one of the most devastating experiences of the soldier at the front. More than once it led to mental breakdowns ranging from moderate fear to successful suicides. The following paragraph will therefore focus on poetry concerned with the most problematic, and at the same time most often concealed, of war's consequences, namely mental illnesses, and the resulting actions of individual soldiers.

4.2.2 Mental

Least graspable of all the consequences of modern war were the many cases of psychological wounds. Before the war, however, the diagnosis of

mental illness was equal to becoming an outcast of society. The Great
War clearly brought a change to this strict division, as more than 12,000
serving soldiers were recognised as being traumatised by the war.[18]
What the war did not remove, however, was the inequalities between
sufferers. Officers were given special treatment, not only in real life,
but also in critical literature dealing with the subject in the war's aftermath. The Workmen's Compensation Act of 1897 had, for the first time,
obliged employers to accept responsibility for accidents to their employ-
ees. The National Health Insurance Act of 1911 further prepared the
way to the modern welfare state through social reforms. But, although
the treatment available to the lower classes did not differ from that of
the rich to such an extent as during the nineteenth century, medicine
was still a costly affair and remained a luxury for the poor. This meant
that, whereas officers were treated in special war mental hospitals,
ordinary privates suffering from mental distress caused by the war were
mostly transferred to public lunatic asylums, if not during the war then
at least after it was over. The divide between classes in British society
was reflected in the distinction of different forms of suffering. Whereas
officers were described to be suffering from anxiety neuroses, so-called
hysterical neuroses afflicted the ranks as a result of their respective
training and position in the army hierarchy. The treatment for both
cases, however, was to engage them in some kind of meaningful occupation in the gardens, workshops or the hospital kitchens.

It is not clear whether the term 'shell-shock' was first invented by medical service personnel or if it was a soldier's phrase, but it was adopted
not only by doctors and nurses but also by sympathisers and the war's
opponents as describing any psychological trauma caused by the war.[19]
The diagnosis of 'shell-shock' was, in some cases, not only a means of
describing the affliction of soldiers, but a convenient way of removing
soldiers from the front when they were regarded as potentially dangerous for the rest of the troop and would otherwise have been severely
punished[20] for their behaviour. Again, it is the battle of the Somme that
functioned as the decisive event for historians, psychologists and literary critics alike. The majority of documented cases of neurasthenia and
shell-shock date from mid-1916 onwards. However, one has to bear in
mind that psychological research was developing fast during the time
and that the illness was not recognised as such before the middle of the
war. Symptoms were rather attributed to different sources, such as her-
editary insanity or venereal disease.[21]

In addition to their illness, as described in poems like Sassoon's
Survivors, or Read's *His wild heart beats with painful sobs*, soldiers diagnosed

as neurasthenic often suffered harsh criticism from both their own company and civilians for their lack of courage and want of 'manly spirit', ineffectual performance and the danger they brought to their division. Their illness was considered a flight from reality, indicating a general weakness of character resulting in a lack of self-control and a childish or womanly attitude towards the dangers of daily life. This attitude among the population of the time might even have increased the symptoms, as fear was suppressed rather than acknowledged, until it finally became overwhelming.

The frequent outbursts of intolerance towards the mentally afflicted before the war had been the result of a misunderstood positivism and had been directed against all social groups considered incapable of contributing to the progress of society. With the beginning of war, soldiers who had broken down were thus easily included in the list of these inefficient groups. Yet it was also assumed that the only cases of real war psychosis were those that recovered quickly when removed from the front. Owen portrays this difference of attitude between the private or junior officer and the senior officer when confronted with such a case. To the senior staff, these men were just 'losses, who might have fought/ Longer' (*Insensibility*, stanza 1, l. 10f.). Additionally, their interest was in the outcome of battle and the possible dangers these soldiers brought onto their own divisions, whereas the serving soldiers had more insight into the causes and thus more sympathy for the afflicted.

Although the suffering soldiers were often accused of cowardice and punished accordingly,[22] in most cases their illness did not indicate a lack of patriotic fervour or deliberate evasion of front line duty, but was a result of the constant shortage of sleep, insufficient rest behind the lines, and living in an atmosphere of decomposing bodies which was heightened by a never-ceasing shelling that strained the nerves of officers and their men alike. This attitude towards suffering gradually changed throughout the war and gave way to hesitancy and respect, as the population learned about the conditions of war.[23] Pensions were granted and dependants were entitled to compensation money. This shift of attitude furthermore prepared the way for mental illnesses to enter the catalogue of literary topics.

For poets like Ivor Gurney, one of the 'sad' cases himself – especially so because he was not an officer – neurasthenia was both a weakness to be cured and a creative force he wanted to use for its artistic potential. This dilemma led him to rebel against the treatments offered to him in public institutions, as he perceived them to be distracting him from the goal providence had provided for him. Gurney also suffered from not being granted a full pension as his condition was judged to be aggravated but not caused by the war.[24] Furthermore, his friends had opted to classify him as an ordinary private patient, instead of as a Service Patient, which would have included an additional grant for clothing and pocket money.

The constant strain of war's horrors on soldiers' minds, however, is only one side of the coin. Even the most cruel war leaders knew that it did not make sense to expose soldiers to continuous danger as this would take away all remaining courage. According to most wartime diaries, soldiers only spent one-third of the year on the front line while the rest of the time was passed with travelling, training, in hospitals or on leave. At the same time, the areas of war differed considerably with regard to the amount of actual fighting. Whereas in some parts it was rather quiet throughout most of the year,[25] other parts of the trenches saw continuous shelling.

In his poem *S.I.W.*, Owen traces the fate of a young man from leaving home, with the (inappropriate) advice of his parents to behave well, until his suicidal death in the trenches. The poem was first drafted in quatrains – a form typical for Sassoon's poetry – but then 'further divided up by means of ironic, literary headings, the style of each section being adjusted appropriately' (Hibberd, 1998, p. 102). In the end, the hopes of the recruit's family are not met, and their son rather dies an unheroic death. What was necessary in the army was what Samuel Hynes calls 'passive courage, a stoic endurance where there is nothing else to be done' (Hynes, 1997, p. 58). Resulting from a lack of this stoicism are the many cases of self-inflicted wounds (as portrayed in Gurney's *Portrait of a Coward*) and suicides. For the frequency of incidents, the abbreviation S.I.W. even became an official term in the English army.

The most striking example of a poem dealing with the consequences of the continuous strain on the souls of men is Sassoon's *The Hero*. The poem not only points out the absurdity of the prevailing concepts of heroism, glory and courage, but also realistically portrays the various possible interpretations of death at war. The title of the poem is already invested with irony as it contrasts the innocently myopic world of the Home Front with the hell of the war in stanzas 2 and 3. *Satires of Circumstance* by Hardy, to whom Sassoon had dedicated *The Old Huntsman and Other Poems* and who had used similar techniques, might have functioned as an ideal for the poem. In a style characteristic of Hardy the situation is presented by a third person narrator, probably the dead son watching the conversation between his mother and the officer from outside. The poem thus qualifies as a 'self-contained dramatic piece' (Lane, 1972, p. 102), strongly relying on the concept of dramatic irony[26] on several layers: the speaker, the officer and the reader know more about the real nature of the son's death than the mother; the mother and the reader, on the other hand, know more about the lies of politicians and war leaders; and finally the reader knows more than all of the poem's characters about the outcome of war in 1918, which was no real victory for any party involved.

Similarly to Owen's *Mental Cases*, Sassoon's treatment of cowardice[27] – similar to desertion, fear or mental illnesses, an unthinkable topic for earlier war poetry – establishes a new form of art without heroes and, in terms of content, without tradition. Line 1 of the poem already rebukes the absurd and misplaced notions of happy-warriorism[28] shared by so many civilians at the time.[29] Contrary to the mother's claim, her boy died unwillingly when he volunteered to join the forces or was forced to do so by conscription; contrary to the colonel's words, he did not die as a hero. At the same time, the mother's sentence remains ambivalent as we do not know whether she really believes what she is saying, or whether she acts as is expected of her by society as a patriotic and dutiful mother. Both officer and mother construct an image of a world that does not exist as such. It is outfaced by front-line realities. Thus the word 'proud' describing the mother's attitude can easily be replaced by 'sad'.

In Sassoon's other poetry, the focus is usually on the death-dealing machinery of war as a whole and the general nature of trench warfare. Here, however, Sassoon singles out one of his own fusiliers for his cowardice. Instead of provoking scorn for the boy's fear and the resulting behaviour, the reader is compelled to feelings of compassion and pity. The officer on the other hand is criticised for spreading lies about the war in accordance with the propaganda press at the time. Yet his words follow the rules of common decency which help to maintain a state of ignorance on the home front, as it was impossible to tell a mother that her son was a 'useless swine'.

The formal phrases of the first stanza are then contrasted ironically in the following stanza when the officer retreats after having done his duty. Both the mother's and the officer's behaviour are thus revealed as following clichés and expected patterns. However, the irony of the poem mainly rests on the verbal oppositions between stanzas 2 and 3: 'triumph', 'joy', 'brave', and 'glorious' clash with words like 'cold-footed', 'useless swine', 'panicked', or 'blown to small bits'. However, the final irony is probably the strongest and drives home Sassoon's point. Nobody will remember or care as nobody can mourn the millions of dead soldiers except the closest relatives. There are simply too many of them. At the same time this is indicative of the uselessness of the soldier's death. The nation for which he gave his life does not care at all. The ironical oppositions on the level of vocabulary are reinforced by the opposition of rhyme schemes. Stanza 2 differs from the rest to emphasise the 'lie about war' by all parties involved: the mother is not proud but sad for the loss of her son, the officer does not tell the truth about his death, nor do the war officials about the number of dead and warfare in general or about the real motives for the continuation of the fighting.

An analysis of the poem following the assumptions of speech act theory and discourse analysis underlines the above interpretation of the poem as ironic. The poem multiplies the communicative situation and thus its complexity by presenting several speech acts. On the internal level, we have to distinguish three different acts, all of which are declaratives. The first one consists of the colonel's letter to the dead soldier's mother, on which we only have her comment, the second speech act is that between the mother and the officer bringing the bad news, and the last internal one is that of the officer talking to himself. All of these internal acts, however, are only partially represented as either the communication partners are absent, as in the case of the letter and the musing officer, or the communication is parallel rather than interactive due to the officer's lies and the mother's role-playing. Sassoon's choice of diction also reveals a clear hierarchy between the patronising officer and the soldier's mother, the 'poor dear' (l. 8). In a striking parallel to this hierarchy, the external imperative speech act also consists of unequal communication partners, the authoritative author and his ignorant readership. On the basis of Sassoon's other work, the message of this external act might be transcribed as follows: 'Stop this war. Then innocent young men will no longer experience such panic and "gallant lies" will not be necessary any more.'

Discourse analysis further reveals the violation of Grice's conversational principles as the main element of the poem's irony. All three speakers more or less violate the maxim of quality as they say something the speakers do not believe to be true. Only in the case of the mother does it remain debatable whether she also violates the quality maxim by saying what is required of her, or whether she strictly follows the maxims and really believes her son to have died a hero. Discourse analysis thus reveals the targets of the poem's irony to be multiple according to the various possible readings. Alternatively, the poet accuses war in general, the women at home, the propaganda machinery, and the war leaders sending boys to their death before they are full-grown men.

In doing so, the poem also criticises the widespread idea that war separates boys from real men.

The mental breakdown of men was not only the result of fear, but also has to be attributed to a strong sense of personal guilt. The state required them to kill, while they had been brought up on the principle that murder was both legally a crime and spiritually a sin. There was also the guilt for the horrors of war in general and the guilt of those on leave for not supporting their comrades. Consequently, Owen's poem *Mental Cases* not only describes in detail the behaviour of these madmen, but, in the second stanza, also indicates the reasons for their insanity. The distressing topic of shell-shocked soldiers, however, belongs to a whole catalogue of themes ignored in the artistic evaluation of previous wars, such as the devastated earth, the corpses, the wounded and feelings of compassion and pity as well as anger at noncombatants. Like the soldier in *Disabled*, who suffers from the physical consequences of war, the mad soldiers are presented as innocent victims. Owen's description of their suffering is based on a language of jaded vocabulary to which he adds elaborate assonances and frequent alliterations. The poem itself follows the form of a dialogue, opening with the questions of stanza 1 which are then answered rudimentarily from the perspective of an external observer in stanzas 2 and 3 – rudimentary because nothing can explain the hell that has already been introduced in the first stanza. It is a hell which men have designed and in which they are now condemned to suffer. However, Lane rightly asks 'But condemned by whom?' and 'Who is responsible for the evil?' (Lane, 1972, p. 154; see the end of the first stanza: 'Who these hellish?'). Owen at least seems to assign this guilt to the reader as an accomplice in the evil and to himself as taking part in it. The mentally disabled are the damned for whom there is no cure and thus no hope of salvation ('always they must see these things and hear them'). However, despite the clash of military orders with civilian values, fear and madness were largely recognised as a problem of psychology rather than morality.

Despite its conventional structure, the poem's description of hell not only recalls Dante, but also reminds the modern reader of Eliot's *The Waste Land*. Furthermore, it also questions the biblical vision of heaven as given in the Book of Revelations 7: 13–17, which begins with the words: 'What are these which are arrayed in white robes? And whence came they?' The passage then focuses on the Christian martyrs and the eternal promises that await them. As in *The Parable of the Old Man and the Young*, 'Owen would seem to be using a well-known Scriptural passage ironically to demonstrate the gap between his civilisation's ideals and its practices' (Hibberd, 1982, p. 339). He achieves this aim by contrasting the mental hospital with heaven, though surprisingly without quoting further from Scriptures. While at first sight the victims of war are equated with the Christian martyrs, further thought reveals them as both damned and saved at the same time. They have lost their minds as a result of the murder they have seen at the front; thus to their victimhood is added the concept of guilt. Differently from Owen's other uses of irony, this case is not geared towards a critique of war in general, but rather of the individual who does nothing to prevent the killing. The concept of 'victim' thus becomes an ambivalent one for the first time.

The general opinion concerning neurasthenia at the time, however, had been a different one. Most psychologists believed that those whose mental problems were caused by the war could easily be nursed back to health once they were removed from the front. In Siegfried Sassoon's *Survivors* we find evidence of this attitude when the speaker says 'No doubt they'll soon get well...They'll soon forget...'.[30] All other cases of long-lasting psychological problems, on the other hand, were believed not to have been triggered by war, but to have their origins in prewar illnesses. W. H. Rivers, treating both Sassoon and Owen at Craiglockhart, had developed three main ideas about the subject: (1) war neurosis was different from the mental disturbances of peacetime; (2) there were no physical origins, so that the term shell-shock is wrong; (3) a distinction between the neuroses of enlisted men and those of their officers was necessary. Soldiers with little responsibility suffered from paralysis, mutism, or anaesthesia, whereas officers and all those having to take difficult decisions were plagued by nightmares, obsessions, and hysteria (see Hynes, 1990, p. 177). For both the first speaker of the poem and the psychologist, the madness is only visible as behavioural symptoms. The speaker's limitation thus represents the limitation of all those who have not shared 'with them in hell the sorrowful dark of hell', including the reader. The poet's sensibility is turned into a plea for understanding, although he knows that the reader's empathy will never replace his lack of experience.

Similarly to some of his other poems (*Disabled/S.I.W./Conscious/ Exposure/Spring Offensive*), Owen chooses its title from a range of impersonal military and medical terms used during the war. The title thus contains an inbuilt ironic effect: one expects neutral clinical descriptions of mentally handicapped people, but the poem instead 'exposes the inhumanity of a purely scientific approach to their fate' (Seeber, 1993, p. 128). Those who have physically survived the war are doomed to live on with destroyed minds, a fate which seems even worse than the bodily harms caused by the war. In order to portray the continuous hell these soldiers live in, Owen reverts traditional symbols of life and hope into images of suffering and death (for example sunlight or dawn). The climax of the poem is consequently reached in the visual image of dawn breaking, like a wound that freshly starts bleeding. 'The method is modern irony and understatement but the feeling behind it is learned from earlier writers, especially Dickens' (Hibberd, 1998, p. 169).

Some people, however, never wanted to forget. Both Ivor Gurney and Robert Graves saw insanity as an inspiration and a source for their artistic work. Thus Miranda Seymour says about Graves, 'He was tortured by his thoughts but he feared the consequences of being cured' (Seymour, 1995, p. 78). One of the poems that provides evidence for the idea that any treatment would dry up the poet's imagination is *The Gnat*, which first appeared in *The Pier Glass* in 1921. The poem compares Graves's mental state to the sensation of an insect boring into the poet's brain. Thus, rather than wishing to be cured, Graves desired a safe refuge in which he could live with his haunting images – understandably a disturbing burden for his wife Nancy, as were the many cases of mental disorders for postwar society.

4.3 Death

Much of what we today call 'antiwar poetry' is directed against the heroic glorification of death at war in patriotic and jingoistic verse, not against the war itself. In the following poems, aesthetic language clashes most strikingly with the ugliness of war to achieve various effects. At the same time, a fascination with death mingles with disgust and fear, as well as anger for the waste of life. Pretending to be cool observers detached from the horrors of war, many of the poets recall the figure of the Greek *eiron* as one who speaks judgement from afar after having observed the scene for a while. Others only hint at it by way of mockery or superficial humour so that its presence only shines through both context and language. This hesitancy in naming death unites them with female authors who hardly mention death in their poetry. Instead, its reality has to be deduced from the argumentation of the poem and almost always remains a vague parallel to the vagueness of the beloved's whereabouts, as shown in Eleanor Farjeon's *Easter Monday* in which lively, springtime nature is opposed to death through a particular choice of imagery. Eggs, apples and the context of Easter not only suggest fertility, but as symbols of life they require praise. Yet joy is already darkened by the coming of the next battle mentioned in the soldier's letter. As such it already foreshadows the end of the poem in which death ends everything: life, joy, hope, praise and the poem itself, as there is nothing more to be said. At the same time, it implies the 'eve' of the young woman's life.

Originating from this constant hovering between the extremes of fear, expectancy, hope and horror, the function of irony in poems on death will be revealed to be a psychological one. Not only does it ease the soldiers' treatment of the topic by offering the necessary detachment, but it also serves as an outlet for any negative emotions, as will be shown in the following sections.

4.3.1   Rotting away

What shocked soldiers most was the fact that it was often impossible to bury the dead of the last attack. Not only did the smell of rotten flesh constantly linger over the trenches, but these corpses were visible reminders of what would probably await all of them sooner or later. In the hot climates of Mesopotamia and Palestine the rotting corpses furthermore attracted myriads of flies carrying dangerous maladies with them so that the smell was generally associated with sickness and suffering. For the relatives at home, the lack of a grave furthermore made it difficult to mourn their dead, whose fates they could only guess. Harold Monro's *Carrion,* the fourth poem of a cycle called 'Youth in Arms', captures the slow process of decay of the dead under the open sky. The poem becomes even more striking for the fact that it was written by a noncombatant. Monro had been declared unfit for military service abroad but was called up in June 1916 to serve as second lieutenant in an anti-aircraft battery. In 1917 he transferred to the Intelligence Department of the War Office. With its inherent critique of the brutality of war the poem vitiates the frequent preference for the soldier's voice over that of civilians for reasons of insight and 'truthfulness' in anthologies of war poetry.

Only gradually does it become obvious that the commentator on the scene is death himself, who does so sardonically. While stanzas 1 and 2 realistically describe death in battle and the rotting away of the corpse somewhere in the mud of Flanders, it is the detached nature of the observer and the coldness of bare facts until line 12 that produce a first hesitancy in the reader. On the basis of the biblical 'dust to dust' motif, Death's arguments are the most repellent as they evoke strong emotions of disgust when associating the daily bread produced from corn with the rotten corpses as fertile soil. This fertility no longer serves as a sign of hope, but is turned into one of destruction and despair. The follow-ing line 13 then represents one of the most sarcastic military phrases: if the soldier had had the time, he would most likely have uttered a cry of fear rather than suppressing it for absurd notions of heroism. The following lines of stanza 3 strongly recall Owen's *Disabled* with their evocation of girls' kisses denied to the dead soldier. However, while the speaker in Owen's poem is full of bitterness for this fact, this no longer makes a difference for the rotting corpse. Before stanza 5 returns to the bleak realism of the battlefield and Death's fear of probably losing his 'prey', stanza 4 leads the whole situation ad absurdum by ironic-ally pointing out the advantages of death in the field without a decent burial. The reader is drawn into his absurd argumentation about the advantages of not being crammed into a coffin and thus retaining one's liberty even in death. The irony of the poem thus not only centres on the personification of death[31] as *eiron,* but also on his mockeries of trad-itional rituals and beliefs.

The introduction of poison gas especially implied a new kind of war in which soldiers ceased to fall in man-to-man combat. Although the use of gas failed to meet the high tactical expectations put into it, the mortality rate of gas casualties was higher than that of any other war wounds, mainly due to the inadequacy of the protective helmets dis-tributed among soldiers. In addition to this, 'some men were overcome by fumes before they were able to fit the complicated gas masks together and an unexpected attack left many helplessly maimed' (Summersgill, 1991, p. 315). Despite the suffocation and pain of gas casualties, the visual display of gas clouds became the object of a certain fascination. Thus Edmund Blunden ironically likens it to another concert party in his poem *Concert Party: Busseboom.* The irony of the poem consists of a peculiar combination of situational and verbal irony, reminding the reader of the light-hearted tone of music hall entertainment while at the same time representing the danger of the situation. The red lights that warn the soldiers of the gas provide a colourful show that seems to invite the soldiers to come closer to the spectacle, and even to dance to the music of battle which ironically clashes with the silence of gas death. The word 'air' in the last line is charged with a double meaning as it refers to a melody and the deadly poisonous air at the same time. Thus the dance inevitably becomes a dance of death.

While some poets describe death as sweet sleep (Thomas, *A Private* and *Lights Out* and Owen, *A Terre,* ll. 52–57) – the two of which can easily be confused as in Sassoon's *The Dug-Out* – or even a love act (as, for instance, in Seeger's *I Have a Rendez-Vous with Death*) by offering an escape from the dreadfulness of war, its ugliness strikes with full blow in Isaac Rosenberg's *Dead Man's Dump*, of which the third stanza has already been discussed in chapter 2. In this poem the different perspectives of the experience of combat culminate in a single snapshot of a cart rolling over dead bodies and by doing so crushing their limbs. Stanzas 1–3 realistically represent the sights and sounds of war, which lead to a series of questions in stanza 4, after which stanza 5 asserts the value of life by evoking the 'honey of youth'. The poem then goes on to name those aspects in the soldiers' environment which conspire against them until stanza 9 focuses on one particular dead soldier. At the end of the poem, the dead are finally, and ironically so, identified by their entire lack of human identity as they are decomposing to become part of mother earth.

Throughout the first half of the poem the dead bodies are described as if human. Their mouths only seem temporarily shut and they are united by sharing the same experience of the conflict. This shared experience includes the speaker, who identifies with his fellow soldiers. In order to show his membership of the group, Rosenberg used first person plural pronouns in nearly all of his poems. This group, however, is neither defined by nationality nor by military rank but includes 'friend and foeman' (l. 10).[32] However, there is a slight incongruity in this thought as stanza 1 suggests the brutality of the enemy while the barbarity of the speaker's own army remains unremarked.

Juxtaposed with the strange humanity of the dead are the limbers, carriages used for the transport of ammunition and equipment, but sometimes also transformed into carriages for the dead. These transport wagons exemplify the indifferent machinery of war as they rape the dead bodies of their dignity,[33] a powerful image for humanity being destroyed by war. The dead do not even seem to hinder them in their paths. On the contrary, in this world of shattered tracks and muddy paths they rather function as planks. In doing so, they enable the limbers to bring further destruction to the front line. The poem thus ends just as it began with the limber crushing the dead.

In between, Rosenberg turns to the wounded as those between the two stages of life and death. Although the transition from one state to the other is not a question of choice, for the wounded there is still some hope to return to the world of the living. The living and the dying, however, are of the same community, existing within touching distance. And this close relationship also decides the fate of the wounded. Instead of their being rescued at the last minute, the only touch that finally comes is that of the cart's wheels, crushing the bones of the wounded together with those already dead. War's machinery is immune to the slight difference between the two. The cry of the man for the stretcher-bearers[34] in the last stanza thus becomes emblematic of the cruel irony of the poem: the failure to reach him is representative of war's inevitable erosion. As the carts pass the dead, all hope is thwarted and survival becomes an illusion.

Although the Somme campaign from July until November 1916 cannot be seen as a turning point from support to disapproval of war, it certainly is representative of modern warfare in the trenches of the Western Front. With the Somme being a slow-moving river in a landscape with low plateaux and ridges, it enabled busy agriculture, yet it was also accountable for the mud that plagued the soldiers in the area. Although it was not the most heavily shelled of the Western Front battlefields, it was the first to see British tanks in action on 15 September 1916. Furthermore, in 1916 the area was new for much of the British army because the British Expeditionary Force had concentrated on Flanders. For the French, it had been an 'inactive' sector as the Germans on the other side of the Front had not put them to trouble before. However, as early as December 1915, plans had been made for a great offensive in the area, and in spring 1916 the necessary infrastructure was created behind the Somme front. The disastrous results of the campaign despite these careful preparations were mainly due to two factors: (1) the British forces believed too strongly in the superiority of their equipment and (2) the battalions were mainly raised by voluntary enlistment, with the result that soldiers were hardly trained for what was awaiting them and were also driven by their readiness for self-sacrifice. When bombardment was opened on 24 June 1916, these amateur soldiers often lacked the skill to fire a shell accurately. Hence, despite the precision of the fire plan, the battlefield was haphazardly cratered. No communication was possible after the troops left their trenches and thus long lines of young men ran towards their own extermination on no-man's-land. Not only did many of the war poets take part in this campaign as volunteers, but also their poems express their evaluation of the Somme as representative of the human tragedy of war as a whole. One of these poems is Wilfred Owen's *Futility*, a poem which does not explicitly mention the war but nevertheless strongly reinforces the despair and consequent anger of the soldiers seeing their comrades die in the middle of their youth.

As with many other poems that were composed during or after the battle of the Somme, Sassoon's *Counter-Attack* centres on the bleak realities of trench warfare, the rotting dead, the mud and rain, and the smoke of exploding shells. Originally drafted in July 1916 at the beginning of the Somme campaign, *Counter Attack* reflects the horror at the Mametz slaughter where some of the dead were deprived of all dignity. The poem makes use of the typical mixture of detachment and humour[35] in order to deal with the horrors of modern war. As a result, 'few other lines in the First World War poetry can equal this passage – with Sassoon's characteristic ironic fillip at the end – in sheer graphic intensity. To the horrors of simple carnage are added the frantic, intermingled, struggling grotesqueries of violent death: the final degradation of the human body which made war such an intolerable outrage to the poets who first confronted its effects' (Johnston, 1964, p. 97). An additional situational irony is the fact that in all this slaughter 'the jolly old rain' (l. 13) sets in – as if all involved have not yet endured enough, the drenching rain comes.

For the English, in this case, the rain really is 'jolly' as it prevents the enemy attack from being continued with high intensity. Yet those who manage not to drown in the mud do so in their own blood, if not in this attack then in the next one. While stanzas 1 and 2 describe the bombardment by enemy fire and the growing sense of panic experienced by one soldier, stanza 3 represents the unsuccessful counterattack ordered in the middle of the confusion by an officer 'blundering down the trench' (l. 26). In the end, the terrified soldier becomes just another corpse when he bleeds to death in a pool of mud, the horror of which is underlined in the matter-of-fact conclusion of the last line, which could equally be found in a volume of military history. However, enemy and friend not only become indistinguishable as corpses,[36] but for those who died the outcome of the attack is absolutely irrelevant.

4.3.2   'Decent taste'

Though most of the men marched forward without questioning, the young man – or rather still a boy – in another of Sassoon's poems, *Suicide in the Trenches*, fails to meet expectations. Together with *The Hero* the poem is one of the rare treatments of the topic in war verse. With its nursery-rhyme style and rhythm opposing the serious subject matter it points out the dehumanising effect of a war which transforms happiness into degradation or even worse, suicidal despair. The impersonal tone of stanza 2 recalls the tragic ballad while the last stanza contains Sassoon's typical anger towards the ignorant civilians who are even made responsible for the suicide. But 'the rhetoric of scorn here prevents the poem from doing its own work. Our attention is drawn away from the material of the poem to the poet, to *his* reaction: we are being *told*.'[37]

The irony in this case is too overt to fulfil its potential. However, as in *How to Die*, *Suicide in the Trenches* marks the discrepancy between heroic and realistic visions of death in war.

In *How to Die* Sassoon again slips from satire into sarcasm in the last stanza through an over-concentration of verbal irony. While stanza 1 at first focuses on a battlefield from afar and slowly zooms in on a dying soldier's last whisper, in stanza 2 neither the speaker nor the situation is clearly defined. Sassoon was most likely thinking of the older generation of civilians with their preconceived notions of the 'Christian soldier'. The term 'lads' in line 10 is not without sympathy for the boys' fate, but the emphasis on decency and taste reveals an entire lack of insight. However, 'by offering only an *ironic* insight into the reality – that soldiers go swearing to their muddy graves – Sassoon permits the misguided public to cleave to their hymn-like vision of "Christian soldiers" who will not only give up their lives for the greater glory of heavenly salvation, but will do so decorously and "with due regard for decent taste"' (Campbell, 1999, p. 164).

Natural words of fear which are not supposed to pass the lips of the dying also feature prominently in *The Leveller* by Robert Graves, which compares the death of an 18-year-old with that of an old professional soldier. While the youth curses God, the old soldier cries for his mother. Löschnigg therefore argues: 'Die letzte Ironie des Todes liegt jedoch darin, daß diese so konträren Todesbilder durch den stereotypen Text des offiziellen Kondolenzbriefs nivelliert werden. In der pietätvollen Verschleierung der Wirklichkeit – nicht nur humanes, sondern auch politisches Gebot – kommt letztlich zum Ausdruck, daß im Krieg der Respekt vor dem individuellen Tod verlorengehen muß' (Löschnigg, 1994, p. 223). As in Sassoon's *The Hero*, truth falls prey to official codes and hollow phrases.

Yet Sassoon, an officer himself, not only pitied his subordinates but also had to deal with and mourn the death of officer friends.[38] *To Any Dead Officer* was composed on the same day as his statement of protest, for which he was sent to Craiglockhart War Hospital. The poem furthermore may serve as an example of the frequent speculations about afterlife as a consolation for those left behind. Its language captures the style of a conversation between friends, including colloquialisms and obscene language revealing the officer's obvious lack of 'decent taste' although he did his job well. The diction of the poem especially creates a sense of intimacy between the chattering subject and his communication partner, who will unfortunately no longer be able to give a response. However, combined with the poem's impersonal title, it emphasises the contrast between the euphemistic jargon of politicians and the meaninglessness of war. The penultimate stanza especially expresses a stark contrast between the official and impersonal language of the casualty lists and the speaker's emotions. 'Wounded and missing' in this respect is a euphemistic phrase that ironically misrepresents the reality of the officer's death in a shell crater. It is the final line that provides the key for the solution of the poem's irony: the First World War is perceived by the speaker as everything but a decent show. Instead of a series of heroic battles, modern technology reduces men to mere machine operators. They die asleep or playing cards, while eating breakfast[39] or when trying to get rid of lice. Or, as Arthur Lane (1972, p. 168) put it: 'They died praying or cursing, weeping or dumb with horror, comforting each other or fighting for shelter. It was pitiable, but it was war.'

The truth about war is conveyed in a final satirical blow typical of Sassoon. In doing so, the poem not only focuses on an individual conclusion but shifts from private sorrow and mourning to a more general statement about the nature of war and a concluding critique directed at the strategists and politicians. The last stanza gives proof of Sassoon's disgust for a nation that deceives its men in order to sacrifice them. However, for Sassoon, his satiric poetry did not convey his sentiments clearly enough. In order to clarify all misunderstandings about his position towards war, he openly voiced his critique in his now famous letter of protest. This clearly shows the limitations of ironic discourse. It fails to have an effect on all those who do not perceive and consequently attempt to decode the irony for reasons of political opinion and/or simple ignorance. In the first case, this might even be a deliberate act; in the second, readers of war poetry might wonder about some of the oddities in style, imagery or diction, but the message behind the poem will be lost on them. The corpus of ironic poems thus might not have had an immediate impact on the public perception of war, but, in the long run, the sheer number of ironies left their traces on the cultural memory of the First World War as the first tragedy of the twentieth century.

4.4   The futility of war

The futility of a war always becomes most obvious after it has ended. It is the product of a slowly emerging idea that it has brought no mentionable results which would cover the losses. Few of the writers examined here lived to see the end of the First World War. For those who did survive the slaughter, war continued in their heads: 'In its defeat Germany dragged down the whole of Europe' (Howard, 2000, p. 27).

Yet bitterness, disappointment, and a sense of betrayal had set in much earlier with the realisation that medals and ribbons were unable to honour the dead and compensate for the suffering (Owen, *A Terre*, l. 8ff.). Even the most heavily bombarded areas of the Western Front saw moments of quietness, times in which soldiers had time to sleep, eat, or think. In doing so, their thoughts wandered back home to loved ones and intact landscapes, but they also remembered previous battles and friends they had lost on the field. Richard Aldington's *Trench Idyll* provides a good example of these reflections. As the reader is gradually taken into the conversation between the two soldiers sitting in a frozen trench, Richard Aldington, line after line, reveals the horrors of the war in graphic detail. The irony of the poem, however, results from the discrepancy in attitudes of readers and speakers towards death. While the reader is shocked by the realistic description of the dead and the fact that they were never buried, the ongoing war has obviously dulled the senses of the conversational partners. They shiver, not so because of their memories, however, but because of the weather. Their resignation prevents them from feeling anything but their own bodily functions and needs. The ironic effect of the poem is further underlined by the light-hearted manner of the conversation, yet it no longer functions as a warning or protest, but rather reveals the futility of any such attempt.

War simply becomes a conversational topic, just as London's nightlife goes on as if nothing has happened or will happen any more, as in Owen's *Exposure*. Here the soldiers are again lying in the trenches at night waiting for a pale winter dawn. To pass the time they watch the lights of exploding shells, listen to the sound of the guns and wonder what they are doing in this hostile environment (stanza 2). Yet although the soldiers are killed in an attack and later carried away by the burying-party, the poem clearly stresses the insignificance of all these events by constantly repeating the phrase 'nothing happens'.

In some cases the attempts to come to terms with the absurdity of war embody traces of the absurd themselves, as in Edgell Rickword's *Trench Poets,* in which a soldier reads classical poetry to his dead comrade. Yet neither Donne nor Tennyson has the power to rouse his friend again. The obvious inappropriateness of the soldier's behaviour ironically reinforces the absurdity of the whole war as immune or contrary to any culture. In the end, the soldier has to give way to his resignation and leave his comrade to the rats and worms.

Of a totally different nature, but no less radical in its attempt to reveal the futility of war, is Robert Graves's *Dead Cow Farm*, a parody of antique creation myths. In its shortness, the poem provides a critical assessment of the situation of Europe, or even the world, after three years of trench warfare: the circle of creation is closed, and chaos reigns again. Graves may have been thinking of Nancy when he wrote the poem in France. She believed in the superior qualities of women and that they had once ruled society (see Seymour, 1995, p. 59). In fact, God in the poem is a woman, but her creation has turned into mud and there is no way of stopping the decay by a sort of rebirth. The fact that Graves chose a cow, a holy animal in Hinduism, to represent the goddess, has been a matter of speculation ever since. Is this blasphemy, or a mockery of religious beliefs? In any case the poem successfully dismantles the idea of a religious revival as well as the hope for a better future through war by comparing the chaos of the trenches with the original state of the earth before the creation of the world as we know it. Ironically, this state with its essentials of mud, stone and rain exactly corresponds to the world of the trenches, with the only exception that this time creation is prevented as the Cow (the creator) is now dead (see also Harold Monro, *The Poets are Waiting*, stanza 6). Mankind is now doomed to live in a 'world grown old, and cold, and weary' (Brooke, *Peace* l. 5).

And mankind has not learned anything from the First World War, as shown in Osbert Sitwell's *The Next War*. The short first stanza of the poem positions the action in the interwar period, when the misery of the trenches slowly sinks into oblivion and the majority of the population are fed up with memories of the war. Nevertheless, some feel obliged to erect memorials in honour of those who gave their lives. However, the whole undertaking is thwarted in the third stanza by one of those in power. The poem successfully combines the various forms of irony that have already been analysed in the course of this book in order to show not only the futility of the First World War from a military perspective, but also its failure to stabilise Europe. Furthermore, the attempts of some of the major war poets to warn the young and thus prevent future wars are revealed as unsuccessful. The situational irony of the attempt 'to make the world safe for the young' by sending the sons of the former 'lost' generation to the front can hardly be stronger, but it is enhanced on a structural level, especially by the isolation of the last word, which works as a deliberate contrast to readers' expectation. In order to stress his point, Sitwell uses imagery of magic such as 'alchemists' (l. 5) and 'wizards' (l. 22) to denote those who have profited from the last war, as they have converted the soldiers' blood into gold. It is thus not surprising that the richest among them argue for another war, of course only as a 'fitting memorial for the fallen' (l. 35), because what they had been fighting for is again endangered. Although Sitwell

strongly resents this chain of argument as two-faced, the older generation are not his only culprits. An equal share of the guilt is attributed
to the young themselves, who follow the new recruitment call without questioning, or rather, without having been 'educated' (l. 21).[40] The
poet here functions as the ultimate ironist, as the one who sees and has
seen in the past, but he is an ironist without power. His only option is
to watch the next generation walk into a new catastrophe without being
able to hinder them, and it seems that he already knows that this coming catastrophe will surpass the former in its horrors.

5
Conclusion

Our memory of the First World War up until today has largely been shaped by a meta-narrative presenting it as the quintessential tragedy of the twentieth century,[1] with the soldier as the primary victim of the tragedy. While there cannot be a clear-cut line between 'fictional' and 'non-fictional' texts about the Great War, what we consider 'fictional' texts came to play a major role in the formation of this meta-narrative. The prose accounts written and published during the interwar period, including the famous autobiographical works by Graves, Sassoon, Blunden and others, provide the majority of this fictional material. However, the most immediate response to war on the fictional level was the poetry analysed in the course of this book. As witnesses, the authors of the poetry of the First World War expressed a partial view, in most cases that of the serving soldier in the various areas of the military, but also that of the nurse, the pilot or the civilian back at home. All of these perspectives are restricted in that they lack an entire vision of war reserved for outsiders or historians.

At the outset of the war, the majority of the population were proud of their nation and its military. Only when the stalemate of modern warfare rendered courage dysfunctional did war turn into the traumatic experience described in many, though not all, of the poems. While writing becomes a defence of life in contrast to war as a constant threat to this life, several difficulties arise out of the witnesses' position. As survivors of war, the witnesses are excluded from fame because, by definition, they cannot have played a decisive role in it or they would not have survived. As dead or lost casualties of war, what remains is their literary legacy, which might be incomplete and/or prone to misinterpretation, even more so if their messages are encoded in ironic discourse. Furthermore, the poets often present themselves as victims and hardly mention the fact that they were, at the same time, potential killers and primary actors of war. The acknowledgement of both roles very rarely forms part of the content of the poetry as it does in such exceptional poems as Wilfred Owen's *Strange Meeting*, in which the speaker is finally united with the enemy on the other side of no-man's-land as his fellow-sufferer, but also as fellow-murderer. Accordingly, Sassoon's poem *Decorated*, another exceptional case, asks the reader to envisage a street scene in which a criminal is about to be brought to justice. In an ironic reversal the newsboy reveals that the centre of attention is 'Corporal Stubbs, the Birmingham V.C.!' By doing so, the poem reveals the absurdity of war, which makes heroes of murderers. This message of the poem was likely to antagonise the establishment, for which reason Sassoon refrained from submitting it to Heinemann for publication.

In presenting their cause, the poets' accounts are undoubtedly true, but one has to be aware of the partial nature of that truth. As the large amount of material has shown, the various perspectives differ immensely from each other and in some cases even led to mutual criticism. Although war undoubtedly implied suffering and pain for many, interviews with veterans over the decades have revealed that, for a large number of soldiers, war did not destroy their lives, either physically or mentally. War remained an exciting experience responsible for both positive and negative memories. The intensity and the challenge of modern warfare were able to provide a release from the boredom of ordinary life, as did the new sexual freedom which at least partly compensated for the horrors of the trenches.

However, both pro- and anti-war poems convey a feeling of a betrayal of expectations. Those who sought adventure and excitement were bored by the static nature of trench warfare; those who expected man-to-man combat experienced a war of equipment which reduced individuals to minute elements in the machinery of war; and those who hoped for a renewal of society were disappointed by the reinforcement of class differences and the rupture of intercultural relationships. In addition to this notion of war as a failure were the daily horrors of bad weather, personal loss and the struggle for survival, which might not have been responsible for an ultimate critique of war, but which in the long run undermined the morale of the troops. All of these experiences led to a transformation of poetic language during the course of the war. Furthermore, many of the famous English war poets tried to position themselves in a world of changing artistic values. While still seeking to support their poetry with traditions of the past, they found that this support did not exist. Consequently, their poetry ranges between the realist mode of description of the nineteenth century, even earlier Romantic imagery, and the artistic notions of modernism brought about and transformed during the war years and their immediate aftermath, in order to show their inappropriateness regarding the reality of war.

This literary positioning, however, is overshadowed by the political implications of war poetry as a direct intervention in the contemporary situation and particularly as an opposition to official propaganda. One might even speak of a fusion of aesthetics with ethics, especially in the cases of Wilfred Owen, for whom 'poetry was in the pity', and Siegfried Sassoon, whose famous statement of protest was supposed to underline and reinforce his position already expressed in his war poetry. However, despite the fact that many of the poems discussed in this study critically confront various aspects of the war, hardly any of the poets qualify as consistent pacifists in both diction and content. Their poems reveal an ambivalent attitude towards violence and a fascination with war as poetic material that might even be called voyeuristic at certain times. The various facets of irony provided the means to represent this ambivalence because irony guaranteed the necessary detachment from the subject of war, even if its reality intruded and shaped the authors' minds. As self-protection against deception and delusion, irony enabled the poets to preserve their integrity. Thus irony's unsettling character in all the poems discussed results from the fact that its main aim as an instrument of 'truth' is to observe and then confront critically. Even if the poets' voices did not have an immediate effect, in the long run their work played a major role in the general perception of war up to the present day.

During the slow, but for many poets inevitable, process of disillusionment during the war, language and with it the various forms of irony and satire experienced a shift in focus. Whereas before the war irony was mainly directed against minor absurdities or cultural peculiarities – Rupert Brooke's *The Old Vicarage, Grantchester* may serve as a brilliant example here – its grand focus shifted during the war from foreign habits onto English society itself. Irony no longer served only to ridicule individuals and their behaviour, but instead became a powerful weapon of sociological criticism. For this purpose it was, on the one hand, used to disguise the critique in rendering it even more successful by emphasising the absurdity of war in opposition to life in peaceful times, as has mainly been pointed out in Chapter 2. On the other hand, in its overt form it directly confronted those considered responsible for the conduct and duration of the First World War, as has been particularly demonstrated in Chapter 3, until it finally turned into bitter sarcasm when focusing on the human side of the war, the wounds, the loss of comrades and the sorrow of the survivors, as shown in Chapter 4. The last chapter has furthermore revealed the limitation of the ironic potential when it comes to factors that could not be helped, such as the weather, the quality of army rations or even the loss of comrades in the futile attempt to gain a few metres of ground. These elements of wartime reality were prone to ridicule or bitter laughter, but the absence of a culprit often prevented irony from functioning as a tool to change the status quo. In these cases, it rather seems to be limited in its potential to merely mentioning these evils.

Yet, as we have seen in the preceding chapters, the purpose of irony cannot be limited to criticism only. This would have made it a powerful weapon in the hands of pacifist poets but rather useless for the large number of others writing at the time. Instead, ironical mockery was employed as a means of increasing awareness of the conditions of modern warfare as well as the inadequacies of everyday language to describe them. Both then and now, irony opposes common sense both linguistically and psychologically by breaking the social boundaries in which language is confined. Irony furthermore served as a possible outlet for personal grief and anger, and at the same time it provided a space for the psychological repression of war experiences, as Chapter 2 has revealed. Where this repression failed, madness was one of the possible consequences, yet this madness in some cases (see, for instance, Ivor Gurney) even provoked the most bitter ironies. Their often biting bitterness does not necessarily look for culprits and scapegoats but is content with revealing the absurdity of the situation as such. As a result, irony became a poetic tool for both soldiers *and* civilians, men *and* women, officers *and* members of the rank.

Accordingly, irony's functions range from, firstly, self-irony as self-reproach, especially when it comes to notions of pride and glory (2.3) and a fascination with technology (2.4), to, secondly, its employment as an argumentative strategy in the hope to better the conditions of life for both soldiers and civilians, as has been demonstrated in Chapters 3.1 (The Establishment), 3.2 (War leaders), 3.4 (Journalism), and 4.1 (The conditions of war), and, thirdly, a dramatic irony presenting the author as the ultimate ironist, as the one who knows, in contrast to the common soldier, ignorant of the fate awaiting him in the 'play'. Despite their superior position, however, the authors remained observers incapable of active intervention. This was particularly shown in Chapters 4.2 (Wounds), 4.3 (Death) and 4.4 (The futility of war) as well as 2.1 (Nature and countryside). With regard to these issues, the authors' hope seems to have rested entirely on their readers' support for their cause, for which they shared their inside knowledge. The ironical de-romantisation of war was thus less a critique of war, and more one of attitude in the face of a realistic evaluation of this war. The authors' ridicule and contempt for wartime society is constantly mingled with an absolute will to live so that irony finally becomes a lifestyle in which humour triumphs over war, death, and destruction.

Yet irony's various functions seem to have required different forms of irony. Thus situational irony was particularly suitable for the portrayal of war's daily absurdities (Chapter 2), whereas verbal irony became an argumentative strategy geared towards raising the population's awareness of wartime conditions. Embedded in satire, irony served to attack those considered responsible for both major and minor drawbacks. And in its most bitter form of sarcasm, irony became the expression of this mixture of despair and anger for which the poetry of the First World War is largely known today.

Although the material has been organised according to its ironical strategy, the sections on poems dealing with comradeship (2.2) and gender issues (3.3) form an exception in that they require a distinction of perspective – insider/outsider or male/female – which again entails ironic variation. Thus, while both comrades and outsiders acknowledge the importance of, as well as the obstacles to, friendship at the front, only outsiders were able to draw an ironic picture of wartime bonds. And whereas male irony often accuses women of supposed superficiality and ignorance, such as Sassoon's *Glory of Women* or Owen's *Disabled*, female irony hardly ever targets male notions of warriorism but instead centres on the experience of war as one of suffering both at home and at the front. Yet the examples have shown that the male–female dichotomy with regard to irony and the war has been overestimated for a long time, as the female focus only differs from that of her male contemporaries with regard to the struggle for survival, home front conditions and violence but is very similar when it comes to wounds or the experience of loss.

For the various possibilities irony offered, it is not surprising that irony and related stylistic or linguistic forms of ambivalence were so frequently used. From the multitude of examples given it becomes clear that the importance of the phenomenon cannot be overestimated. The various manifestations of irony in the poetry of the First World War have revealed that it had by no means ceased to play a major role in the literature of the twentieth century. On the contrary, irony experienced a revival as well as a transformation of focus and function unparalleled since the times of European Romanticism. Not only did the poets draw on its ancient origins as a rhetorical device (Quintilian irony) or mode of existence (Socratic irony), but they also made use of romantic theories on irony as enabling them to detach themselves from the subject of war as well as the artistic work itself. It is exactly that indeterminateness of irony which rendered it powerful as a psychological, literary, or even philosophical tool, but which at the same time makes it so difficult to grasp in one single comprehensive theory.

Yet the lack of a clear-cut definition by no means advanced a misuse of the term *ironic* as synonymous with *incongruous* or *coincidental*. A situation classified as a mere coincidence by those involved will inevitably become ironic if it is elevated to the level of a literary text which deliberately plays with the expectations of its readers. Owen's *Inspection* provides us with a good example here: it is a mere coincidence that the soldier is dirty on a parade and that the dirt is detected and the soldier punished by the sergeant. From Owen's portrayal of the scene, the reader at first perceives the sergeant's reaction as a just one. Only when the spot is identified as the soldier's own blood in l. 8 can we speak of situational irony.

As this study has aimed to demonstrate, irony must be located on the communicatory level and works due to a combination of linguistic, contextual and situational elements, among which the organisation of the material plays a major role. In addition to this, the popularity of the term *irony* mainly results from its inclusion of what we might call ironies of fate. However, this is by no means a recent development, but one that began in the late eighteenth century and became particularly useful in the context of the First World War (see Chapter 4). Furthermore, every study of irony is one reading among others. However, it is one that has to be able to account for the properties which inspire the ironic interpretation, which might be of a formal, logical or ontological nature.

While sarcasm represents one particular variant of irony, satire and irony do not necessarily have anything to do with each other. Satire may use irony as one of its 'weapons', but this is by no means an exigency, as has been demonstrated in Chapter 3. However, as the main focus has been on irony, the majority of poems analysed in that chapter were manifestations of the particular relationship between satire and irony. Sarcasm, on the other hand, can be qualified as a sharp ironic utterance that captures the bitterness of the speaker, or in our case the poet. As such, it was of particular value to the later generation of war poets fighting in the trenches of the Western Front as it enabled them to deal with adverse conditions as well as to speak up for their comrades against the supposed ignorance of English society.

This study has revealed the large variety of ironic discourse in the English poetry of the First World War as well as the individual background for its usage, by applying a general communicatory model to literature according to which

> literary works can exemplify the potentiality for change: change within the self, and change to society at large. Even a profoundly disturbing text may also be inspiring and eclectically life-affirming, thanks to its writer's having made an impressive effort of co-adaptation in the first place. But such exemplary force would never carry across to readers unless writers had faith: the sheer faith to write; faith in their own co-adaptive grapplings with circumstance; faith in readers; faith in the final outcome of the communication. (...) As long as people go on exchanging words, there is still a chance that problems will be solved. Even a bitter pessimist, by going public, may be challenging others to steel themselves to endurance, or perhaps turn over a new leaf. (Sell, 2000, p. 246)

With regard to communicative purposes, irony creates a situation of double bonding in which two or more persons – the author and his/her readers – engage in a relationship of particular psychological or even physical importance. By creating this bond through irony, the author draws the reader into an argumentative and/or emotional struggle which strongly determines the communicative success.

As the aim was to analyse the functions and underlying techniques of irony in the English poetry of the First World War by applying a text-oriented conversational approach, other aspects have had to be left open for future research. Not only does this include a comparison of the English ironic literary heritage of war with that of other countries involved such as France, Germany or Russia, but it would also be interesting to take an empirical approach in order to grasp the cultural potential of ironic war poetry. While psychological studies have largely concentrated on mapping the interpretational process as based on individual language skills, a statistical analysis of the readers' reactions towards ironic war poetry is still lacking. Furthermore, questions of developmental psychology such as the understanding of irony by children and teenagers have hardly been answered. While Ellen Winner's study, *The Point of Words. Children's Understanding of Metaphor and Irony* (1988), distinguished between the metaphor as requiring logical–analytical skills in contrast to irony which requires social–analytical skills – both of which need to be acquired as part of a cultural-specific competence – she concentrates entirely on oral irony. However, with regard to the poetry of the First World War, a text-based study would be of particular interest as many of the poems can be found in the curriculum of the nations' literature classes. Furthermore, it remains open to historical research to investigate the Wirkungsgeschichte as well as the position of ironic poetry of the First World War in both national and international literary canons as a result of changing political, cultural and social coordinates.

Lloyd George's task in the last year of war had been to restore England to the bright idealism of 1914, but that was utterly impossible after what had happened at the various fields of battle. Attacking pacifists, however, was no use as they were not the cause of the growing resistance, but only a symptom of England having lost its focus. In the end, there was no option other than to continue, whether for good or for bad. The general bitterness no longer affected only the soldier poets, but the population as a whole. Feelings of dislocation, exploitation and of having lost precious time gave way to a general pessimism that spoiled victory when it finally came on 11 November 1918. For large parts of the population it was impossible to understand that the end of war had come although nothing had really been achieved. This feeling of failure was captured in many literary works of the interwar period, most notably in poems like Hardy's *And there was a great calm* and Sassoon's *Aftermath*. However, in the evaluation of generations of literary critics, the transformation of language and imagery became the major achievement of this first modern war. It was a transformation that not only dominated much of the interwar period, but has had a lasting influence up until today on any aesthetic discourse concerned with the experience of war. A comparative analysis of this lasting impact with regard to the aesthetic legacy of the major wars of the last century, be it the Second World War or the wars in Vietnam, Korea or Iraq, would finally reveal the scope of irony to be widening even further, while at the same time sharing most of the communicative functions unveiled and analysed in the course of this study.

Notes

1 Introduction

1. See, for example, the Italian army at Caporetto in November 1917; the open mutiny of the Imperial Russian army in February 1917; the French army in May and June 1917; and the German navy refusing to continue fighting in the autumn of 1918. For a thorough treatment of the breaking apart of the armies see Keegan, 1999, ch. 9.
2. See, for instance, Sir Edward Grey's famous sentence: 'The lamps are going out all over Europe. We shall not see them lit again in our time' and Roger Fry's observation in a letter to a friend in August 1914: 'It is over with all our ideas.'
3. Winter, 1995, p. 2. See also Quinn, 1994, p. 23: 'writing poetry became a form of mental therapy to expiate the haunting memories of the front and the nagging guilt at having survived'.
4. See Eksteins, 1989, p. 219 and Stephen, 1996, p. 200: 'It is sometimes assumed that irony broke upon British poetry in 1916 like the plague on London in 1665. In fact the image is a valid one: irony, like the plague, had been around long before, but after the war achieved a strength and prevalence it had not reached for many centuries.' However, Stephen also points out the indebtedness of many poets to the English Romantic movement that did not automatically cease with the war.
5. Some of the main features of modernist poetry and painting – concentration, focus on processes of perception, fragmentariness – are already used extensively as means of intensification of expression. Despite the fact that many of the poets of the Great War cannot be called innovators in the strict sense of poetic technique or imagery, their role in the development of twentieth century poetry may nevertheless be qualified as decisive, as the poets were faced with subject matter that violently demanded new representational approaches.
6. A. P. Herbert, *Open Warfare*, ll. 1–3, however, describes the contrary: 'I like a trench, I have no lives to spare;/And in those catacombs, however cramping,/ You did at least know vaguely where you were...'
7. The distinction of several phases of poetic responses to the war had largely been underlined by various anthologies up to the late 1970s. To avoid the suggestion of a linear development of antiwar sentiments, the most recent anthologies organise their material according to its topic or area of production rather than its attitude towards the war, a principle which should also be adhered to in this book.
8. Nevertheless, irony had already played a major role in the critical anti-Boer War poetry of Thomas Hardy, admired by both Rupert Brooke and Siegfried Sassoon, among many others.
9. This emphasis on the subject of the poetry not only rendered it attractive for many generations, it also evoked severe criticism. W. B. Yeats, for example,

did not see war as an appropriate subject for poetry. On the basis of aesthetic criteria he excluded all war poems from his *Oxford Book of Modern Verse*. Whether one takes this position or not, any evaluation of poetry from the Great War must face the difficulties posed by the importance of its subject matter.

10. Grubb, 1965, p. 95, however, argued to the contrary: 'Any artist who does not herald war – anyone who *thinks* critically about force outside war – argues for peace.' And later on the same page: 'Owen and Rosenberg are pacifists in an active state (...) They transcend "pacifism" and reach one of the strangest, and to the creative mind most indispensable, truths of life: the only way to convict evil with any authority worth respect is to suffer it yourself.'

11. Hutcheon, 1994, p. 118, therefore rejects intentional/non-intentional as a false distinction and argues that all irony happens intentionally either on the side of the ironist or on the side of the interpreter.

12. Speech act theory underlines the performative aspect of language in emphasising that speakers are *doing* something when using language, an assumption preparing the way for Sell's communicative theory. Following Austin's and Searle's description of speech acts, one of the main questions of speech act theory with regard to irony is whether the irony affects the level of locution or illocution. However, for a long time literature has not been perceived as a 'real' speech act between writer and reader, but as a fictional imitation of a speech act on the level of implied author and implied reader, or rather between various characters.

13. Grice, 1975, pp. 41–58. The principle is based on the distinction between conventional (semantic content of an utterance) and conversational implicature, of which the latter is of special relevance with regard to the cooperative nature of discourse. By removing the 'safety net' for conversations that words mean what they say, irony makes people feel uneasy. For a combination of speech act theory and psychology with regard to irony see Groeben and Scheele, 1984.

14. Muecke distinguishes between three 'grades of irony' (overt, covert and private) and four modes (impersonal, self-disparaging, ingénu and dramatised), all of which may be used in poetry as they are not genre-related.

15. For this reason, Fabb, 1997, p. 264, calls irony 'a culturally specific notion rather than a universal'.

16. Whereas Derrida – together with Machin and Norris, 1987, pp. 3, 7 – concludes from this uncontrollability of readings that every interpretation can only be a misinterpretation, Sell argues that any readable text can be understood repeatedly by different readers in different circumstances (see also Culler, 1982, p. 176). Fabb, 1997, p. 259, takes a middle position here by focusing on the text itself: 'It is always necessary to remember that texts do not determine their interpretations, but only provide evidence for them.'

17. Jacobson's model consists of six factors and their respective functions: sender (expressive), message (poetic), receiver (conative), context (referential), contact or channel (phatic), code (meta-linguistic). Hutcheon, 1994, p. 6, considers the sender and the receiver to be the most important among these factors as they function as ironist and interpreter. The interpreter, however, does not necessarily need to be the intended addressee of the

ironist's utterance, but he is the one to attribute irony and to interpret the particular ironic meaning of the utterance.

18. Thus Fabb and Durant, 1987, p. 6 have argued against structuralist assumptions by proclaiming that 'it is difficult to identify any formal properties of literary language which do not also appear in non-literary language'. This argumentation is strengthened by the frequent occurrence of code-switching between different registers in literary works, including language usually classified as non-literary. Both literary and non-literary kinds of discourse, they continue, 'share a common range of properties when considered pragmatically, from the point of view of the kinds of communicative acts they perform'.

19. Although Sell draws on Habermas's communicative theory in most of his arguments, he differs from Habermas in this aspect. The latter qualifies literary works as incomplete speech acts because they are robbed of their illocutionary force (1999, p. 390). According to Habermas, the only illocutionary force of literature is mimesis, that is the imitation of several speech acts.

20. See Hutcheon's attempt (1994, p. 2), to theorise irony's social as well as formal dimensions on the basis of verbal and structural ironies (rather than situational irony or irony of fate): 'Unlike metaphor or allegory, which demand similar supplementing of meaning, irony has an evaluative edge and manages to provoke emotional responses in those who "get" it and those who don't, as well as in its targets and in what some people call its "victims".'

21. Habermas, 1987, p. 376: 'Schließlich ist kommunikatives Handeln auf situative Kontexte angewiesen, die ihrerseits Ausschnitte aus der Lebenswelt der Interaktionsteilnehmer darstellen.'

22. See also Habermas, 1999, p. 396: 'It [literary criticism] is, however, not merely an esoteric component of a culture of experts but, over and above this, has the task of mediating between the cultures of experts and the everyday world.' Habermas calls this the 'bridging function' of art criticism.

23. See Sartre, 1995, p. 229: 'This is the measure we propose to the writer: as long as his books arouse anger, discomfort, shame, hatred, love, even if he is no more than a shade, he will live.'

24. Sell, 2000, p. 26f.: 'Whereas readers, if they are going to be affected, must obviously be still alive, there is nothing to prevent them from being affected by a writer who is already dead, and by a cultural formation no longer extant.'

25. Fabb, 1997, p. 264: ' "Irony" is a name for various kinds of communication where the speaker dissociates herself from the thoughts communicated. The communicated thought is attributed to a third party, who may or may not be specified, and at the same time the speaker communicates one of a particular range of attitudes of dissociation towards the set of thoughts. The dissociation might be mild disbelief or fierce disapproval.'

26. Habermas identified 'Verständigung' ('understanding') as the main purpose of human communication in his *Theorie des kommunikativen Handelns*, 1987, p. 387: 'Verständigung wohnt als Telos der menschlichen Sprache inne.' Whereas understanding between communication partners is usually achieved by a straightforward use of language (direct understanding), certain situative contexts require interpretation of figurative language and

irony (indirect understanding). The various functions of irony identified in the following chapters may thus be subsumed under the primary aim of understanding. To underline this distinction between direct and indirect understanding, Habermas draws on Austin's differentiation between illocutionary and perlocutionary speech acts. Accordingly, indirect understanding is identified as a result of the perlocutionary force of an utterance, its strategic potential via emotions.

27. Johansen, 2002, p. xiii: 'The author wants to represent and insist on something in addressing his or her listeners or readers, although what is said transcends what has been intended. Literary texts (...) seem to contain a surplus of meaning. The matter of literature is, broadly speaking, the human condition as it is seen – or in the case of literature, just as much imagined – by the uttering subject. Since such a perspective is grounded in time and space, the historical context of uttering is important to the understanding of the texts.'

28. In the Military Service Act of January 1916 and its revised form of May that year, George V not only introduces conscription but also appreciates the great number of volunteers. See Great Britain, *Public General Statutes*, 5&6/ George V, c.104.

29. Great Britain, *Public General Statutes*, LIII, 21–22: 5/George V, c.8.

30. Booth, 1974, p. 13, argues to the contrary by stating that irony creates 'amiable communities' between the ironist and interpreter who experience the pleasure of joining together in language. Thus for him irony is a 'communal achievement'.

31. Thus the years 1964–1968 constituted a period of cultural reassessment of the war. The polarity of responses can be seen in two major works of the time, the political satire *Oh what a lovely war*, and Britten's *War Requiem* (grief and pity vs. withdrawal and protest). During the 1970s, every year saw the publication of at least one significant new book on the war with a new appeal to personal memory in order to replace popular myth with 'objective' analysis. The following decade was then marked by the politics of the Thatcher Era, while studies and anthologies from the 1990s onwards became more and more influenced by recent trends in historiography and cultural studies.

32. See also Hecker, 2005, pp. 136–148. The author asks for a critical re-evaluation of the impact of Wilfred Owen's poetry of the First World War on the reception of other war poems which have often been dismissed because they fail 'to function as poetry of pity' (p. 137) and 'are not overtly activist' (p. 138).

33. Parfitt, 1990, p. 63, distinguishes four varieties of representation of war for the ordinary soldier: (1) total elision; (2) poetry of men who served in the ranks although they were not 'ranker class'; (3) real 'ranker'poets; and 4. the three special cases of Wilfrid Gibson, Isaac Rosenberg and Ivor Gurney.

34. The historical authenticity of many of the representations of war experience, however, has been questioned ever since Douglas Jerrold's 1930 pamphlet *The Lie About the War*. The question of authenticity, or even historical accuracy, will not be answered here; it will not even be asked. What is important, however, is an awareness of the high degree of subjectivity that becomes obvious in the authors' chosen point of view.

35. See also Hynes, 1997, p. xii: 'And so if we would understand what war is like, and how it feels, we must turn away from history and its numbers, and seek the reality in the personal witness of the men who were there.' Hynes, however, still omits the valuable narratives of those women 'who were there' as well and those who experienced and documented war at home.

36. Adams, 1985, p. 26, argues that poetry – other than the novel or the drama as purely fictional genres – straddles fiction and non-fiction.

37. For information on war in the air and at sea, see Keegan (1993); Halpern (1994); Campbell (1986); and Hough (1983). Stephen, 1993, p. 218f., also points out the difference between the two areas of warfare with regard to writing: 'The air war was new; there was no tradition for poets to fall back on either when involved in it, or when writing about it from back at home. The opposite was true of the war at sea. The country took tremendous and overwhelming pride in its Navy, and pre-war writers had not been backward in producing a significant quantity of stirring stuff about Britain's Pride.˙(...) Poetry about the war at sea therefore tends either to be heroic and romantic, or rather low-key, although this did not stop some fine pieces being written.'

38. The results of a comparative perspective can be found in various publications, such as Marsland (1991); Field (1991); Klein (1978) and Stanzel/ Löschnigg (1993).

39. Hynes, 1990, ch. 5: 'A Turn of Speech'.

40. This lack of irony might be due to several reasons: (1) Australian and New Zealand volunteers were supposed to be shipped to England first. However, they were instead embarked in Alexandria to support the Gallipoli campaign. Thus the ANZAC forces were mainly involved in the East, so that the features of poetry from the Eastern Front are also valid in this case. (2) Australians did not accept the traditional British military hierarchy. Thus, instead of mocking their superiors behind their backs, Australians expressed open criticism immediately and therefore did not need to draw on irony in this case. (3) After the failure of the Gallipoli campaign, the ANZAC troops were shifted to Palestine and Mesopotamia, where poetry writing was influenced by the rich myths about the Holy Land and the Psalms rather than an ironic tradition. Thus, although Australia and New Zealand armies each suffered the highest proportion of casualties sustained by any nation during the war (82 percent casualty rate), the poetry to deal with the experience draws on other sources than irony and satire.

41. See also Bowman (2003) and Haughey (2002).

42. Brearton, 2000, p. 10: 'Theoretically, both the Ulster and the Irish National Volunteers enlisted in loyal support of Britain's war aims; in reality, the leaders of both sides volunteered their troops in an attempt to influence British policy. The 'opponent' in each case, paradoxically, was England.'

43. See also Bloom, 2002, p. 9: 'I wonder though if a complex irony, rather than pity, is not Owen's true mode.' And one page further: 'Perhaps a fatal irony is the essence of war poetry.'

44. Quinn, 1994, p. 21: 'Sassoon had a knack for transforming the negative emotions of horror and disgust into accusatory verse. It gave his poetry not only a didactic flavour, but also an unmistakable taste of irony that was meant to shock his complacent respectable readers into awareness of the

actualities of the front.' Campbell, 1999, p. 25, thus describes Sassoon's technique of writing as one of 'ironic juxtaposition with an unexpected switch of emphasis in the last line' for the sake of a concentrated effect. However, irony is not limited to the last line but often embedded in the main body of the poem, as in the case of Wilfred Owen's works. Rather than confronting the reader with the reality of war in general, his poetry mainly expresses sympathy and pity with war's victims via general ironical overtones. As Lane, 1972, p. 151, puts it: 'The overall tone of the poem [in this case *Disabled*] is the blend of irony and compassion characteristic of Owen.'

2   Evasion

1. See also Moore, 1969, p. 205: 'At first, even at the front, poetry was for Sassoon an escape into a more pleasant world rather than a means to comprehend and convey the world he was caught up in.'
2. Whereas Spear, 1979, p. 67, still argues that 'realism had completely superseded the romantic attitude for those who had had the experience of battle', Stephen, 1996, p. 201, speaks of a continuation of the romantic mode throughout the whole of the war.
3. Beginning with the *Romance of the Rose* (translated by Chaucer into English), the rose features prominently in English love lyrics from Shakespeare's sonnets to the Romantics such as Blake's *My Pretty Rose Tree*.
4. For the anglophone world, this distinction largely follows that of Thirlwall (1833), who differentiated between three forms of irony: verbal irony, dialectic irony, and practical irony. Kierkegaard even claimed the existence of an 'irony of nature', a general tragic inherent in the world, as a subcategory of practical irony.
5. See, for example, Geoffrey Faber, *The Eve of War*, stanza 2: 'But here through bending trees blows a great wind;/Through torn cloud-gaps the angry stars look down./Here have I heard this night the wings of War,/His dark and frowning countenance I saw./What dreadful menace hangs above our town?'
6. Wilson, 1975. For a comparison of Rosenberg's Jewishness with that of Sassoon, see Avi Matalon, 2002, pp. 25–43.
7. See Owen, *A Terre*, l. 37ff.: 'Not worse than ours the lives rats lead –/Nosing along at night down some safe rut,/They find a shell-proof home before they rot.'
8. For a comparison between Rosenberg's and Shelley's treatment of the lark see Hendry, 1992, pp. 67–69.
9. See Motion, 1980, p. 92 and Pikoulis, 1987, p. 129, who argues that Thomas's poetry 'illuminates war – and more than war – in ways that are not dependent on (...) having seen active service'.
10. See Pikoulis, 1987, p. 119: 'Thomas was the reluctant or hesitant suicide, one who lacked the courage (or single-mindedness) to finish himself off and who found in the war a miraculous release from his private dilemma.'
11. Longley, 2005, p. 73: 'If Owen's poetry-as-history is anthropocentric, Thomas's is ecocentric, ecological. Thomas, too, rejected Christianity but

humanity ("a parochial species") became less, not more, central to his vision.'

12. Stephen, 1996, pp. 221 and 222: '[N]ature has a power that the war can suspend but never destroy.'

13. Stephen, 1996, p. 197, does not interpret this clash of diction with reality as deliberately ironic: 'The chariot is an emblem for a type of warfare far removed from the bolt-action rifle and gas-attack, and with its Roman associations is an image of honour, glory and victory, precisely the glorious image of warfare that Owen seems to wish to avoid.'

14. Graves, 1969, p. 217: 'We no longer saw the war as one between trade-rivals: its continuance seemed merely a sacrifice of the idealistic younger generation to the stupidity and self-protective alarm of the elder.'

15. Quinn, 1994, p. 22 and Stephen, 1996, p. 209: 'If not drifting from the war into fantasy Graves is more usually found retreating at the first opportunity into memories of a pre-war pastoral idyll.'

16. See also Hynes, 1997, p. 8, on the external origins of that idea: 'War turns landscape into anti-landscape, and everything in that landscape into grotesque, broken, useless rubbish – including human limbs.'

17. For the debate on some authors' homoeroticism see Caesar (1993); Santanu (2006); Taylor (1998); and the early essay by Cohen, 1965, pp. 253–268.

18. Following her argumentation 'Friendship and comradeship are not allied forms (...), but antagonists' (p. 77). Hynes, 1997, p. 9, also distinguishes these terms but locates the difference in the nature of war: 'Friendship, (...), is different there – different enough to need another name: *comradeship*. The first thing to be said of comradeship is that it is accidental.' Despite this accidental nature of comradeship, it is a very intense form of friendship but at the same time the most fragile as it is constantly threatened by death.

19. For a detailed history of war at sea, see Hough (2003).

20. See also Jeffery Day's poem *North Sea* describing life and death on board a battleship.

21. Stephen, 1996, p. 220: 'Poetry about the war at sea lacked the war-revulsion that we have seen as typifying trench poetry, and so has often been ignored.'

22. Both the fascination and the horrors of air warfare provide the topic of Charles M. Schulz's famous comic strips on Snoopy the Flying Ace and the Red Baron in his *Peanuts* series.

23. Plett, 1982, p. 83, in this context is talking about 'sekundäre Ironisierung'. The example he gives is a critique of the New Critics, for, in his view, inappropriate ironic reading of many texts that were not intended to be ironic in the first place. However, we have to bear in mind that this kind of secondary ironisation is already employed by certain authors themselves, which might even lead to a 'tertiary' ironisation when readers today analyse their works. An example of this development can be found in Owen's use of the earnest Horatian 'Dulce et decorum est pro patria mori' in the sarcastic end of his poem. A modern reader, however, might read even more into the sentence than Owen originally intended.

24. The main focus here is on Grice's cooperative principle as a guarantee for successful communication which he developed in his essay 'Logic and Conversation'. According to his theory, irony mainly violates the maxims

of manner and relevance. However, texts may contain several irrelevancies without being ironic and in cases of subversive irony none of the maxims are violated. For a direct critique of Grice's theory with regard to irony see Holdcroft, 1983, pp. 493–511, who argues for a necessary distinction between the irony in a text (in the form of trope irony) and irony as attitude, for which speech act theory is doomed to fail.

25. Frye, 1957, p. 41, differentiated between naive and sophisticated irony: 'the naive ironist calls attention to the fact that he is being ironic, whereas sophisticated irony merely states, and lets the reader add the ironic tone himself'. But, in order for the reader to be able to do this, he or she needs additional information, such as the context of the utterance.

26. For the concept of implied author and reader see also Booth, 1961, pp. 71 and 73f.

27. Müller, 1995, p. 124ff., furthermore lists five advantages of literary texts as opposed to spoken language: (1) texts are 'real' attempts at successful communication as their authenticity is guaranteed; (2) texts are complete entities which contain a complete set of information; (3) the horizon of interpretation is the same for any average reader of the same cultural background and education; (4) every author adapts his text to culture-specific norms so that the precision of the text is guaranteed (the possibilities of chance irony are thus limited); (5) literary texts have a natural representativeness, which means that their irony resembles the irony used in everyday life.

28. Sperber and Wilson, 1995, ch. 4, sections 4–9 and Eun-Ju Noh, 1998, ch. 2.

29. For the historical development of the idea of fragmentariness see Fietz (1994). While fragmentariness was formerly perceived as inherent in human nature, Fietz, p. 214, argues that a major paradigmatic change took place in the late nineteenth and twentieth centuries so that from then on fragmentariness is seen as resulting from external factors such as society and economy. In addition to these two, the fast development of (military) technology that began in the prewar years and continued during the twentieth century plays a major role.

30. See, for example, the report on 16 September 1916 in the *Times* on 'The mysterious "Tanks": Our Latest Military Weapon' describing the weapons as an 'army of unearthly monsters'. See also Mary Borden, *The Hill*, perceiving the movement of tanks as one of a 'regiment of monsters' moving slowly 'along on their stomachs'.

31. Hibberd, 2002, p. 387, claims that *Soldier's Dream* 'had satirised the Americans for ensuring that the war would continue'. However, I would argue that the poem rather follows Owen's technique of playing with biblical material in order to reflect on the generational conflict as mirrored in the quarrel between Jesus and his father.

32. Löschnigg, 1994, p. 158: 'Die von Brooke 1914 artikulierte Erwartung einer mit dem Krieg verbundenen Purifikation führt das spätere Gedicht Owens in den entstellenden Kontortionen des Gasopfers *ad absurdum*.'

33. Hipp, 2002, p. 36ff., argues that for Owen the poem served as an early step towards coming to terms with his psychological trauma. 'The first half of the poem, then, has charted new psychological territory for Owen by immersing him in the memory that haunts him while writing. But the second half,

with its rhetoric of anger, illustrates that like the unresolved sonnet embedded within, the poet's crisis of responsibility, though exposed poetically, remains an open wound.'

34. Norgate, 1989, p. 521, however, argues that read in the context of soldier poetry an even sharper irony is at work as 'Owen's poem [is] now speaking also to those who *have* participated, who must have watched and heard, but who apparently still do not really *see*; those – such as the Soldier Poets – who, having experienced warfare in the trenches, can still (for whatever reason) "lie" about it.'

3 Confrontation

1. The author even identifies the twentieth century as a 'satirical age' (p. 223).
2. See also Weiß (1982) who argues that the choice of genre always follows the satirical aim.
3. See Parsons, 1965, p. 20: 'Human beings seek relief from insupportably nerve-racking experiences...by satirizing them.'
4. 'Old Men' was not only a generational, but also a class term. The anger at the older generation was directed not against workers or farmers, but against those in a position with power to send young men to war, namely bishops, generals, admirals, politicians and journalists. They represented the power of the past over the present and it was this (Victorian) past that was made responsible for the war. Robert Graves' *Good-bye to All That* can be seen as symbolic of this rejection of the past, including the war itself.
5. Frye, 1957, p. 223: 'The chief distinction between irony and satire is that satire is militant irony: its moral norms are relatively clear, and it assumes standards against which the grotesque and absurd are measured.' Frye furthermore identified two main ingredients of satire, namely wit or humour (not necessarily irony!), and an object of attack.
6. See, for instance, Hutcheon, 1981, pp. 140–155. However, as Connery and Combe, 1995, p. 9, rightly point out: '[I]n general usage, "satire" remains less an identifiable genre than a mode, and an astonishingly wide range of vastly varied works have been placed under its rubric'.
7. Nilsen, 1988, pp. 1–10, mentions several 'necessary conditions' that distinguish satire, namely irony, negativity, distortion, humour, and the fact that satire unifies its audience against the common enemy. Highet, 1962, p. 15f., also points out special features on the basis of which satires could be recognised: (1) a generic definition might be given by the author himself; (2) the author may produce a pedigree that includes other satires or authors of satire; (3) choice of a traditionally satiric subject and its treatment as such; (4) the quotation of another distinguished satirist by the author. To all of these lists, the context of the text has to be added as a decisive criterion.
8. Connery and Combe, 1995, p. 6: 'Perhaps more that any other genre, satire is constructed or structured on the basis of oppositions or hierarchies; in satire, these oppositions are represented in their extremes in order to achieve maximum tension. The most common rhetorical figures of satire – irony, paradox, and oxymoron (all three are based upon opposites) – are

those that maximize the imaginative tension of the text and produce in the reader a consequent sense of discomfort.'

9. For that reason, satire criticism can only gain by the recent developments in historicism after having been neglected by a large group of scholars who wished to exclude history from literary criticism.

10. For a collection of the 'weapons of satire' see Highet, 1962, p. 18.

11. See also Connery and Combe, 1995, p. 1: 'Satire establishes oppositions between good and evil, text and reader, reader and society, even between the reader and herself. In aligning ourselves with the satirist, we find ourselves in unattractive company and subject to the fear and loathing of the society of dulness (sic!) the satirist opposes. Conversely, in aligning ourselves in opposition to the satirist, we risk being derided as hypocrites.'

12. In 1599 the Archbishop of Canterbury and the Bishop of London issued an order prohibiting the printing of any satires. At the same time, all existing satirical works were to be burned. In the twentieth century, the publication of satires might lead to financial losses for the publisher and in some countries satirists still risk being sentenced to death. In the context of war, satirists had to be aware of military sanctions in addition to censorship of personal letters.

13. Connery and Combe, 1995, p. 5: '[S]atire's own frequent formlessness forces it to inhabit the forms of other genres (...), and makes satire resistant to simplistic versions of a formalist approach.'

14. Freeman, 1963, pp. 307–322. She furthermore identifies detachment as a major problem of parody as 'the emotional context in which the style was once used has to be treated with extreme delicacy or its value will be lost'. See also Hutcheon (1981).

15. Buitenhuis, 1987, p. xvii: 'The enthusiasm and loyalty of the British authors were sufficient to carry them through until late 1916 when it became evident that the war was going to be a long drawn-out and costly affair. Although they continued to write propaganda, some of them began to think sceptically about British leadership and the alleged bestiality of the Germans. Such doubt appears in the ironic fiction of H. G. Wells (*Mr. Britling Sees It Through*), Arnold Bennett (*The Pretty Lady*), John Galsworthy (*Saint's Progress*), and Ford Madox Hueffer (*Zeppelin Nights*).'

16. Löschnigg, 1994, p. 27: 'Kritischen englischen und deutschen Frontgedichten gemeinsam ist der Gedanke, dass auch im Hinterland ein Feind sitzt, in den Stabsquartieren, den Zeitungsredaktionen und an den Schaltstellen der politischen Macht.'

17. 'Religion' or 'faith' in this chapter will include the various possible attitudes towards God, of the churches and their clergy, but also of individuals, dogma, doubt, and other personal modes of religious thinking. However, due to the focus on British poetry in this book, the analysis of 'religion' will be limited to Christianity as other beliefs only played a minor role at the time. Yet the concentration on Christianity will by no means exclude the texts of such famous authors as Isaac Rosenberg, a Jew, or Siegfried Sassoon, son of a Jewish father and an Anglican mother.

18. Only the most recent investigations into the role of Christianity during the First World War now challenge this misconception. For a new perspective on the importance of religion see Snape (2005) and Schweitzer (2003).

19. This is what Snape, 2005, ch. 1, calls 'diffusive Christianity'. Whilst other historians have argued for a decline of religious beliefs in British society during the first half of the twentieth century, Snape sees the various forms of religious practices and beliefs as the outcome of a personalisation of religion that had its origin in the prewar decades but was furthered by the war experience. At the same time, the religious diversity, according to Snape, mirrors the soldiers' ethnic, regional, social and generational differences.

20. This argument gained special importance for the Irish involvement in the war as part of the British Army despite their political struggles for Irish home rule. Belgium's fate seemed to resemble that of Israel in Biblical times as well as that of the early Christian communities persecuted by the Roman Empire. Thus Wilkinson, 1978, p. 30, points out: 'Whereas a respected minority, both inside and outside the Churches, had opposed the Boer War, few voiced any opposition to the Great War once it had broken out.'

21. Charles H. Sorley was among those who saw very early that this war was not the right way to fight evil. See Sorley, 1978, p. 262: 'What we are doing is casting out Satan by Satan.'

22. Interestingly enough, the American clergy, in contrast to their British colleagues, opted for neutrality, respecting their president Wilson's policy of non-involvement, at least until the sinking of the *Lusitania* in 1915.

23. For Owen's mockery of the concept see his poem *Greater Love* and the earlier *At a Calvary Near the Ancre* in which he accuses the Church to be a disciple of the Devil for its hatred of Germany as true love does not hate. He strongly expresses the opinion that 'pure Christianity will not fit in with pure patriotism'. (See Owen and Bell, 1967, p. 461.)

24. Winter, 1985, p. 291, therefore proposed that 'it is perhaps best to understand most of the war literature (...) less as a literature of warning, than first as a literature of separation and bereavement, and secondly as a literature of the guilt of the survivor'.

25. Wilkinson, 1978, p. 174, even reckons that 30 percent of British officers were the sons of Anglican clergymen.

26. For Graves's religious development see Seymour (1995) and Graves (1987).

27. See also Marrin (1974). For the longer-lasting results of war on religion in Britain see also Heyck (1996). However, one should not neglect the fact that even before the war, the Church of England was disunited and split into various groups (Evangelicals, Liberals, Anglo-Catholics and others). Even if the war momentarily united these groups under a common cause, in the long run it increased the gap between them as they accused each other of misrepresenting Christianity. For the reaction against these drawbacks see Wilkinson, 1978, pp. 80–90.

28. See Gassenmeier, 1994, p. 203. It is the cry of desperation that ends the sonnet before its form is complete.

29. Wilson, 1998, p. 410, argues to the contrary: 'His usual irony is missing, though the poem does end with one of his typical soldier's curses.'

30. In its form, the poem is similar to *Sick Leave*, a poem composed at roughly the same time. Wilson, 1998, p. 410, attributes both form and technique to the influence of Owen.

31. Wilkinson, 1978, p. 158: 'One odd legacy of the widespread knowledge of hymns was that well-known tunes were available to be set to comic or bawdy words.'

32. The comparison of the dying soldiers with Christ according to John 15:13 in this poem was added at a later stage of revision, as the critical edition shows. Contrary to most other scholars, Hibberd, 1998, p. 160, argues that the religious imagery here should not be interpreted as a sign of faith. Its function is instead 'to reveal the beauty and bitterness of man's life on earth'. This corresponds with his angry statement concerning the profiteers on 31 March 1918 using John 3:16 as basis: 'God so hated the world that He gave several millions of English-begotten sons, that whosoever believeth in them should not perish, but have a comfortable life.' See Owen and Bell, 1967, p. 544. I myself would argue that, by using a passage frequently quoted by both critics and supporters of the war, Owen shows his awareness of both possible interpretations. Whereas the soldier may indeed have found consolation in the passion of Christ, it is the misuse of the concept that Owen condemns here. God the Father, on the other hand, is portrayed in unsympathetic terms as a non-caring God, but this does not contradict the religious truth of Christ's sacrifice. For the poem's use of romantic imagery see Freeman, 1963, pp. 318–322.

33. Although Owen did not share Sassoon's enthusiasm for Graves when they met at Craiglockhart War Hospital in summer 1917, he was nevertheless interested in his work and probably knew *Goliath and David* before composing the *Parable of the Old Man and the Young*.

34. Note that some manuscripts read 'The Parable of the Old M*en* and the Young'.

35. In a letter to Osbert Sitwell in 1918 he identifies Christ on the cross with the soldier while he himself takes responsibility for their crucifixion: 'I...inspected his feet to see that they should be worthy of the nails'.

36. See also his ironical poem *Soldier's Dream* in which Jesus stops the war by destroying and blocking the weapons. However, when the dream ends, the soldier awakes to find that the archangel Michael empowered by God has repaired them, so that the war can continue.

37. See also Grubb, 1965, p. 95: '[T]he only way to convict evil with any authority worth respect is to suffer it yourself'.

38. See also Norgate, 1989, p. 529: '"At a Calvary" confronts the implications of true sacrifice and recognizes the war as continuing evidence of man's inability to comprehend "the greater love".'

39. Wilkinson, 1978, p. 116: 'Through his experiences of the war, his understanding of God and of Christ became more ironic and more profound, richer and wider in scope than anything he could have received from his evangelical upbringing.'

40. Norgate, 1989, p. 522f., draws a parallel between Owen's poem and *A Soldier's Cemetery* by J. W. Streets, which was published posthumously in 1917, arguing that 'Owen's sonnet bitterly contradicts the central premiss of "A Soldier's Cemetery"' by dismissing all consolatory possibilities as mockeries. As such, it refuses 'not only the memorializing rituals of organized religion itself, but also the rhetorical tradition which offers poetic memorials as either complementary to, or a substitute for, religion'.

41. Kerr, 1993, p. 157: 'Weapons (...) provide a metallic and chemical commentary on the slaughter, in the absence of human voices to mourn'.
42. Hibberd, 1998, p. 110, however, had argued that the often criticised allusions to romantic poetry are intended to show the battlefield as a demented *parody* of the Romantic landscape by using Keatsian language.
43. For the ironic connotations of 'bugles' see also Bloom, 2002, p. 36: 'The same bugles that now sound the "Last Post" for the fallen soldiers were the ones that previously called them to colors. Church and state are thus both implicated in the betrayal of the soldiers.'
44. See also Laurence Binyon, *For the Fallen*, which uses the expression in order to suggest continuous remembrance.
45. For Owen's ideas on the humanity and intensity of mourning see also *Futility*. Hibberd, 1998, p. 110, furthermore argued that the poem does not say whether the rites of the bereaved families in England are right or wrong. Instead, the poem identifies them as the only option available. Wilkinson, 1978, p. 173, however, points out that even at home full mourning after a while became impossible because of the great number of the bereaved. Additionally, 'too ostentatious a display of mourning was thought unpatriotic and bad for morale'. On the other hand, public prayer for the dead had been uncommon in the Church of England in 1914 but became widespread by the end of the war.
46. In another of Sassoon's poems, *Memorial Tablet (Great War)*, the dead speaker recalls how one of the clerical nationalists had pressed him to enlist without knowing or caring what fate would await the boy at the front. The poem thus ends with the bitterly ironic question: 'What greater glory could a man desire?' Only after the war did the poet return to organised religion and in 1957 he converted to Roman Catholicism.
47. Proof for this can be found in the collection of essays published in 1918 by a group of British chaplains and laymen with the title speaking for itself: *The Church in the Furnace.*
48. See Budd (1977) and Wilkinson, 1978, p. 162f.: 'Fatalism seemed to be of more help to many soldiers than Christianity. "If your name is on the shell you will get it" was a frequently asserted opinion among troops. Fatalism steadied the nerves. "Soldiers are fatalists; otherwise they would be madmen," declared a lance-corporal.' (...) 'The fact that there seemed no providential pattern discernible, when one was killed and another saved, encouraged fatalism or notions of predestination.' For soldiers taking part in séances see Wilkinson, 1978, p. 179f.
49. Wilson also sees the title as an ironic reference to the opening of Virgil's *Aeneid.*
50. In addition to his traits of character and wrong decisions he made, this conviction of the importance of the cavalry was seen by many as a proof for Sir Douglas Haig's lack of military competence. For a summery of the critical scientific positions concerning Haig see Stephen, 1996, pp. 57–69.
51. Quinn, 1994, p. 182: 'Verbal irony abounds in the poem from the first line.'
52. Quinn, 2001, p. 231: 'This juxtaposition between the chummy greeting and the evidence of the general's incompetence is exposed ironically in the first two lines of the triplet as we listen to the kindly words of the innocent

slogging off to the slaughter. The message is driven home in the last line, when the reader realizes that the two glum heroes, Harry and Jack, will be deprived by yet another bungled attack of ever seeing the future.'

53. According to Paulson, 1967, p. 4, this is characteristic for the genre of satire as it 'judges man not for what he is but for what he did and, indeed, makes the ultimate error (...) of equating the two'.

54. Gibson, 2001, p. 193: 'These voices enable the poet to realize his professed aims of pleading and warning.'

55. O'Keefe, 1972, p. 76: 'The dramatic irony in the poem depends upon the obtuseness of the sergeant-speaker, concerned only with the ritual of cleanliness and not with the meaning of the bloodstains he finds on the soldier's uniform during an inspection.'

56. See also Gibson, 2001, p. 196: 'In so far as we might take this at its face value, we are, theologically speaking, in the presence of original sin, but the epithet "Field-Marshal" applied to God insists that we read the whole passage ironically.'

57. See Marcus, 1989, p. 249. In her work she contradicts Gilbert, 1987, pp. 197–226, who argues that the Great War served to empower women psychologically, economically, and sexually.

58. At the request of the Belgian authorities, an exception was made for Mairi Chisholm and a Mrs Knocker who had set up an advanced dressing-post immediately behind the Belgian front line. As a reward, they later became 'Chevaliers of the order of Leopold'. They remained the only British women living not at the base camps but right behind the trenches.

59. Bergonzi (1965) lacks any reference to female writers. Fussell (1975) only lists about a dozen women as recipients of letters and only two of the four major anthologies of the 1960s contained any poetry by women.

60. For a detailed analysis of the suffragist movement during First World War see Smith (2005).

61. The poem personifies war and peace as brothers that are close to each other. See Byles, 1995, p. 72f.: 'The poem also elaborates the familiar metaphor of war as a monster that devours fathers and sons, ironically supporting the theme of the dualism of war and peace by suggesting that in peace we fatten and nourish our loved ones only to feed this monster.'

62. In all of these poems Ford stresses 'her conviction that if women had had an active part in the formulation of laws they would have dispensed with war'. See Khan, 1988, p. 84. A similar opinion is expressed by Mary Gabrielle Collins in *Women at Munition Making* portraying women's change of role as an enforced one and war as a male activity in opposition to everything natural. However, the poem fails to convince as it fails to question women's culpability. More successful in this respect is Margaret Sackville's poem *Nostra Culpa* admitting women's complicity.

63. However, she believed that 'patriotism and militarism took precedence over the emancipation issue for the duration of the war'. See Byles, 1995, p. 27.

64. Wilson, 1986, p. 707, even speaks of a form of sexual exploitation here as women assigned 'members of the opposite sex to the risk of acute physical suffering. Further, males were being required to play out a warrior role imposed upon them by virtue of their sex, when this role did not necessarily accord with their particular natures'.

65. Higgonet (1987) even argues that the First World War did not change gender roles at all, but rather highlighted women's privileged status as noncombatants.
66. As Byles, 1995, p. 51, states, women's place being in the home was ironically challenged by air raids in cities and towns. Home was then the most dangerous place one could imagine.
67. See, for example, Kitchener's famous recruitment poster slogan 'Women of England say "Go"!' which not only spoke of women's necessity for the war but even directly addressed them.
68. See for instance the remarks of an anonymous soldier on leave at home in *The Nation* of 21 October 1916 that speak of a 'reticence as to the obvious physical facts of the war'. The perception of this gulf, however, was not a male issue only. A very late poem by Vera Brittain, *Lady into Woman* (1953), equally speaks of war as separating men from women due to the difference of experience.
69. Reilly in her bibliography lists 532 women poets, some of whom were established writers before the war, such as Charlotte Mew, Edith Nesbitt and May Sinclair. Others were beginning to establish themselves as writers when the war broke out, as for example Mary Webb and Edith Sitwell, while still others only became famous after the war or because of the war, as for example Margaret Postgate Cole, Vera Brittain and Rose Macauley.
70. See also Connery and Coombe, 1995, p. 12: 'Satire, as a literature of power and attack, has been seen as radically masculinist, and in fact a form of power excerted frequently against women.'
71. See also the entirely different tone of Gibson's poem about a father whose son goes off to war and who worries 'what stranger would come back' to him.
72. Despite his anger Sassoon perceived that knitting for the soldiers was not only a typically female, but also a therapeutic, activity to deal with the war experience of waiting and loss. Only by producing comfort for others were many women able to keep their sanity.
73. Tylee, 2000, p. 257: 'Their heroes do not use the bayonet. No-Man's-Land is not portrayed as a killing-zone, a battlefield. The taboo on murder, the stigma on the murderer, acts like a shutter on women's imagination, preventing them from exploring this essential aspect of men's experience of war. It is part of the forbidden zone on which they do not trespass.'
74. Wilson, 1986, p. 731, points out the difficulties of the term: it can be any form of communication that 'propagates the course of one side and discredits that of its opponents. However, the term does not distinguish between strictly factual information and invention or between different tones of propaganda, which may range from scrupulous to obscene and sensationalist.'
75. See Wilson, 1998, p. 347: 'The War Correspondent's phrase is as dead and meaningless as the corpses, as the contrast between his words (again in direct speech) and the narrator's reactions (in indirect speech) reveals.'
76. O'Keefe, 1972, p. 79: 'In the final stanza the poem expands to condemn the noisy war propagandists in contradistinction to the quiet soldiers who offer their lives in love, like Christ. (...) The scribes and pharisees correspond perfectly to the war propagandists because both groups protest too much about their fervor.'

4 Resignation

1. Keegan, 1998, p. 7: 'Perhaps the worst afflicted were the victims of disfiguring facial wounds, some of whom were so awful to behold that secluded rural settlements were established, where they could holiday together.'
2. A line of an anonymous poem thus places the enemy on the same level as sand and armour: 'Our little fights are nameless,/with Turk and sand and gun.' See Stephen, 1998, p. 185.
3. Food prices rose immensely from autumn 1916 onwards, any empty area was converted to grow food, and the Women's Land Army was created to do the work in the fields.
4. Müller, 1995, p. 177ff., talks of 'Anspielungsironie' which might be of an intertextual nature and thus refer to individual texts or a whole genre, but also includes references to cultural memory. In the case of *The Poet and the Butcher*, both variants are used. Not only does the style of the poem recall an epoch of cultural flourishing as opposed to the present wartime situation, but the reference to Milton underlines the political impact of the topic.
5. This tradition is most commonly associated with Germany and the so-called 'Jena Romantics': August Wilhelm and his brother Friedrich Schlegel, Ludwig Tieck, Karl Wilhelm Ferdinand Solger and Novalis with their journal *Athenaeum*.
6. Mellor, 1980, p. vii: 'The romantic ironist's enthusiastic response to process and change terminates where the perception of a chaotic universe arouses either guilt or fear.'
7. Mellor, 1980, p. 187: 'Historically, however, romantic irony was born from the upheavals of the French and Industrial Revolutions, flourished during the early nineteenth century, and was seriously weakened by the violence of First World War. By 1918, the fear of sudden change that had overwhelmed the timid Lewis Carroll had become a widely shared cultural paranoia. To many people, change meant only destruction.' Thus after the devastation of the Great War, 'the romantic ironist's enthusiastic celebration of process and change seemed callow or philosophically absurd.'
8. For the technique of ironic detachment see Mücke, 1969, p. 216f. Mücke furthermore argues that this technique guarantees the objectivity of the ironic observer as opposed to the unreflexive subjectivity of the victim, because what the ironist sees from his high position is contrary to his own position. Thus the archetypal victim is trapped in time and matter, blind and unfree, whereas the archetypal ironist (God) is omniscient, free, absolute and infinite. In his simultaneous immanence and transcendence, the ironic author resembles God, yet remains himself vulnerable to irony as he finds himself in exactly the same situation as the victim he observes.
9. Schlegel, 1958ff., KA 11, p. 9: 'Weil aber alle Erkenntnis des Unendlichen wie ihr Gegenstand immer unendlich und unergründlich, also nur indirekt sein kann, wird sinnbildliche Darstellung nötig, um das, was nicht im ganzen erkannt werden kann, doch teilweise erkennen zu können. Was nicht in einen Begriff zusammengefaßt werden kann, läßt sich vielleicht durch ein Bild darstellen; und so führt dann das Bedürfnis der Erkenntnis zur Darstellung, die Philosophie zur Poesie.' See also Mellor, 1980, p. 10: 'This awareness of the limitations of the self is what Schlegel meant by philosophical "irony" or the "critical faculty" (a Kantian term).'

10. This duality goes back to Socrates, who, by being constantly aware of his own weaknesses and failures, but also of his strength, was able to appear both serious and playful at the same time. By knowing the limitations of his own knowledge, from the viewpoint of the absolute he knew nothing.

11. See Hibberd, 1998, p. 114 and 1979, p. 333. Isaac Rosenberg equally used a version of the slogan in *Dead Man's Dump*.

12. A direct allusion can be found in l. 10. Sassoon, *The Death-Bed*, l. 7 reads: 'Someone was holding water to his mouth.'

13. See also Sassoon's wounded soldier on his way back home in *Stretcher Case*, l. 15: ' "If I were dead," he mused, "there'd be no thinking –".'

14. See Wilson, 1998, p. 407: 'The speaker is condemned out of his own mouth for even asking if they [amputation, blindness, madness] matter.'

15. Thus Thorpe, 1966, p. 26, made a point when he claimed: 'In *showing* the dreadfulness of the War, in its surface aspects, he preceded Owen and surpasses him and all English poets who had previously written of war. His satires have, quantitatively, greater "bite" than those of his fellow war-poets and a sheer brutality of utterance that matches the reality. No English satirist since Byron had had such power of invective ... He relieved the pressure of his emotion by *speaking* the brutality, over and over again.'

16. See Wilson, 1998, p. 285: '[I]nstead of raging against the loss of a leg, [the soldier] is grateful for the amputation which restores him to safety'.

17. In this respect Sassoon's Jewish background might be of interest as cripples and amputees are denied access to some of the religious offices in Judaism.

18. Due to increasing recruitment and the need for a large number of volunteers, however, the medical selection process had in most cases only been superficial so that a large number of young men were admitted to the army who had been suffering from mental illnesses before the outbreak of war and whose condition then deteriorated under the conditions of war.

19. For the application of the term see Leese (2002) and Mosse, 2000, pp. 101–108.

20. Punishment in some cases even included shooting of the respective panicking soldier. See Corns and Hughes-Wilson (2001).

21. Sauerteig, 1999, pp. 167–188. See also Shephard (2000).

22. Many of those so-called lunatics were considered a danger to the troops both morally and militarily so that severe punishment seemed justified. See, for example, Frankau, *The Deserter*, or Gibson, *His Mate*, in which a soldier is shot by one of his comrades for singing, or rather yelling a nursery tune while sitting on a heap of dead bodies. It remains questionable whether this is supposed to be an act of mercy or a kneejerk reaction for fear of attracting enemy fire.

23. Barham, 2004, p. 124, even speaks of a 'remoralization of lunacy', which even included mental disorders unrelated to the war. And on p. 127 he perceives 'a new and radically expanded understanding of normality, in which the neurotic is no longer the deviant or the isolate but everyman'.

24. When Ivor Gurney finally died in 1937 no money was left behind to pay his funeral expenses or debts. However, as Barham, 2004, p. 265, states: 'His pauperization was a product of a proud and well-intentioned, but ultimately myopic, effort to support this distraught genius with only limited recourse

to the state, as though to ensure that he conformed to the type of the lonely suffering artist, spurned by the society which he had yearned to serve.'
25. Before summer 1916 the Somme, for instance, was a rather peaceful and largely neglected part of the front.
26. Dramatic irony is based on the distinction between reality and appearance. However, this distinction is only obvious for the reader or spectator of a particular situation but not so for the characters immediately involved. In order to detect the irony, the reader must be aware of the various possible layers of meaning in both language and action. See Cuddon, 1999, pp. 237, 427–432. See also Muecke, 1969, p. 104ff.
27. The charge of cowardice unfortunately led to the military execution of 345 British men by March 1920.
28. See also Herbert Read, *The Happy Warrior*, in which madness is the only possible source of happiness. Happy is only the one who in his insanity does not question the brutality of war. Whereas Wordsworth idealised the soldier in *The Character of the Happy Warrior*, Read's warrior is reduced to a bestial or rather mechanistic actor. As such, his behaviour no longer follows the rules of civilisation or Christian ethics.
29. Campbell, 1999, p. 117, argues: 'In "The Hero" irony resides in the mother's proud conviction that her "glorious boy" has died a hero's death.'
30. Spear, 1979, p. 131: '[T]he irony is obvious; they were the words of the sacrificers, not of the victims.' Like Owen's *Mental Cases* the poem suggests that these mental cases will not recover sanity.
31. A similar personification of death, though without ironic intent, can be found in Sassoon, *The Death-Bed*, in which death claims his prey (see the last stanza of the poem) in the hospital ward.
32. Wilfred Owen, *Strange Meeting*, suggests a similar unity of friend and foe as the basis of new hope for a future peaceful world. In Rosenberg's poem, however, I would rather see the contrary, namely that all hope is futile.
33. See Bloom, 2002, p. 85: 'In his measured, unflinching gaze at human pain, Rosenberg is able to achieve one of the fullest understandings of human dignity.'
34. Hibberd, 1979, p. 333, points out the similarity of the man's cry to a slogan on a recruiting poster asking 'Will they never come?' See also the cry of the maimed soldier in Wilfred Owen, *Disabled*.
35. Wilkinson, 1978, p. 171: 'A mixture of detachment and humour was one defence against such horrors.'
36. See also the mutilated corpse in May Plowman, *Going into the Line*, as emblem for the anonymous killing.
37. Lane, 1972, p. 111. Thus 'sneak home' is qualified by Lane as 'an instance of anger over-riding art, a making of a point by insult instead of observation'
38. For the death of officers see also Davies and Maddox (1995).
39. Compare Gibson, *Breakfast*, in which one soldier is killed as a result of a breakfast bet about who would dare to raise his head during shell-fire.
40. See also Owen, *Arms and the Boy*, in which children are playing soldiers. The poem clearly reveals that the provision of man-made arms and ammunition by society is against nature. Yet, as long as this fascination with weaponry will last, war will continue to destroy both youth and beauty.

5   Conclusion

1. It is important to note here that the evaluation of the First World War varies according to national ideology. While for many German scholars the First World War became the disastrous beginning of another 'Thirty Years War' as a result of the denial of the armistice of 1918 as defeat, its identification as the 'Great War' or 'Grande Guerre' in England and France implies its ideological superelevation as 'war to end all wars'. According to Reimann, 2004, pp. 3038, both versions fall short as they fail to take into account the long industrialisation process of the nineteenth century. Under the perspective of a continuation of this technological age, the First World War becomes both the culmination point as well as the catalyst of the resulting aggressive potential.

Bibliography

Ackroyd, L. (1997) 'Nonconformity at War', *Stand To! The Journal of the Western Front Association*, 48, 17–21.

Adams, H. (1992) *Critical Theory since Plato* (London/Toronto/Washington: Washington University).

Adams, J.-K. (1985) *Pragmatics and Fiction* (Amsterdam/Philadelphia, PA: John Benjamins).

Adams, R. J. Q. (1990) *The Great War 1914–18: Essays on the Military, Political and Social History of the First World War* (London: Macmillan).

Alford, S. E. (1984) *Irony and the Logic of the Romantic Imagination* (New York: Peter Lang).

Allemann, B. (1969) *Ironie und Dichtung*, 2nd edn (Pfullingen: Neske).

Allemann, B. (1970) 'Ironie als literarisches Prinzip' in A. Schaefer (ed.) *Ironie und Dichtung. Sechs Essays* (München: C.H. Beck), 22–37.

Allemann, B. (1973) 'Aufriß des ironischen Spielraums' in H.-E. Hass/ G. A. Mohrlüder (eds) *Ironie als literarisches Phänomen* (Köln: Kiepenheuer & Witsch), 39–46.

Allen, C. A./Stephens, G. D. (1962) *Satire: Theory and Practice* (Belmont: Wadsworth).

Allitt, P. (1997) *Catholic Converts. British and American Intellectuals turn to Rome* (Ithaca, NY: Cornell University Press).

Amante, D. J. (1981) 'The Theory of Ironic Speech Acts', *Poetics Today*, 2/2, 77–96.

Anderson, O. (1971) 'The Growth of Christian Militarism in Mid-Victorian Britain', *The English Historical Review*, January, 46–72.

Aristoteles (1959) *Rhetorik an Alexander*, ed. by P. Gohlke (Paderborn: Schöningh).

Aristoteles (1985) *Nikomachische Ethik*, ed. by G. Bien, 4th edn (Hamburg: Meiner).

Arntzen, H. (1989) *Satire in der deutschen Literatur, Geschichte und Theorie*, vols 1 and 2 (Darmstadt: WBG).

Ashworth, T. (2000) *Trench Warfare 1914–1918. The Live and Let Live System* (London: Pan).

Austin, J. L. (1962) *How to Do Things With Words* (Oxford: Oxford University Press).

Austin-Smith, B. (1990) 'Into the Heart of Irony', *Canadian Dimension*, 27/7, 51–52.

Bachtin, M. M. (1990) *Literatur und Karneval. Zur Romantheorie und Lachkultur* (Frankfurt: Fischer).

Bainton, R. H. (1960) *Christian Attitudes Toward War and Peace. A Historical Survey and Critical Re-Evaluation* (New York/Nashville: Abingdon Press).

Baker, K. (1996) *The Faber Book of War Poetry* (London: Faber).

Barbe, K. (1995) *Irony in Context* (New York: John Benjamins).

Barham, P. (2004) *Forgotten Lunatics of the Great War* (New Haven/London: Yale University Press).

Barker, J. (1987) *The Art of Edward Thomas* (Bridgend: Seren Books).
Barlow, A. (2000) *The Great War in British Literature* (Cambridge: Cambridge University Press).
Basire, B. (1985) 'Ironie et Métalangage', *Revue de Linguistique*, 32, 129–50.
Baßler, M. (1995) *New Historicism. Literaturgeschichte als Poetik der Kultur* (Frankfurt: Fischer).
Baßler, M. (2001) *New Historicism. Literaturgeschichte als Poetik der Kultur* (Tübingen: A. Francke).
Bayliss, G. M./Moberly, F. J. (1987) *Operations in Persia, 1914–19* (London: Imperial War Museum).
Beaver, P. (1973) *The Wipers Times* (London: Macmillan).
Bebbington, G. (1973) 'Jessie Pope and Wilfred Owen', *Ariel. A Review of International English Literature*, 3/4, 82–93.
Becker, A. (1998) *War and Faith. The Religious Imagination in France, 1914–1930* (New York: Berg Publishers).
Beckett, I. F. W./Simpson, K. (1985) *A Nation in Arms. A Social Study of the British Army in the First World War* (Manchester: Manchester University Press).
Beckett, I. F. W. (2002) *The First World War. The Essential Guide to Sources in the UK National Archives* (Public Record Office).
Beckett, I. F. W. (2005) *Ypres. The First Battle 1914* (New York: Longman).
Behler, E. (1971) 'Techniques of Irony in the Light of Romantic Theory', *Rice University Studies*, 57/4, 1–17.
Behler, E. (1972) *Klassische Ironie, Romantische Ironie, Tragische Ironie. Zum Ursprung dieser Begriffe* (Darmstadt: WBG).
Behler, E. (1990) *Irony and the Discourse of Modernity* (Seattle, WA: University of Washington Press).
Behler, E. (1997) *Ironie und literarische Moderne* (Paderborn/München/Wien/ Zürich: Schöningh).
Berg, W. (1978) *Uneigentliches Sprechen. Zur Pragmatik und Semantik von Metapher, Metonymie, Ironie, Litotes und rhetorischer Frage* (Tübingen: TBL Verlag Gunter Narr).
Bergonzi, B. (1965) *Heroes' Twilight. A Study of the Literature of the Great War* (London: Constable).
Berntsen, D./Kennedy, J. M. (1996) 'Unresolved contradictions specifying attitudes – in metaphor, irony, understatement and tautology', *Poetics*, 24, 13–29.
Berry, P./Bostridge, M. (1995) *Vera Brittain. A Life* (London: Chatto & Windus).
Bet-El, I. (1999) *Conscripts. Lost Legions of the Great War* (Stroud: Sutton Publishing).
Bloom, E. A./Lilian, D. (1979) *Satire's Persuasive Voice* (Ithaca, NY: Cornell University Press).
Bloom, H. (2002) *Poets of World War I. Wilfred Owen & Isaac Rosenberg* (Broomall, PA: Chelsea House).
Bodel, B. (1995) 'Satire: As the Twentieth Century Closes', *Satire*, 2/3, 54–56.
Bogacz, T. (1986) ' "A Tyranny of Words." Language, Poetry, and Antimodernism in England in the First World War', *The Journal of Modern History*, 58/3, 643–668.
Bond, B. (1999) *Look to Your Front. Studies in the First World War* (Staplehurst: Spellmount).

Bond, B./Cave, N. (1999) *Haig. A Reappraisal Sventy Years On* (Barnsley: Pen & Sword).

Bond, B. (2002) *The Unquiet Western Front. Britain's Role in Literature and History* (Cambridge: Cambridge University Press).

Bonnici, T. (1991) 'Sassoon's Criticism of War', *Revista Unimar*, 13/1, 119–126.

Booth, A. (1996) *Postcards from the Trenches: Negotiating the Space between Modernism and the First World War* (Oxford: Oxford University Press).

Booth, W. C. (1961) *The Rhetoric of Fiction* (Chicago: University of Chicago Press).

Booth, W. C. (1974) *A Rhetoric of Irony* (Chicago/ London: University of Chicago Press).

Borgmeier, R. (1985) 'Konzeption und Funktion der Natur in der modernen englischen Kriegsdichtung' in G. Ahrends/H. U. Seeber (eds) *Englische und amerikanische Naturdichtung im 20. Jahrhundert* (Tübingen: Narr), 50–68.

Bornadeo, A. (1989) *Mark of the Beast. Death and Degradation in the Literature of the Great War* (Lexington, KY: University Press of Kentucky).

Bosanquet, N./Whitehead, I. (2000) 'Casualties and British Medical Services' in P. Liddle/J. Bourne/I. Whitehead (eds) *The Great World War 1914–45, vol. 1. Lightning Strikes Twice* (London: Harper Collins), 329–354.

Bourne, J. M. (1989) *Britain and the Great War: 1914–1918* (London/New York/ Melbourne/Auckland: Edward Arnold).

Bouyssou, R. (1966) 'Le Messianisme de Wilfred Owen', *Caliban*, 3, 235–248.

Bouyssou, R. (1982) 'Wilfred Owen's War Poetry and the Bible', *Caliban*, 19, 45–57.

Bowman, T. (2003) *The Irish Regiments in the Great War. Discipline and Morale* (Manchester: Manchester University Press).

Boylan, G. M. (1999) 'Wilfred Owen's Response to Propaganda, Patriotism and the Language of War', *Revista Canaria de Estudios Ingleses*, 38, 151–164.

Bracco, R. M. (1993) *Merchants of Hope. British Middlebrow Writers of the First World War, 1919–1939* (Oxford: Berg).

Brearton, F. (2000) *The Great War in Irish Poetry. W.B. Yeats to Michael Longley* (Oxford: Oxford University Press).

Breen, J. (1974) 'Wilfred Owen "Greater Love" and Late Romanticism', *English Literature in Transition (1880–1920)*, 17, 173–183.

Bridgwater, P. (1987) 'German and English Poetry of the First World War. A Comparative View', *Sprachkunst*, 18, 208–226.

Bridgwater, P. (1993) 'Discovering a Post-Heroic War Poetry' in F. K. Stanzel/ M. Löschnigg (eds) *Intimate Enemies. English and German Literary Reactions to the Great War 1914–1918* (Heidelberg: Winter), 43–58.

Brooks, C. (1951) 'Irony as a Principle of Structure' in M. D. Zabel (ed.) *Literary Opinion in America* (New York: Harper and Brothers), 729–741.

Brooks, C. (1973) 'Ironie und "ironische" Dichtung' in H. E. Hass/G.-A. Mohrlüder (eds) *Ironie als literarisches Phänomen* (Köln: Kiepenheuer & Witsch), 31–38.

Brophy, J. D. (1971) 'The War Poetry of Wilfred Owen and Osbert Sitwell. An Instructive Contrast', *Modern Language Studies*, 1/2, 22–29.

Brown, M. (2001) *The Death of Christian Britain* (London: Routledge).

Bruce, S. (1992) *Religion and Modernization. Sociologists and Historians Debate the Secularization Thesis* (Oxford: Clarendon).

Budd, S. (1977) *Varieties of Unbelief. Atheists and Agnostics in English Society 1850–1960* (London: Heinemann).

Bühler, K. (1934) *Sprachtheorie* (Jena: Gustav Fischer).

Buitenhuis, P. (1987) *The Great War of Words. British, American and Canadian Propaganda and Fiction 1914–1933* (Vancouver: University of British Columbia Press).

Burke, S. (1995) *Authorship: From Plato to the Postmodern. A Reader* (Edinburgh: Edinburgh University Press).

Byles, J. M. (1995) *War, Women and Poetry: 1914–1945. British and German Writers and Activists* (Newark: University of Delaware Press).

Caesar, A. (1993) *Taking It Like a Man. Suffering, Sexuality and the War Poets. Brooke, Sassoon, Owen, Graves* (Manchester/New York: Manchester University Press).

Campbell, J. (1986) *Jutland. An analysis of the Fighting* (London: Lyons Press).

Campbell, J. (1999) 'Combat Gnosticism: The Ideology of First World War Poetry Criticism', *New Literary History*, 30, 203–215.

Campbell, K. S. (1979) 'Irony Medieval and Modern and the Allegory of Rhetoric', *Allegorica*, 4/1–2, 291–300.

Campbell, M. (2001) 'Poetry and War' in N. Roberts (ed.) *A Companion to Twentieth-Century Poetry* (Oxford: Blackwell), 64–75.

Campbell, P. (1999) *Siegfried Sassoon. A Study of the War Poetry* (Jefferson, NC/London: Mc Farland & Co. Inc.).

Campbell, P. (2001) ' "Thoughts That You've Gagged All Day": Siegfried Sassoon, W.H.R. Rivers and "[The] Repression of War Experience" ' in P. J. Quinn/S.Trout (eds) *The Literature of the Great War Reconsidered. Beyond Modern Memory* (Houndsmills: Palgrave Macmillan), 219–229.

Cano Echevarra, B. (1995) 'Victims and Victimizers in Wilfred Owen's Poetry', *Focus on Robert Graves and His Contemporaries*, 2/3, 21–24.

Carpenter, R. H. (1995) *History as Rhetoric. Style, Narrative and Persuasion* (Columbia, SC: University of South Carolina Press).

Carretta, V. (1983) *The Snarling Muse. Verbal and Visual Political Satire from Pope to Churchill* (Philadelphia, PA: University of Pennsylvania Press).

Carter, D. N. G (1993) ' "Two Fusiliers": Robert Graves and Siegfried Sassoon' in F. K. Stanzel/M. Löschnigg (eds) *Intimate Enemies. English and German Literary Reactions to the Great War 1914–1918* (Heidelberg: Winter), 73–82.

Cave, N. (1999) 'Haig and Religion' in B. Bond/N. Cave (eds) *Haig: A Reappraisal 70 Years On* (Barnsley: Pen and Sword), 240–260.

Cecil, H. (1995) *The Flower of Battle. British Fiction Writers of the First World War* (London: Secker & Warburg).

Cecil, H./Liddle, P. (1996) *Facing Armageddon. The First World War Experienced* (London: Leo Cooper).

Chambers, R. (1990) 'Irony and the Canon', *Profession*, 90, 18–24.

Champion, N. (2002) *Poets of the First World War* (Oxford: Heinemann).

Chapman, G. (1937) *Vain Glory. A Miscellany of the Great War, 1914–18* (London: Cassell) 1937.

Church of England (1931) *Thirty-Nine Articles*, 32nd edn (London: Church Book Room).

Clark, B. (1996) 'Stylistic Analysis and Relevance Theory', *Language and Linguistics*, 5, 163–178.

Clark, H. H./Gerrig, R. J. (1984) 'On the Pretense Theory of Irony', *Journal of Experimental Psychology*, General 113/1, 121–126.

Clark, J. R./Motto, A. L. (1973) *Satire – That Blasted Art* (New York: Putnam and Capricorn).

Clark, J. R. (1983) 'Satire. Language and Style', *Special Issue of Thalia: Studies in Literary Humour*, 5/1, 1–49.

Clark, J. R. (1991) *The Modern Satiric Grotesque and its Traditions* (Lexington, KY: University of Kentucky Press).

Clarke, D. (2004) *The Angel of Mons. Phantom Soldiers and Ghostly Guardians* (Chichester: Wiley).

Clarke, P./Sauers, J. (1996) *Pundemonium. The Step-by-Schlep Guide to Humour's Lowest Form* (Port Melbourne: Heinemann).

Cohen, D. (2001) *The War Come Home. Disabled Veterans in Britain and Germany 1914–39* (Berkeley, CA: University of California Press).

Cohen, J. (1960) 'The War Poet as Archetypal Spokesman', *Stand*, 4/3, 23–27.

Cohen, J. (1965) 'Owen Agonistes', *English Literature in Transition*, 8/5, 253–268.

Cohen, J. (1975) *Journey to the Trenches. The Life of Isaac Rosenberg 1890–1918* (London: Robson Books).

Cohen, M. A. (2001) 'Fatal Symbiosis: Modernism and the First World War' in P. J. Quinn/S. Trout (eds) *The Literature of the Great War Reconsidered. Beyond Modern Memory* (Houndsmills: Palgrave), 159–171.

Cole, S. (2001) 'Modernism, Male Intimacy, and the Great War', *ELH*, 68, 269–500.

Combe, K. (1995) 'The New Voice of Political Dissent: The Transition from Complaint to Satire' in B. A. Connery/K. Combe (eds) *Theorizing Satire. Essays in Literary Criticism* (New York: St Martin's Press), 73–94.

Comer, K. (1996) *Strange Meetings. Walt Whitman, Wilfred Owen and Poetry of War* (Lund: Lund University Press).

Coombs, R. (1998) 'Church and Religion in World War I', *Relevance*, 3.

Copp, M. (2002) *An Imagist at War. The Complete War Poems of Richard Aldington* (Madison, NJ: Fairleigh Dickinson University Press).

Cork, R. (1994) *A Bitter Truth. Avant-Garde Art and the Great War* (New Haven/ London: Yale University Press).

Corns, C./Hughes-Wilson, J. (2001) *Blindfold and Alone. British Military Executions in the Great War* (London: Weidenfeld Military).

Corrigan, D. F. (1973) *Siegfried Sassoon. The Poet's Pilgrimage* (London: Victor Gollancz).

Coste, D. (1989) *Narrative as Communication* (Minneapolis, MN: University of Minnesota Press).

Cox, J. (1982) *The English Churches in a Secular Society. Lambeth 1870–1930* (Oxford: Oxford University Press).

Crawford, F. D. (1988) *British Poets of the Great War* (Selinsgrove: Susquehanna University Press).

Cross, T. (1988) *The Lost Voices of World War I. An International Anthology of Writers, Poets, and Playwrights* (London: Bloomsbury).

Cuddon, J. A. (1999) *The Penguin Dictionary of Literary Terms and Literary Theory*, 4th edn (London/New York/Victoria a.o.: Penguin).

Culler, J. (1982) *On Deconstruction. Theory and Criticism after Structuralism* (Ithaca, NY: Cornell University Press).

Cyr, M. D. (1991) *In Different Skies. The War Poetry of Wilfred Owen* (University of Washington PhD thesis).

Cyr, M. D. (1994) 'Formal Subversion in Wilfred Owen's "Hospital Barge,"' *Style*, 28/1, 65–73.

Dane, J. A. (1980) 'Parody and Satire. A Theoretical Model', *Genre*, 13, 145–159.

Dane, J. A. (1991) *The Critical Mythology of Irony* (Athens: University of Georgia Press).

Davidson, M. (1972) *The Poetry is in the Pity* (London: Chatto & Windus).

Davies, F./Maddox, G. (1995) *Bloody Red Tabs. General Officer Casualties of the Great War, 1914–1918* (London: Leo Cooper).

Day, G. (1994) 'The Poets. Georgians, Imagists and Others' in C. Bloom (ed.) *Literature and Culture in Modern Britain*, vol. 1 (New York: Longman).

De Groot, G. (1996) *Blighty. British Society in the Era of the Great War* (Harlow: Longman).

Derottignies, J. (1988) *Ecritures Ironiques* (Lille: Presses Universitaires).

Devine, K. (1994) 'Silkin: Sassoon and the Imagery of Loss', *Focus on Robert Graves*, 2/2, 35–38.

Dollar, M. (2004) 'Ghost Imagery in the War Poems of Siegfried Sassoon', *War, Literature, and the Arts. An International Journal of the Humanities*, 16/1–2, 235–245.

Downie, J. A. (1986) 'Defoe's Shortest Way with the Dissenters: Irony, Intention and Reader-Response', *Prose Studies*, 9, 120–139.

Dyer, G. (1994) *The Missing of the Somme* (London: Hamish Hamilton).

Dyson, A. E. (1967) *The Crazy Fabric. Essays in Irony* (London: Macmillan).

Ebbatson, R. (2005) *An Imaginary England. Nation, Landscape and Literature 1840–1920* (London: Ashgate).

Eksteins, M. (1989) *Rites of Spring. The Great War and the Birth of the Modern Age* (London/New York/Toronto u.a.: Bantam Press).

Eliot, T. S. (1951) *Selected Essays*, 3rd edn (London: Faber).

Elliott, R. C. (1954) 'The Satirist and Society', *ELH*, 21, 237–248.

Elliott, R. C. (1970) *The Power of Satire: Magic, Ritual, Art* (Princeton, NJ: Princeton University Press).

Ellis, J. (1976) *Eye-Deep in Hell. Trench Warfare in World War I* (Baltimore, MD: John Hopkins University Press).

Empson, W. (1930) *Seven Types of Ambiguity* (London: Chatto & Windus).

Englert, J. M./ Kern, J. J. (1685) *Dissertatione philologica Ironiam/censurae comittunt praeses Joh. Matthaeus Englert et respondens Johann Jeremias Kern* (Wittenbergae: Brüning).

Enright, D. J. (1986) *The Alluring Problem. An Essay on Irony* (Oxford: Oxford University Press).

Fabb, N./Attridge, D./Durant, A./MacCabe, C. (1987) *The Linguistics of Writing. Arguments between Language and Literature* (Manchester: Manchester University Press).

Fabb, N. (1997) *Linguistics and Literature* (Oxford: Blackwell).

Farwell, B. (1987) *The Great War in Africa* (London: Norton & Co.).

Featherstone, S. (1995) *War Poetry. An Introductory Reader* (London/New York: Routledge).

Feinberg, L. (1965) *The Satirist: His Temperament, Motivation, and Influence* (New York: Citadel).

Feinberg, L. (1967) *Introduction to Satire* (Ames, IA: Iowa State University Press).

Ferguson, M./Salter, M. J./Stallworthy, J. (1996) *The Norton Anthology of Poetry*, 4th edn (New York/London: Norton).

Ferguson, N. (1999) *The Pity of War. Explaining World War I* (New York: Basic Books).

Fichte, J. G. (1965) *Gesamtausgabe*, Reihe I, vol. 2, ed. by R. Lauth and H. Jacob (Stuttgart: Frommann-Holzboog).

Field, F. (1991) *British and French Writers of the First World War. Comparative Studies in Cultural History* (Cambridge: Cambridge University Press).

Fielden, K. C. (2005) *The Church of England in the First World War* (Dissertation East Tennessee State University) [http://etd-submit.etsu.edu/etd/theses/available/etd-1104105-090538/]

Fietz, L. (1994) *Fragmentarisches Existieren. Wandlungen des Mythos von der verlorenen Ganzheit in der Geschichte philosophischer, theologischer und literarischer Menschenbilder* (Tübingen: Niemeyer).

Finlay, M. (1988) *The Romantic Irony of Semiotics. Friedrich Schlegel and the Crisis of Representation* (Berlin/New York/Amsterdam: Mouton de Gruyter).

Firchow, P. (1971) *Friedrich Schlegel's Lucinde and the Fragments* (Minneapolis, MN: University of Minnesota Press).

Fish, S. (1980) *Is there a text in this class? The Authority of Interpretive Communities* (Cambridge, MA/London: Harvard University Press).

Fish, S. (1983) 'Short People Got no Reason to Live: Reading Irony', *Daedalus*, 112/1, 175–191.

Fitzgerald, G. (1986) 'The Satiric Use of Setting', *Studies in Contemporary Satire*, 13, 2–4.

Fletcher, M. D. (1987) *Contemporary Political Satire. Narrative Strategies in the Post-Modern Context* (New York: University Press of America).

Freeman, R. (1963) 'Parody as a Literary Form. George Herbert and Wilfred Owen', *Essays in Criticism. A Quarterly Journal of Literary Criticism*, 13/4, 307–322.

Fromkin, D. (2005) *Europe's Last Summer. Why the World Went to War in 1914* (Oxford: Heinemann).

Frye, N. (1957) *Anatomy of Criticism. Four Essays* (Princeton, NJ: Princeton University Press).

Furtounov, S. (1989) *Eighth International Biennial of Humour and Satire in the Arts* (Gabrovo, Bulgaria: House of Humor and Satire).

Fussell, P. (1975) *The Great War and Modern Memory* (New York/Oxford: Oxford University Press).

Gardner, B. (1964) *Up the Line to Death. The War Poets 1914–18* (London: Methuen).

Gassenmeier, M. (1994) 'The Propagation and the Deconstruction of a Martial Myth: Zur englischen Kriegsdichtung 1914–1918' in T. Stemmler (ed.) *Krieg und Frieden in Gedichten von der Antike bis zum 20. Jahrhundert* (Tübingen: Narr), 175–223.

Gaunt, S. (1989) *Troubadours and Irony* (New York/London: Cambridge University Press).

George, W. (1989) 'Teaching Satire and Satirists', *English Journal*, 78/3, 38–43.

Gerster, R. (1988) *Big-Noting: The Heroic Theme in Australian War Writing* (Melbourne: Melbourne University Press).

Gibson, J. (2001) 'Mother's Boy and Stationmaster's Son: The Problem of Class in the Letters and Poems of Wilfred Owen' in P. J. Quinn/S. Trout (eds) *The Literature of the Great War Reconsidered. Beyond Modern Memory* (Houndsmills: Palgrave), 189–204.

Giddings, R. (1988) *The War Poets* (London: Bloomsbury).

Giese, R. (1982) *Die Versdichtung Edmund Blundens. Traditionalistischer Ansatz und moderne Wirklichkeitserfahrung* (Bochum: Brockmeyer).

Gilbert, M. (1994) *First World War* (London: Harper Collins).

Gilbert, S./ Gubar, S. (1989) *No Man's Land. The Place of the Woman Writer in the 20th Century* (New Haven, CT: Yale University Press).

Gilbert, S. M. (1987) 'Soldier's Heart: Literary Men, Literary Women and the Great War' in M. Higgonet (eds) *Behind the Lines: Gender and the Two Wars* (New Have, CT: Yale University Press), 197–226.

Gilbert, S. M. (1999) ' "Rats' Alley": The Great War, Modernism and the (Anti) Pastoral Elegy', *New Literary History*, 30/1, 179–201.

Goetsch, P. (2002) 'The Fantastic in Poetry of the First World War' in B. Korte/ R. Schneider (eds) *War and the Cultural Construction of Identities in Britain* (Amsterdam/New York: Rodopi), 125–141.

Goldensohn, L. (2004) *Dismantling Glory. Twentieth-Century Soldier Poetry* (New York/Chichester: Columbia University Press).

Götze, M. (1999) *Ironie und absolute Darstellung. Philosophie und Poetik in der Frühromantik* (Paderborn/München/Wien/Zürich: Schöningh).

Graham, D. (1984) *The Truth of War. Owen, Blunden, Rosenberg* (Manchester: Carcanet Press).

Graves, R. (1969) *Goodbye to All That*, 4th edn (London: Cassell).

Graves, R. (1988) *Poems about War* (London: Cassell).

Graves, R. P. (1987) *Robert Graves. The Assault Heroic, 1895–1926* (New York: Viking Penguin).

Gray, M. (1995) 'Lyrics of the First World War: Some Comments' in G. Day/ B. Docherty (eds) *British Poetry 1900–50. Aspects of Tradition* (London: Macmillan) 48–64.

Greenblatt, S. (1990) 'Resonance and Wonder' in P. Collier/R. H. Geyer (eds) *Literary Theory Today* (Cambridge: Cambridge University Press), 74–90.

Gregson, J. M. (1976) *Poetry of the First World War* (London: Edward Arnold).

Grice, H. P. (1975) 'Logic and Conversation' in P. Cole/J. L. Morgan (eds) *Syntax and Semantics 3: Speech Acts* (New York: Academic Press), 41–58.

Grimm, R./Hermand, J. (1991) *Laughter Unlimited: Essays on Humour, Satire and the Comic* (Madison, WI: University of Wisconsin Press).

Groeben, N./Scheele, B. (1984) *Produktion und Rezeption von Ironie* (Tübingen: Narr).

Grubb, F. (1965) *A Vision of Reality: A Study of Liberalism in Twentieth-Century Verse* (London: Chatto and Windus).

Gurewitsch, M. (1994) 'Ironists, Satirists, and Humorists' in Ibd. *The Ironic Temper and the Comic Imagination* (Detroit, MI: Wayne State University Press), ch. 2: 85–142.

Gurney, I. (1984) *Collected Poems*, ed. by P. J. Kavanagh (Oxford: Oxford University Press).

Habeck, M. R. (2000) 'Technology in the First World War: The View from Below' in J. Winter/ G. Parker/M. R. Habeck (eds) *The Great War and the Twentieth Century* (New Haven, CT/London: Yale University Press).

Habermas, J. (1987) *Theorie des kommunikativen Handelns*, vols 1 und 2, 4th edn (Frankfurt: Suhrkamp).

Habermas, J. (1999) *On the Pragmatics of Communication*, ed. by M. Cooke (Cambridge: Polity Press), ch. 9: On the Distinction between Poetic and Communicative Uses of Language, 383–401.

Hagen, P. L. (1992) *The Rhetorical Effectiveness of Verbal Irony* (Pennsylvania State University PhD thesis).

Halpern, P. (1994) *A Naval History of World War I* (Annapolis, MD: Naval Institute Press).

Hamilton, R. F./Herwig, H. H. (2003) *The Origins of World War I* (Cambridge: Cambridge University Press).

Hamilton, R. F./Herwig, H. H. (2005) *Decisions for War. 1914–1917* (Cambridge: Cambridge University Press).

Hammer, S. B. (1990) *Satirizing the Satirist* (New York: Garland).

Hart-Davis, R. (1983) *Siegfried Sassoon: Diaries 1915–1918* (London: Faber & Faber).

Harvey, A. D. (1998) *A Muse of Fire. Literature, Art and War* (London: Hambeldon Press).

Haughey, J. (2002) *The First World War in Irish Poetry* (Lewisburg, PA: Bucknell University Press).

Hecker, W. (2005) 'Finding Wilfred Owen's Forwarding Address: Moving Beyond the World War One Paradigm', *Forum of Modern Language Studies,* 41/2, 136–148.

Hegel, G. W. F. (1952) *Phänomenologie des Geistes*, 6th edn (Hamburg: Felix Meiner).

Hendry, D. (1992) 'Up with the Lark(s)', *Critical Survey,* 4/1, 67–69.

Heyck, T. W. (1996) 'The Decline of Christianity in Twentieth-Century Britain', *Albion,* 28, 437–454.

Hibberd, D. (1979) 'Some Contemporary Allusions in Poems by Rosenberg, Owen and Sassoon', *Notes and Queries,* 224, 333–334.

Hibberd, D. (1979) 'Wilfred Owen and the Georgians', *Review of English Studies, New Series,* 30/117, 28–40.

Hibberd, D. (1981) *Poetry of the First World War. A Casebook* (London: Macmillan).

Hibberd, D./Onions, J. (1986) *Poetry of the Great War. An Anthology* (London: Macmillan).

Hibberd, D. (1990) *The First World War* (Basingstoke: Palgrave Macmillan).

Hibberd, D. (1992) *Wilfred Owen: The Last Year 1917–1918* (London: Constable & Co.).

Hibberd, D. (1993) 'Attitudes to Germany in the Work of Wilfred Owen and Other British Poets of the First World War' in F. K. Stanzel/M. Löschnigg, Martin (ed.) *Intimate Enemies. English and German Literary Reactions to the Great War 1914–1918* (Heidelberg: Winter), 223–234.

Hibberd, D. (1998) *Owen the Poet* (London: Macmillan).

Hibberd, D. (2003) *Wilfred Owen. A New Biography* (London: Phoenix).

Hickman, T. (1995) 'The Importance of Violence in the Visceral Imagery of World War I Soldier Poets' in W. Wright/S. Kaplan (eds) *The Image of Violence in Literature, the Media, and Society* (Pueblo, CO: University of Southern Colorado), 91–95.

Higgonet, M. (1987) *Behind the Lines: Gender and the Two World Wars* (New Haven, CT: Yale University Press).

Highet, G. (1962) *The Anatomy of Satire* (Princeton, NJ: Princeton University Press).

Hindmarsh, R. (1980) *Cambridge English Lexicon* (Cambridge: Cambridge University Press).

Hipp, D. W. (1999) *Expressions of War Experience. Shell Shock, Poetic Identity and Psychological Healing in the Work of Owen, Gurney, and Sassoon* (Vanderbuilt University PhD thesis).

Hipp, D. W. (2002) '"By Degrees Regain[ing] Cool Peaceful Air in Wonder." Wilfred Owen's War Poetry as Psychological Therapy', *Journal of the Midwest Modern Language Association*, 35/1, 25–49.

Hirst, D. (1997) 'Private David Jones and Private Isaac Rosenberg', *Chesterton Review. The Journal of the G.K. Chesterton Institute*, 23/1–2, 139–145.

Hodgart, M. (1969) *Satire* (New York: McGraw-Hill).

Holdcroft, D. (1983) 'Irony as a Trope, and Irony as Discourse', *Poetics Today*, 4/3, 493–511.

Holmes, R. (1999) *The Western Front* (London: BBC Publications).

Holmes, R. (2004) *Tommy. The British Soldier on the Western Front 1914–1918* (London: Harper Collins).

Hough, R. (1983) *The Great War at Sea* (Oxford: Oxford University Press).

Housman, L. (2002) *War Letters of Fallen Englishmen* (Philadelphia, PA: University of Pennsylvania Press).

Howard, M. (2000) 'The First World War Reconsidered' in J. Winter/G. Parker/ M. R. Habeck (eds) *The Great War and the Twentieth Century* (New Haven, CT/ London: Yale University Press), 13–29.

Howes, D. (1996) 'A Word Count of Spoken English', *Journal of Verbal Learning and Verbal Behavior*, 5, 572–604.

Howes, C. (1986) 'Rhetorics of Attack: Bakhtin and the Aesthetics of Satire', *Genre*, 18, 215–243.

Hurd, M. (1978) *The Ordeal of Ivor Gurney* (Oxford: Oxford University Press).

Hutcheon, L. (1978) 'Ironie et Parodie. Stratégie et Structure', *Poétique*, 36, 467–477.

Hutcheon, L. (1981) 'Ironie, Satire, Parodie. Une approche pragmatique de l'ironie', *Poétique*, 46, 140–155.

Hutcheon, L. (1994) *Irony's Edge. The Theory and Politics of Irony* (London/ New York: Routledge).

Hynes, S. (1990) *A War Imagined: The First World War and English Culture* (London: Bodley Head).

Hynes, S. (1997) *The Soldiers' Tale. Bearing Witness to Modern War* (New York: Viking).

Iser, W. (1972) *Der implizite Leser. Kommunikationsformen des Romans von Bunyan bis Beckett* (München: Fink).

Iser, W. (1978) *Der Akt des Lesens. Theorie ästhetischer Wirkung* (München: Fink).

Jackendoff, R. (1987) *Consciousness and the Computational Mind* (Cambridge, MA: MIT Press).

Jakobson, R. (1960) 'Linguistics and Poetics' in T. Sebeok (ed.) *Style in Language* (Cambridge, MA: MIT Press), 350–377.

Jakobson, R. (1974) *Form und Sinn. Sprachwissenschafliche Betrachtungen* (München: Wilhelm Fink).

Japp, U. (1983) *Theorie der Ironie* (Frankfurt a.M.: Klostermann).

Jauss, H. R. (1982) *Towards an Aesthetic of Reception* (Brighton: Harvester).

Jeffery, K. (2000) *Ireland and the Great War* (Cambridge: Cambridge University Press).

Johansen, J. D. (2002) *Literary Discourse. A Semiotic-Pragmatic Approach to Literature* (Toronto/Buffalo/London: University of Toronto Press).

Johansson, S./Hofland, K. (1989) *Frequency Analysis of English Vocabulary and Grammar*, vols 1, 2 (Oxford: Clarendon Press).

Johnston, J. H. (1964) *English Poetry of the First World War* (Princeton, NJ: Princeton University Press).

Jorgensen, J./Miller, George A./Sperber, D. (1984) 'Test of the Mention Theory of Irony', *Journal of Experimental Psychology*, General 113/1, 112–120.

Kaufer, D. S. (1977) 'Irony and Rhetorical Strategy', *Philosophy and Rhetoric*, 10/2, 90–110.

Kaufer, D. S. (1983) 'Irony, Interpretive Form, and the Theory of Meaning', *Poetics Today*, 4/3, 451–464.

Kaufer, D. S./Carley, K. M. (1993) *Communication at a Distance. The Influence of Print on Sociocultural Organization and Change* (Chicago/London: University of Chicago Press).

Kedzierska, A. (1995) 'Nature and War in the Trench Poems of Isaac Rosenberg (1890–1918)', *Lubelskie Materialy Neofilologiczne*, 19, 21–35.

Keegan, J. (1988) *The Face of Battle. A Study of Agincourt, Waterloo and the Somme* (London: Jonathan Cape).

Keegan, J. (1993) *Battle at Sea* (London: Pimlico).

Keegan, J. (1998) *The First World War* (London: Pimlico).

Keegan, P./Hollis, M. (2003) *101 Poems Against War* (London: Faber & Faber).

Kendall, T. (2003) 'The Pity of War?', *Phylon Review*, 30/1, 30–32.

Kenner, H. (1986) 'Irony of Ironies', *TLS*, 17 October, 1151–1152.

Kernan, A. P. (1962) *Modern Satire* (New York: Harcourt, Brace and World).

Kernan, A. P. (1965) *The Plot of Satire* (New Haven, CT: Yale University Press).

Kerr, D. (1991) 'Wilfred Owen and the Social Question', *English Literature in Transition (1880–1920)*, 34/2, 183–195.

Kerr, D. (1992) 'The Disciplines of War. Arm Training and the Language of Wilfred Owen', *The Modern Language Review*, 87/2, 286–299.

Kerr, D. (1993) *Wilfred Owen's Voices. Language and Community* (Oxford: Clarendon Press).

Khan, N. (1988) *Women's Poetry of the First World War* (Lexington, KY: University of Kentucky Press).

Kierkegaard, S. (1976) *Über den Begriff der Ironie. Mit ständiger Rücksicht auf Sokrates* (Frankfurt a.M.: Suhrkamp).

Kingsbury, C. M. (2002) *The Peculiar Sanity of War. Hysteria in the Literature of World War I* (Lubbock, TX: Texas Tech University Press).

Kingsley, J./Boulton, J. T. (1966) *English Satiric Poetry* (London: Edward Arnold).

Klein, H. (1978) *The First World War in Fiction* (London: Macmillan).

Klein, H. (1993) 'Comrades? – The Enemy as Individual in First World War Poetry' in F. K. Stanzel/M. Löschnigg (eds) *Intimate Enemies. English and German Literary Reactions to the Great War 1914–1918* (Heidelberg: Winter), 181–200.

Knight, C. A. (2004) *The Literature of Satire* (Cambridge: Cambridge University Press).

Knox, N. (1961) *The Word Irony and its Context: 1500–1755* (Durham, NC: Duke University Press).

Knox, N. (1972) 'On the classification of ironies', *Modern Philologies*, 70, 53–72.

Knox, N. (1973) 'Die Bedeutung von "Ironie": Einführung und Zusammenfassung', in H. E. Hass/G.-A. Mohrlüder (eds) *Ironie als literarisches Phänomen* (Köln: Kiepenheuer & Witsch), 21–30.

Konstantinovic, Z. (1980) *Literary Communication and Reception* (Innsbruck: Verlag des Instituts für Sprachwissenschaft der Universität).

Kreuz, R. J./Roberts, R. M. (1993) 'On Satire and Parody: The Importance of Being Ironic', *Metaphor and Symbolic Activity*, 8/2, 97–109.

Kuiper, K. (1984) 'The Nature of Satire', *Poetics*, 13, 459–475.

Lakoff, G./Johnson, M. (1980) *Metaphors we live by* (Chicago: University of Chicago Press).

Lane, A. E. (1972) *An Adequate Response: The War Poetry of Wilfred Owen and Siegfried Sassoon* (Detroit: Wayne State University Press).

Lang, C. D. (1988) *Irony/Humour: Critical Paradigms* (Baltimore/London: John Hopkins University Press).

Lapp, E. (1992) *Linguistik der Ironie* (Tübingen: Gunter Narr).

Larsen, E. (1980) *Wit as a Weapon* (London: Muller).

Leavis, F. R. (1962) *The Common Pursuit* (Harmondsworth: Penguin).

Leavis, F. R. (1964) *Revaluation: Tradition and Development in English Poetry* (Harmondsworth: Penguin).

Leech, G. N./Short, M. H. (1983) *A Linguistic Guide to English Fictional Prose* (London: Longman).

Leed, E. J. (1979) *No Man's Land. Combat and Identity in World War I* (London/ New York: Cambridge University Press).

Leese, P. (2002) *Shell Shock. Traumatic Neurosis and the British Soldiers of the First World War* (London: Palgrave Macmillan).

Lehmann, J. (1980) *Rupert Brooke. His Life and His Legend* (London: Weidenfeld & Nicolson).

Lehmann, J. (1981) *The English Poets of the First World War* (London: Thames & Hudson).

Leonard, J. (1986) 'The Catholic Chaplaincy' in D. Fitzpatrick (ed.), *Ireland and the First World War* (Dublin: Trinity History Workshop).

Lessenich, R. P. (1999) *Where Death Becomes Absurd and Life Absurder. Literary Views of the Great War 1914–1918* (Erfurt Electronic Studies in English).

Lessenich, R. P. (2003) 'Homoerotik in der Englischen Schützengrabenlyrik des Ersten Weltkriegs', *Forum*, 43, 25–42.

Lewandowski, T. (1984/1985) *Linguistisches Wörterbuch*, 4th edn (Heidelberg: Quelle & Mayer).

Leyburn, E. (1956) *Satiric Allegory: Mirror of Man* (New Haven, CT: Yale University Press).

Liddle, P./Cecil, H. (1995) *At the Eleventh Hour. Reflections, Hopes and Anxieties at the Closing of the Great War. 1918* (London: Leo Cooper).

Liddle, P. H. (1997) *Passchendaele in Perspective* (London: Leo Cooper).

Light, A. (1991) *Forever England. Femininity, Literature and Conservatism between the Wars* (London: Routledge).

Livesey, A. (1996) *The Viking Atlas of World War I* (Middlesex: Penguin).

Lloyd, A. (1976) *The War in the Trenches* (London: Hart-Davis/MacGibbon).

Lockwood, T. (1974) 'On the Relationship of Satire and Poetry after Pope', *Studies in English Literature 1500–1900,* 14, 387–402.

Loe, T. (1990) 'Design and Satire in Decline and Fall', *Studies in Contemporary Satire,* 17, 31–41.

Longley, E. (2005) 'The Great War, History and the English Lyric' in V. Sherry (ed.) *The Cambridge Companion to the Literature of the First World War* (Cambridge: Cambridge University Press), 57–84.

Löschnigg, M. (1994) *Der Erste Weltkrieg in deutscher und englischer Dichtung* (Heidelberg: Winter).

Love, H. (2004) *English Clandestine Satire (1660–1702)* (Oxford: Oxford University Press).

Ludwig, H.-W. (1998) *Arbeitsbuch Romananalyse* (Tübingen: Narr).

Macdonald, L. (1983) *Somme* (London: Michael Joseph).

Machin, R./Norris, C. (1987) *Post-Structuralist Readings of English Poetry* (Cambridge: Cambridge University Press).

Machinek, A. (1986) 'Smile, Smile, Smile. The Study of Laughter in Wilfred Owen's Poetry' in *Kwartalnik Neofilologiczny,* 33/4, 525–537.

Macleod, J. (2004) *Reconsidering Gallipoli* (Manchester: Manchester University Press).

Mahler, A. (1992) *Moderne Satireforschung und elisabethanische Verssatire. Texttheorie, Epistemologie, Gattungspoetik* (München: Schoeningh).

Marcus, J. (1989) 'Afterward' in H. Z. Smith (ed.) *Not So Quiet…Stepdaughters of War* (New York: Feminist).

Marrin, A. (1974) *The Last Crusade. The Church of England in the First World War* (Durham, NC: Duke University Press).

Marsland, E. A. (1991) *The Nation's Cause. French, English and German Poetry of the First World War* (London/New York: Routledge).

Martin, G. D. (1983) 'The Bridge and the River or: The Ironies of Communication', *Poetics Today,* 4/3, 415–435.

Martin, W. R. (1979) 'Bugles, Trumpets and Drums. English Poetry and the Wars', *Mosaic. A Journal for the Interdisciplinary Study of Literature,* 13/1, 31–48.

Marwick, A. (1991) *The Deluge. British Society and the First World War,* 2nd edn (London: Macmillan).

Massie, R. K. (2003) *Castles of Steel: Britain, Germany, and the Winning of the Great War at Sea* (New York: Random House).

Matalon, A. (2002) 'Difference at War. Siegfried Sassoon, Isaac Rosenberg, U.Z. Grindberg, and the Poetry of the First World War', *Shofar. An Interdisciplinary Journal of Jewish Studies,* 21/1, 25–43.

McIlroy, J. F. (1974) *Wilfred Owen's Poetry. A Study Guide* (London: Heinemann).

Mellor, A. K. (1979) 'On Romantic Irony, Symbolism and Allegory', *Criticism,* 21, 217–229.

Mellor, A. K. (1980) *English Romantic Irony* (Cambridge, MA/London: Harvard University Press).

Mews, S. P. (1967) *The Effects of the First World War on English Religious Life and Thought* (University of Leeds M.A. thesis).

Mews, S. P. (1973) *Religion and English Society in the First World War* (University of Cambridge PhD dissertation).

Meyers, A. R. (1974) 'Toward a Definition of Irony' in R. Fasold/R. Shuy (eds) *Studies in Language Variation* (Washington, DC: Georgetown University Press).

Middlebrook, M. (1971) *The First Day of the Somme* (London: Allen Lane/ Penguin).

Moeyes, P. (1997) *Siegfried Sassoon Scorched Glory. A Critical Study* (Basingstoke: Macmillan).

Moore, L. H. (1969) 'Siegfried Sassoon and Georgian Realism', *Twentieth Century Literature*, 14/4, 199–209.

Mosse, G. (2000) 'Shell Shock as a Social Disease', *Journal of Contemporary History*, 35, 101–108.

Motion, A. (1980) *The Poetry of Edward Thomas* (London: Routledge & Kegan Paul).

Motto, A. L./Clark, J. R. (1994) 'Kill 'em All. An Ancient and Modern Satiric Theme', *Thalia: Studies in Literary Humour*, 14/1–2, 40–49.

Moynihan, M. (1983) *God On Our Side. The British Padres in World War I* (London: Leo Cooper).

Muecke, D. C. (1969) *The Compass of Irony* (London: Methuen & Co LTD).

Muecke, D. C. (1970) *Irony* (London: Methuen &Co. Ltd.).

Muecke, D. C. (1973) 'The Communication of Verbal Irony', *Journal of Literary Semantics*, 2, 35–42.

Muecke, D. C. (1983) 'Images of Irony', *Poetics Today*, 4/3, 399–413.

Muir, K. (1993) 'Connotations of "Strange Meeting"', *Connotations. A Journal for Critical Debate*, 3/1, 26–36.

Müller, M. (1995) *Die Ironie. Kulturgeschichte und Textgestalt* (Würzburg: Königshausen & Neumann).

Murray, L. (1980) 'Isaac Rosenberg', *Quadrant*, 24/3, 52–55.

Musil, C. (1986) 'Wilfred Owen and Abram', *Women's Studies. An Interdisciplinary Journal*, 13/1–2, 49–61.

Muster, H.-P. (1992) *Who's Who in Satire and Humour* (Basel: Wiese).

Najarian, J. (2001) '"Greater Love": Wilfred Owen, Keats, and a Tradition of Desire', *Twentieth Century Literature*, 47/1, 20–38.

Nathan, D. O. (1982) 'Irony and the Artist's Intentions', *British Journal of Aesthetics*, 22, 245–256.

Newman, H. E. (1973) 'Die Identifikation der Ironie' in H. E. Hass/G.-A. Mohrlüder (eds) *Ironie als literarisches Phänomen* (Köln: Kiepenheuer & Witsch), 47–56.

Newman, V. B. E. (2004) *Women's Poetry of the First World War. Songs of Wartime Lives* (Colchester: University of Essex PhD thesis).

Nilsen, A. P./Nilsen, D. L. F. (2000) 'Satire' in *Encyclopedia of Humor and Comedy* (Phoenix, AZ: Oryx Press), 258–260.

Nilsen, D. L. F. (1988) 'Satire – The Necessary and Sufficient Conditions – Some Preliminary Observations', *Studies on Contemporary Satire*, 15, 1–10.

Noakes, V. (2004) *The Poems and Plays of Isaac Rosenberg* (Oxford: Oxford University Press).

Noh, E.-J. (1998) *The Semantics and Pragmatics of Metarepresentation in English: A Relevance-Theoretic Approach* (London: University of London).

Norgate, P. (1987) 'Shell. Shock and Poetry. Wilfred Owen at Craiglockhart Hospital', *English. The Journal of the English Association*, 36, 1–35.

Norgate, P. (1989) 'Wilfred Owen and the Soldier Poets', *Review of English Studies. A Quarterly Journal of English Literature and the English Language (RES)*, New Series, 40/160, 516–530.

Norgate, P. (1990) 'Soldier's Dreams. Popular Rhetoric and the War Poetry of Wilfred Owen', *Critical Survey*, 2/2, 208–215.

Novalis (1960ff) *Schriften*, ed. by R. Samuel (Stuttgart/Berlin/Köln: Kohlhammer).

Ohmann, R. (1971) 'Speech Acts and the Definition of Literature', *Philosophy and Rhetoric*, 4, 1–19.

Ohmann, R. (1973) 'Literature as Act' in C. Seymour (ed.) *Approaches to Poetics. Selected Papers from the English Institute* (New York: Columbia University Press), 81–107.

O'Keeffe, T. (1972) 'Ironic Allusion in the Poetry of Wilfred Owen', *Ariel. A Review of International English Literature*, 3/4, 72–81.

Ong, W. J. (SJ) (1982) 'From Mimesis to Irony: The Distancing of Voice' in P. Hernadi (ed.) *The Horizon of Literature* (Lincoln: University of Nebraska Press), 11–42.

O'Prey, P. (1982) *In Broken Images: Selected Letters of Robert Graves* (London: Hutchinson).

Owen, H./Bell, J. (1967) *Wilfred Owen. Collected Letters* (London: Oxford University Press).

Palmer, A. (1992) *The Decline and Fall of the Ottoman Empire* (New York: Barnes & Noble Books).

Panichas, G. A. (1968) *Promise of Greatness. The War of 1914–18* (London: Cassell).

Papiór, J. (1989) *Ironie. Diachronische Begriffsentwicklung* (Poznan: UAM).

Parfitt, G. (1990) *English Poetry of the First World War – Context and Themes* (New York/London/Toronto: Harvester Wheatsheaf).

Parker, P. (1987) *The Old Lie. The Great War and the Public School Ethos* (London: Constable & Co.).

Parsons, I. M. (1931) 'The Poems of Wilfred Owen (1893–1918)', *New Criterion*, 10, 658–669.

Parsons, I. (1965) *Men Who March Away. Poems of the First World War* (London: Chatto & Windus).

Parsons, I. (1979) *The Collected Works of Isaac Rosenberg* (London: Chatto & Windus).

Paulson, R. (1971) *Satire: Modern Essays in Criticism* (Englewood Cliffs, NJ: Prentice-Hall).

Pearsall, R. B. (1974) *Rupert Brooke – The Man and Poet* (Amsterdam: Rodopi).

Pikoulis, J. (1987) 'Edward Thomas as War Poet' in J. Barker (ed.) *The Art of Edward Thomas* (Bridgend: Seren Books), 113–130.

Pilkington, A. (2000) *Poetic Effects. A Relevance Theory Perspective* (Amsterdam/ Philadelphia, PA: John Benjamins).

Pittock, M. (2001) 'The War Poetry of Wilfred Owen. A Dissenting Reappraisal' in P. J. Quinn/S. Trout (eds) *The Literature of the Great War Reconsidered. Beyond Modern Memory* (Houndsmills: Palgrave), 205–218.

Plett, H. (1982) 'Ironie als stilrhetorisches Paradigma', *Ars Semeiotica*, 4/5, 1, 75–89.

Pollard, A. (1970) *Satire* (London: Methuen).

Porter, P. (2002) 'The Sacred Service. Australian Chaplains and the Great War', *War and Society*, 20/2, 23–52.

Potter, J. (2006) *Boys in Khaki, Girls in Print. Women's Literary Responses to the Great War 1914–1918* (Oxford: Oxford University Press).

Powell, A. (1993) *A Deep Cry. A Literary Pilgrimage to the Battlefields and Cemeteries of First World War British Soldier-Poets Killed in Northern France and Flanders* (Aberporth: Sutton Publishing).

Pratt, M. L. (1977) *Toward a Speech Act Theory of Literary Discourse* (Bloomington, IN: Indiana University Press).

Prier, A./Gillespie, G. (1997) *Narrative Ironies* (Amsterdam: Rodopi).

Prior, R./Wilson, T. (1992) *Command on the Western Front* (Oxford: Blackwell).

Prior, R./Wilson, T. (1994) 'Paul Fussell at War', *War in History,* 1, 63–80.

Prior, R./Wilson, T. (2005) *The Somme* (New Haven, CT: Yale University Press).

Public General Statutes, LIII, 21–22: 5 / George V, c. 8.

Quendler, C. (2001) *From Romantic Irony to Postmodernist Metafiction. A Contribution to the History of Literary Self-Reflexivity in its Philosophical Context* (Frankfurt/New York: Lang).

Quinn, P. J. (1994) *The Great War and the Missing Muse. The Early Writings of Robert Graves and Siegfried Sassoon* (Selinsgrove: Susquehanna University Press).

Quinn, P. (1999) *Dictionary of Literary Biography: 216 British Poets of the Great War* (Detroit, MI: Thomson Gale).

Quinn, P. J. (2001) 'Siegfried Sassoon: The Legacy of the Great War' in P. J. Quinn/S. Trout (eds) *The Literature of the Great War Reconsidered. Beyond Modern Memory* (Houndsmills: Palgrave Macmillan), 230–238.

Quinn, P. J./Trout, S. (2001) *The Literature of the Great War Reconsidered. Beyond Modern Memory* (Houndsmills: Palgrave Macmillan).

Reilly, C. W. (1978) *English Poetry of the First World War. A Bibliography* (London: George Prior).

Reilly, C. W. (1981) *Scars upon my heart. Women's Poetry and Verse of the First World War* (London: Virago).

Reimann, A. (2004) 'Der Erste Weltkrieg – Urkatastrophe oder Katalysator', *Beilage zur Wochenzeitung Das Parlament,* 12 Juli 2004, 30–38.

Rety, J. (2003) *In the Company of Poets* (London: Hearing Eye).

Reznick, J. S. (2005) *Healing the Nation. Soldiers and the Culture of Caregiving in Britain during the Great War* (Manchester: Manchester University Press).

Richards, I. A. (1924) *Principles of Literary Criticism* (London: Routledge and Kegan Paul).

Richards, I. A. (1929) *Practical Criticism: A Study of Literary Judgement* (London: Routledge and Kegan Paul).

Richter, D. H. (1981) 'The Reader as Ironic Victim', *Novel,* 14, 135–151.

Riley, D. (2000) *The Words of Selves. Identification, Solidarity, Irony* (Stanford, CA: Stanford University Press).

Robbins, K. (1985) *The First World War. The Outbreak, Events and Aftermath* (Oxford/New York: Oxford University Press).

Roberts, B. E. (1996) 'The Female God of Isaac Rosenberg. A Muse for Wartime', *English Literature in Transition,* 39/3, 319–332.

Roberts, D. (1998) *Minds at War,* 4th edn (Burgess Hill: Saxon Books).

Roberts, J. S. (1999) *Siegfried Sassoon (1886–1967)* (London: Richard Cohen Books).

Romero, S. J. (1983) *Religion in the Rebel Ranks* (Lanham/New York/London: University Press of America).

Rorty, R. (1989) *Kontingenz, Ironie und Solidarität* (Frankfurt a.M.: Suhrkamp).

Rosenberg, I. (1962) *The Collected Poems of Isaac Rosenberg*, ed. by G. Bottomley/ D. Harding (London: Chatto and Windus).

Rosenheim, E. W. (1963) *Swift and the Satirist's Art* (Chicago: University of Chicago Press).

Roshwald, A./Stites, R. (1999) *European Culture in the Great War. The Arts, Entertainment and Propaganda. 1914–1918* (Cambridge: Cambridge University Press).

Sanders, M./Taylor, P. M. (1982) *British Propaganda during the First World War. 1914–1918* (London: Macmillan).

Santanu, D. (2006) *Touch and Intimacy in First World War Literature* (Cambridge: Cambridge University Press).

Sartre, J. P. (1995) 'Writing For One's Age' in S. Burke (ed.) *Authorship: From Plato to the Postmodern. A Reader* (Edinburgh: Edinburgh University Press), 223–229.

Sassoon, S. (1973) *Siegfried's Journey. 1916–1920* (London: Faber & Faber).

Satterfield, L. (1981) 'Toward a Poetics of the Ironic Sign' in L. Satterfield/R. T. De George (eds) *Semiotic Themes* (Laurence, KA: University of Kansas Press).

Sauerteig, L. D. H. (1998) 'Sex, Medicine and Morality during the First World War' in R. Cooter/M. Harrison/S. Sturdy (eds) *War, Medicine and Modernity* (Stroud: Sutton Publishing), 167–188.

Scannell, V. (1976) *Not without Glory: Poets of the Second World War* (London: Woburn Press).

Scates, B./Frances, R. (1997) *Women and the Great War* (Cambridge/New York/ Melbourne: Cambridge University Press).

Schaefer, A. (1970) *Ironie und Dichtung* (München: Beck).

Schiller, F. (2002) *Über naive und sentimentalische Dichtung* (Stuttgart: Reclam).

Schlegel, F. (1958ff) *Kritische Schlegel Ausgabe (KA)*, ed. by E. Behler/J.-J. Anstett/ H. Eichner (Paderborn/München/Wien: Schoeningh).

Schlegel, F. (1988) *Kritische Schriften und Fragmente*. Studienausgabe in 6 Bänden, ed. by E. Behler/H. Eichner (Paderborn: Schoeningh).

Schmidt, M. (1998) 'The Land of Lost Content' in M. Schmidt (ed.) *Lives of the Poets* (London: Weidenfeld & Nicolson), 505–532.

Schneider, U. (1986) 'Die literarische Verarbeitung des Ersten Weltkriegs in Wilfred Owen's "Smile, Smile, Smile"' in K. J. Höltgen/L. Hönninghausen/ E. Kreutzer/G. Schmitz (eds) *Tradition und Innovation in der englischen und amerikanischen Lyrik des 20. Jahrhunderts* (Tübingen, Niemeyer), 41–55.

Schweitzer, R. (1998) 'The Cross and the Trenches. Religious Faith and Doubt among Some British Soldiers on the Western Front', *War and Society*, 16, 33–57.

Schweitzer, R. (2003) *The Cross and the Trenches. Religious Faith and Doubt among British and American Great War Soldiers* (Westport, CT/London: Praeger).

Searle, J. R. (1969) *Speech acts. An Essay in the Philosophy of Language* (Cambridge: Cambridge University Press).

Searle, J. R. (1975) 'Indirect Speech Acts' in P. Cole/J. L. Morgan (eds) *Syntax and Semantics, vol. 3: Speech Acts* (New York: Academic Press), 59–82.

Seeber, H. U. (1993) 'Modernization, Violence and Modern Poetry. Comments on Wilfred Owen, August Stramm and Lascelles Abercrombie' in F. K. Stanzel/ M. Löschnigg (ed.) *Intimate Enemies. English and German Literary Reactions to the Great War 1914–1918* (Heidelberg: Winter), 121–136.

Sell, R. D. (2000) *Literature as Communication. The Foundations of Mediating Criticism* (Amsterdam/Philadelphia, PA: John Benjamins).

Sell, R. D. (2001) *Mediating Criticism. Literary Education Humanised* (Amsterdam/Philadelphia, PA: John Benjamins).

Seymour, M. (1995) *Robert Graves. Life on the Edge* (London/New York/Toronto a.o.: Doubleday).

Shaftesbury, A. A. C., 3rd Earl of (1981) *Standard Edition. Sämtliche Werke, ausgewählte Briefe und nachgelassene Schriften. In englischer Sprache mit paralleler deutscher Übersetzung*, ed. by W. Benda/C. Jackson-Holzberg/F. A. Uehlein/E. Wolff (Stuttgart: Frommann-Holzboog).

Sheffield, Gary D. (2000) *Leadership in the Trenches. Officer-Man Relations, Morale and Discipline in the British Army in the Era of the First World War* (Basingstoke: Macmillan).

Sheffield, Gary D. (2001) *Forgotten Victory. The First World War: Myths and Realities* (London: Headline).

Sheffield, G. D./Bourne, J. (2005) *Douglas Haig. War Diaries and Letters 1914–1918* (London: Weidenfeld & Nicholson).

Shelton, C. (1992) 'War Protest, Heroism and Shellshock. Siegfried Sassoon: A Case Study', *Focus on Robert Graves*, 1/13, 43–50.

Shephard, B. (2002) *A War of Nerves. Soldiers and Psychiatrists. 1914–1994* (London: Pimlico).

Sherry, V. (2005) *The Cambridge Companion to the Literature of the First World War* (Cambridge: Cambridge University Press).

Silkin, J. (1972) *Out of Battle – The Poetry of the Great War* (Oxford/London a.o.: Macmillan).

Silkin, J. (1979) *The Penguin Book of First World War Poetry* (Harmondsworth: Penguin).

Silkin, J. (1993/94) ' "Strange Meeting," a Fragment? A Reply to Muir's "Owen" ', *Connotations. A Journal for Critical Debate*, 3/2, 186–192.

Sillars, S. (1987) *Art and Survival in First World War Britain* (Basingstoke: Macmillan).

Sim, S. (2002) *Irony and Crisis. A Critical History of Postmodern Culture* (Cambridge: Icon Books Ltd.).

Simkins, P. (1988) *Kitchener's Army. The Raising of Britain's New Armies (1914–16)* (Manchester: Manchester University Press).

Simpson, D. (1979) *Irony and Authority in Romantic Poetry* (London: Macmillan).

Simpson, M. (1990) 'Only a Living Thing – Some Notes Towards a Reading of Isaac Rosenberg's "Break of Day in the Trenches" ', *Critical Survey*, 2/2, 131–132.

Sitwell, O. (1919) *Argonaut and Juggernaut* (London: Chatto & Windus).

Smith, A. K. (2000) *The Second Battlefield. Women, Modernism and the First World War* (New York: Manchester University Press).

Smith, A. K. (2005) *Suffrage Discourse in Britain during the First World War* (London: Ashgate).

Smith, L. V. (2000) 'Narrative Identity at the Front: "Theory and the Poor Bloody Infantry" ' in J. Winter/G. Parker/M. R. Habeck (eds) *The Great War and the Twentieth Century* (New Haven (CT)/London: Yale University Press).

Snape, M. (2002) 'British Catholicism and the British Army in the First World War', *Recusant History*, 26, 314–358.

Snape, M. (2005) *God and the British Soldier. Religion and the British Army in the First and Second World Wars* (London: Routledge).

Solger, K. W. F. (1926) 'Beurteilung der Vorlesung über dramatische Kunst und Literatur' in L. Tieck/F. von Raumer (eds) *Nachgelassene Schriften und Briefwechsel*, vol. 2 (Leipzig: Brockhaus), 493–628.

Sorley, C. H. (1985) *Collected Poems*, ed. by J. M. Wilson (London: Cecil Woolf).

Stallworthy, J. (1974) 'Owen and Sassoon. The Craiglockhart Episode', *New Review*, 1/4, 5–17.

Spear, H. D. (1975) ' "I Too Saw God." The Religious Allusions in Wilfred Owen's Poetry', *English. The Journal of the English Association*, 24, 35–40.

Spear, H. D. (1979) *Remembering, We Forget, A Background Study to the Poetry of the First World War* (London: Davis-Poynter).

Spear, H. D. (1984) 'Not Well Content. Wilfred Owen's Dislocation of the Sonnet Form', *Durham University Journal*, 77/1, 57–60.

Sperber, D./Wilson, D. (1981) 'Irony and the use-mention distinction' in P. Cole (ed.) *Radical Pragmatics* (New York: Academic Press), 295–318.

Sperber, D. (1984) 'Verbal Irony: Pretense or Echoic Mention?', *Journal of Experimental Psychology*, General 113/1, 130–136.

Sperber, D./Wilson, D. (1995) *Relevance. Communication and Cognition*, 2nd edn (Oxford: Blackwell).

Spurlin, W. J./Fischer M. (1995) *The New Criticism and Contemporary Literary Theory. Connections and Continuities* (New York/London: Garland).

Stallworthy, J. (1977) *Wilfred Owen. A Biography* (London: Oxford University Press).

Stallworthy, J. (1984) *The Oxford Book of War Poetry* (Oxford: Oxford University Press).

Stallworthy, J. (2002) *Anthem for Doomed Youth. Twelve Soldier Poets of the First World War* (London: Constable).

Stallworthy, J. (2003) *The Poems of Wilfred Owen*, 16th edn (London: Chatto & Windus).

Stanzel, F. K. (1979) *Theorie des Erzählens* (Göttingen: Vandenhoek & Ruprecht).

Stanzel, F. K. (1987) 'Englische und deutsche Kriegsdichtung 1914–1918. Ein komparatistischer Versuch', *Sprachkunst*, 18, 227–244.

Stanzel, F. K. /Löschnigg, M. (1993) *Intimate Enemies. English and German Literary Reactions to the Great War 1914–1918* (Heidelberg: Winter).

Stanzel, F. K. (1993) ' "The Beauty of the Bayonet": Hand-to-hand Combat in English and German Poetry' in F. K. Stanzel/M. Löschnigg (eds) *Intimate Enemies. English and German Literary Reactions to the Great War 1914–1918* (Heidelberg: Winter), 83–98.

Stead, C. K. (1964) *The New Poetic. Yeats to Eliot*. Ch. 4: 1909–16: 'Poetry' versus 'Life'. Imperialists; Georgians; War Poets (London: Hutchinson), 67–95.

Steel, N./Hart, P. (2001) *Passchendaele: The Sacrificial Ground* (London: Cassell).

Stempel, W.-D. (1976) 'Ironie als Sprechhandlung' in W. Preisendanz/R. Warning (eds.) *Das Komische* (München: Fink).

Stephen, M. (1996) *The Price of Pity. Poetry, History and Myth in the Great War* (London: Leo Cooper).

Stephen, M. (1998) *Poems of the First World War. 'Never such Innocence'* (London: Everyman).

Stevenson, D. (2004) *1914–1918: The History of the First World War* (London: Allen Lane).

Stevenson, R. (1992) *Modernist Fiction. An Introduction* (New York/London/ Toronto a.o.: Harvester Wheatsheaf).

Stone, N. (1975) *The Eastern Front 1914–17* (New York: Scribner).

Strachan, H. (2004) *The First World War in Africa* (Oxford: Oxford University Press).

Stryker, L. S. (1992) *Languages of Sacrifice and Suffering in England in the First World War* (University of Cambridge PhD dissertation).

Sühnel, R. (1996) 'Wilfred Owen's Anthem for Doomed Youth' in S. Horlacher/ M. Islinger (eds) *Expedition nach der Wahrheit. Poems, Essays and Papers in Honour of Theo Stemmler* (Heidelberg: Winter), 243–248.

Suleiman, S. (1976) 'Interpreting Ironies', *Diacritics*, 6/2, 15–21.

Summersgill, S. A. (1991) 'Poison Gas and the Poetry of War', *Essays in Criticism. A Quarterly Journal of Literary Criticism*, 41, 308–323.

Sutherland, J. (1958) *English Satire* (Cambridge: Cambridge University Press).

Sutherland, W. O. S. (1965) *The Art of the Satirist* (Austin, TX: University of Texas Press).

Swift, J. (1958) *The Poems*, vol. 2, ed. by H. Williams (Oxford: Clarendon).

Symons, J. (1942) *An Anthology of War Poetry* (London: Penguin).

Tanaka, R. (1973) 'The Concept of Irony: Theory and Practice', *Journal of Literary Semantics*, 2, 43–56.

Taylor, M. (1998) *Lads. Love Poetry of the Trenches*, 2nd edn (London: Duckworth).

Test, G. A. (1991) *Satire: Spirit and Art* (Gainesville, FL: University of South Florida Press).

Thibault, P. J. (1991) *Social Semiotics as Praxis. Text, Social Meaning Making, and Nabokov's ADA* (Minneapolis, MN: University of Minnesota Press).

Thirlwall, C. (1833) 'On the Irony of Sophocles', *The Philological Museum*, II, 483–536.

Thomas, D. (1954) 'Wilfred Owen' in Ibd. *Quite Early One Morning* (London: Dent & Sons LTD), 91–105.

Thomas, E. (1978) *Collected Poems*, ed. by R. G. Thomas (Oxford: Clarendon).

Thomas, R. G. (1995) *Edward Thomas. Selected Letters* (Oxford: Oxford University Press).

Thompson, E. P. (1994) *Making History. Writings on History and Culture* (Cambridge: Cambridge University Press).

Thornton, R. K. R. (1984) *Ivor Gurney. War Letters* (London: Hogarth Press).

Thurley, G. (1974) *The Ironic Harvest. English Poetry in the Twentieth Century* (London: Edward Arnold Ltd.).

Tindale, C. W./Gough, J. (1987) 'The Use of Irony in Argumentation', *Philosophy and Rhetoric*, 20/1, 1–17.

Todorov, T. (1990) *Genres in Discourse* (Cambridge: Cambridge University Press).

Tomlinson, A. (1993) 'Strange Meeting in Strange Land. Wilfred Owen and Shelley', *Studies in Romanticism*, 32/1, 75–95.

True, M. (1985) ' "The Topography of Golgotha." Wilfred Owen, the Church, and the First World War', *Spectrum*, 1/1, 23–30.

Turner, F. (1926) *The Element of Irony in English Literature* (Cambridge: Cambridge University Press).

Tylee, C. M. (1990) *The Great War and Women's Consciousness. Images of Militarism and Womanhood in Women's Writings 1914–64* (London: Macmillan).

Tylee, C. M. (2000) *Women, the First World War and the Dramatic Imagination. International Essays (1914–1999)* (Lewiston, ME: Mellen Press).

Van Wienen, M. W. (2002) *Rendezvous With Death. American Poems of the Great War* (Urbana, IL: University of Illinois Press).

Veeser, A. (1989) *The New Historicism* (London: Routledge).

Vossins, I. (1978) 'Rhétorique de l'Ironie', *Poétique*, 36, 495–508.

Walter, G. (2003) *Rupert Brooke and Wilfred Owen* (London: Phoenix).

Walter, G. (2004) *In Flanders Fields. Poetry of the First World War* (London: Allen Lane).

Ward, C. (1997) *World War One British Poets* (London: Dover).

Warner, P. (2003) *Field Marshall Earl Haig* (London: Cassell).

Watkins, B. (2000) *Remembering Armageddon. Reflections on a Century of War* (Saint Paul, MN: Little Leaf Press).

Watzlawick, Janet H. Beavin and Don D. Jackson (1969) *Menschliche Kommunikation. Formen, Störungen, Paradoxien* (Bern/New York: Huber).

Webb, B. (1990) *Edmund Blunden. A Biography* (New Haven, CT: Yale University Press).

Weiß, W. (1982) *Die englische Satire* (Darmstadt: WBG).

Weiß, W. (1992) *Swift und die Satire des 18. Jahrhunderts. Epoche – Werke – Wirkung* (München: Beck).

Welland, D. S. (1978) *Wilfred Owen. A Critical Study* (London: Chatto & Windus).

White, G. M. (1969) *Wilfred Owen* (New York: Twayne).

Wilkinson, A. (1978) *The Church of England and the First World War* (London: SPCK).

Wilkinson, A. (1986) *Dissent or Conform. War Peace and the English Churches 1900–1945* (London: SCM Press).

Williams, D. (1984) 'An Outline of Satire' in M. Helitzer (ed.) *Comedy Techniques for Writers and Performers* (Athens, OH: Lawhead Press), 70–79.

Williams, J. C. (1982) 'The Myth of the Lost Generation. The British War Poets and Their Modern Critics', *Journal of Literature, History, and the Philosophy of History*, 12, 45–56.

Williams, J. P. (1984) 'Does Mention (or Pretense) Exhaust the Concept of Irony?' *Journal of Experimental Psychology*, General 113/1, 127–129.

Williams, M. (1993) *Wilfred Owen* (Melksham: Cromwell).

Wilson, D./Sperber, D. (1992) 'On Verbal Irony', *Lingua*, 87/1, 53–76.

Wilson, J. M. (1975) *Isaac Rosenberg: Poet and Painter* (London: Cecil Woolf).

Wilson, J. M. (1985) *Charles Hamilton Sorley. A Biography* (London: Cecil Woolf).

Wilson, J. M. (1998) *Siegfried Sassoon. The Making of a War Poet – A Biography (1886–1918)* (London: Duckworth).

Wilson, T. (1986) *The Myriad Faces of War. Britain and the Great War, 1914–1918* (Cambridge: Polity Press).

Wimsatt, W. K. (1955) *The Verbal Icon. Studies in the Meaning of Poetry* (London: Methuen).

Winner, E. (1988) *The Point of Words. Children's Understanding of Metaphor and Irony* (Cambridge, MA: Harvard University Press).

Winter, D. (1979) *Death's Men* (London: Penguin).

Winter, J. M. (1985) *The Great War and the British People* (Basingstoke: Macmillan).

Winter, J. M. (1992) 'Catastrophe and Culture: Recent Trends in the Historiography of the First World War', *Journal of Modern History*, 64/3, 525–532.

Winter, J. M. (1995) *Sites of Memory, Sites of Morning, The Great War in European Cultural History* (Cambridge: Cambridge University Press).

Winter, J. M./Parker, G./Habeck, M. R. (2000) *The Great War and the Twentieth Century* (New Haven, CT/London: Yale University Press).

Wolffe, J. (1994) *God and Greater Britain. Religion and National Life in Britain and Ireland 1893–1945* (London: Routledge).

Worcester, D. (1960) *The Art of Satire* (New York: Russell & Russell).

Wordsworth, W. (1974) 'Preface to Lyrical Ballads' in W. J. B. Owen/J. W. Smyser (eds) *The Prose Works of William Wordsworth* (Oxford: Clarendon Press).

Wormleighton, S. (1990) 'Something in Sassoon's Style. Notes on Owen's "The Dead-Beat" and other Late-1917 Poems', *Notes and Queries*, 37/1, 65–67.

Young, A. (1999) 'W. H. R. Rivers and the War Neuroses', *Journal for Historical Behavioristic Science*, 35, 359–378.

Yu, C. (2004) *Nothing to Admire. The Politics of Poetic Satire from Dryden to Merrill* (Oxford: Oxford University Press).

Index

Made in the USA
Las Vegas, NV
21 October 2024

10192159R00122